HISTORY OF ACTUARIAL SCIENCE

Published in association with the Institute of Actuaries

HISTORY
OF
ACTUARIAL SCIENCE

Edited by
STEVEN HABERMAN
and
TREVOR A. SIBBETT

VOLUME III

Life Insurance Mathematics

Part 1

LONDON
WILLIAM PICKERING
1995

Published by Pickering & Chatto (Publishers) Limited

21 Bloomsbury Way, London, WC1A 2TH

Old Post Road, Brookfield, Vermont 05036, USA

BRITISH LIBRARY CATALOGUING IN PUBLICATION DATA
A catalogue reference for this book
is available from the British Library
Set ISBN 1 85196 143 7
This volume ISBN 1 85196 162 3

LIBRARY OF CONGRESS CATALOGING-IN-PUBLICATION DATA
History of actuarial science / edited by Steven Haberman and Trevor A. Sibbett.
p. cm.
Includes bibliographical references (p.).
ISBN 1-85196-143-7 (set)
1. Actuarial science—History. I. Haberman, Steven, 1951– . II. Sibbett, Trevor A., 1935–. .
HG8781.H57 1995
368′.01—dc20 95-21353
CIP

Typeset by Waveney Typesetters
Norwich

Printed and bound in Great Britain by
Antony Rowe Limited
Chippenham

CONTENTS

ANNUITIES

UPON

LIVES:

OR,

The VALUATION of ANNUITIES upon any Number of LIVES; as alſo, of REVERSIONS.

To which is added,

An APPENDIX concerning the EXPECTATIONS of LIFE, and Probabilities of SURVIVORSHIP.

By A. DE MOIVRE. F. R. S.

LONDON,
Printed by WILLIAM PEARSON, over-againſt *Wright's-Coffee-Houſe* in *Alderſgate-Street*. MDCCXXV.

Abraham de Moivre, *Annuities on Lives: or, The Valuation of Annuities upon any Number of Lives; as also, of Reversions. To which is added, an appendix concerning the expectations of life, and probabilities of survivorship*, London, William Pearson (1725).

In this book, which is the first textbook on life contingencies, de Moivre develops a considerable number of important results. There is a good definition of expectation of life, published in English for the first time. (Nicholas Bernoulli published a definition and calculations, some based on Graunt's 1662 Life Table, in 1709 – *De Usu Artis Conjectandi in Jure*, Basle. Bernoulli's new contribution in this work was to consider the expectation of life of the longest living of a group of lives.) De Moivre uses uniform decrements to approximate to Halley's table over the middle range of ages and this has become known as de Moivre's law. De Moivre also explains how to derive annuity values using the relationship $a_x = v\ p_x \ddot{a}_{x+1}$. Euler derived this relationship independently in 'Sur Les Rentes Viagères,' *Mémoires de l'Academie Royale des Sciences*, Berlin (1767).

There are few tables in the work. De Moivre expected his readers to undertake the mathematics when they wished to know annuity values or other information. The reality was probably that de Moivre asked too much of his readers.

There were four separately published editions and pp. 261 onwards in the third edition of de Moivre's *The Doctrine of Chances, 1756* are effectively a final and fifth edition. The second edition, 1743, covers annuities payable with a proportionate payment to the date of death – page 86. Temporary annuities are examined in 'A letter from Mr Abraham de Moivre, FRS to William Jones, Esquire, FRS concerning the easiest method for calculating the value of annuities upon lives, from tables of observations', *Philosophical Transactions of the Royal Society*, no. 473 (1744).

The first table of annuities upon lives available generally in the United Kingdom is on p. 20 of *Tables for Renewing & Purchasing of the Leases of Cathedral-Churches and Colleges* (1686), sometimes wrongly attributed to Isaac Newton. It does not differentiate lives by age. The author, quoted by Augustus de Morgan in *Journal of the Institute of Actuaries*, Vol. 9, p. 185 (1861) was George Mabbot, a caterer (mancipium) at King's College, Cambridge. Another short table for annuities on eight or more lives is in Gerhard Malynes *Consuetudo, vel, Lex Mercatoria*, London (1622). Isolated cases of annuities on lives are found in mediaeval times.

TO

THE MOST HONOURABLE

THOMAS

EARL of MACCLESFIELD,

Lord High Chancellour

OF

Great Britain.

MY LORD,

I Should not presume to inscribe the following Piece to your Lordship, were it not that the Subject it treats of has been made the Entertainment of some of Your leisure Hours.

As this Eſſay is founded partly on Mathematical Reaſoning, and partly on thoſe Probable Conjectures that may be derived from Fact and Experience; I thought I could not ſubmit to a better Judge than Your Lordſhip, the Truth of this Theory, the Conſequences that flow from it, and their Agreeableneſs to the Rules of that Equity which ought to preſide in Contracts.

I am incouraged to hope for a favourable reception of this Performance, both from Your Lordſhip's known Goodneſs, and your noble Inclination to promote Arts and Sciences, of which Your Lordſhip has upon all Occaſions ſhewn Your ſelf the Great and Glorious Patron.

THESE Motives, which of themſelves were more than ſufficient to induce me to give Your Lordſhip this Teſtimony of my humble Reſpects, are alſo hightened from the Conſideration of thoſe Excellent Qualities which ſo Eminently diſtinguiſh Your Lordſhip, and thoſe Singular Virtues of which the Influence is ſo univerſally Beneficial.

I ſhall no longer detain Your Lordſhip, but only requeſt that You would be pleaſed to look upon the Liberty of this Addreſs, as an effect of that high Veneration which I have conſtantly profeſſed for Your Lordſhip, and of the earneſt deſire I ever had of declaring my ſelf,

MY LORD,

Your Lordſhip's

moſt Obedient, and

moſt Devoted

Humble Servant,

Jan 1. 172$\frac{4}{5}$.

A. DE MOIVRE.

PREFACE.

THE Method of Calculating the Values of Annuities upon Lives, seems never to have been perfectly understood 'till Dr. HALLEY first published the Rules of it; which may be seen in the Philosophical Transf. N°. 196.

ALTHOUGH there is some Ground to believe that what he writ upon that Subject was partly occasional; yet there appears in it the same exquisite Judgment and Sagacity that has always shewn it self in all his other Productions.

AS this Calculation chiefly depends on the various Degrees of Probability which Lives of different Ages have to continue in Being, so it was previously necessary that a Table should be constructed which might at one View exhibit the State of Life in Respect to its probable Duration: Such a Table was accordingly constructed in the best Form that could be contrived, out of five Years Observations upon the Bills of Mortality of Breslaw the Capital of Silesia.

BUT notwithstanding the Pains taken by that excellent Mathematician in fitting a true Algebraic Calculation *to his Table of Observations, yet he was sensible that both his Table and Calculations, were capable of farther Improvement; of this he expressed his Sense in the following Words:* Were this Calculus founded on the Experience of a very great Number of Years, it would very well be worth the while to think of Methods to facilitate the Computation of Two, Three or more *Lives.*

FROM whence it appears that the Table of Observations, being only the Result of a few Years Experience, is not so entirely to be depended upon as to make it the Foundation of a fixt and unalterable Valuation of Annuities *for* Life, *and that even admitting such a Table could be obtained as might be grounded on the Experience of a very great Number of Years, still the Method of applying it to the Valuation of several* Lives *would be extreamly laborious, considering the vast Number of Operations that would be requisite to combine every Year of each* Life *with every Year of all the other* Lives.

I own, that in the Method which I have taken to make the Calculation of Lives *easy, I have not made use of any other Table than of that which has been constructed by Dr.* HALLEY; *for which Reason, I am contented it should be thought that the Values of* Annuities, *as deduced from my Calculation, are still liable to some Exceptions, and need not therefore prejudice any established Practice of Estimation.*

WHEREFORE all I can in Justice pretend to, is to have contrived such Rules as will make the Valuation of Lives *easy, whenever it shall so happen that a Table is produced that can be depended upon, as to the Sufficiency of the Number of Observations on which it is built, the Accuracy of the Observers, and the Skill of those who construct the Table from the Observations.*

I have been very particular in all the Questions that can be formed about Lives, *and have rather chosen to insert in this Tract some few* Problems *that do not so immediately relate to Practice, than omit any Thing which might be thought essential to my Subject.*

AFTER I have shewn how to estimate the Value of One Life, *I proceed to the Consideration of Two, Three or as many* Lives *as may be assigned, and determine by an easy Calculation,* 1st, *The Values of* joint Lives, *that is, the Value of an* Annuity *which is to continue so long as the* Lives *concerned are all of them subsisting together;* 2dly, *The Value of the* longest Life, *that is, the Value of an* Annuity *which is to continue so long as any One of the given* Lives *are in Being;* 3dly, *The Value of all Sorts of* Reversions, *whether of* One Life *after* One, *of* One *after* Two, *of* Two *after* One, *&c. whether those* Reversions *be for* Lives *nominated at the Time of the first Possession, or to be nominated when the first Possession expires.*

WHAT is chiefly to be regarded in the Rules above mentioned, is the Justness of their Conclusions; for admitting that several Lives *singly taken are rated at their proper Values; then the Value of an* Annuity *upon all those* joint Lives, *or upon the* longest *of them, is determined by necessary Consequence; thus if Two* Lives *singly taken, be each of them worth* 10 *Years Purchase, and the* Rate *of* Interest *be* 5 per Cent, *then it will follow that an* Annuity *upon the* longest *of them will be worth* 13.44; *and in the same Manner, if Three* Lives *singly taken, be each of them worth* 10 *Years Purchase; then an* Annuity *upon the* longest *of them will be worth* 15.14.

TO the End, that the Rules by me delivered may be of use to all Sorts of Readers, they have been expressed in Words at length, and the greatest Part of them illustrated by proper Examples ; *as for the* Demonstration *of those Rules, it will easily be apprehended by those who being conversant in* Algebra, *are also acquainted with the First Rudiments of the* Doctrine of Chances.

AFTER I have proceeded thus far, I subjoin an Appendix that has a very natural Connexion with the Things before demonstrated ; it contains a Method whereby taking still the Table of Observations to be our Guide, the Expectations *of* Life, *and Probabilities of* Survivorship *are easily determined.*

THE Expectation *of* Life, *is that Duration which may justly be expected from a* Life *of a given* Age; *and is properly a* Medium *between the longer and shorter* Durations *of a great Number of preceeding* Lives, *from the Time of their having attained the Age given, to the Time of their Extinction. With the present Value of this* Expectation, *the Proprietor of a* Life *may be said, in some Sense, to have purchased an* Annuity *for* Life, *of which the Rent is paid him in actual Duration, and thereby to have taken his Chance of an uncertain Duration, as an Equivalent for that fixt Duration he is entituled to by the Right of his* Expectation.

TO facilitate the Computations relating to that Subject, I resume an Hypothesis which I had begun to introduce in the first Part of this Tract : It consists in supposing that the Number of Lives *existing of any Age is proportional to the Number of Years intercepted between the Age given, and the Extremity of Old Age ; thus if there be* 36 Lives *of the Age of* 50, *we may imagin that in the succeeding Years, there will remain respectively* 35, 34,

33, 32, &c. 'till they be all extinct in the 86th Year, which is supposed to be the utmost Term of Life. This Hypothesis will appear in several Respects to have some Foundation in Nature; 1st, As it assigns a Term to human Life, which is very rarely exceeded; 2dly, As it makes Life more and more obnoxious to decay; 3dly, As it has a near Conformity with the Table of Observations. After this Hypothesis has been established, I find Means to correct its Conclusions by help of the Table it self, and to bring them to so near a Degree of Coincidence with those deduced Year by Year from the Table, that it may be a doubt whether the Difference arising from the Comparison be not a Balance for some Unaccuracy that will still remain in the best Observations.

THE Conclusions derived immediately from my Hypothesis have a very great degree of Simplicity, of which to give some Instances; suppose 1° it be required to find the Expectation of a Life of which the Age is given; the Rule for finding it, is expressed in these few Words; take the Half Difference between the Age given, and the Extremity of Old Age supposed at 86, and that half Difference is the Thing required; thus if the Age be 50, then the Difference between 50 and 86 being 36, whereof the Half is 18; it may be concluded that 18 Years is the Duration which a Life of 50 may justly expect; but if the End of that Interval once happens to be attained by the Life in Question, then it acquires a farther Expectation of 9 Years, and so on: 2° let it be required to find the joint Expectation of Two equal Lives; the Rule will be to take one third of the Difference between their common Age and 86; thus if Two Lives be each of them 50, it may be expected that both of them together may continue in Being during an Interval of 12 Years; and if the Number of equal Lives be Three, Four, or Five, &c. then the Time due to their joint Continuance is respectively expressible by $\frac{1}{4}$, $\frac{1}{5}$, $\frac{1}{6}$,

&c. *of the Difference between their common Age and* 86; 3° *If there be ever so many equal* Lives, *then the Time due to the longest of them, that is the Time due to that* Life *which survives all the rest, may also be determined; for if there be Two, Three or Four equal* Lives, *then* $\frac{2}{3}$, $\frac{3}{4}$, $\frac{4}{5}$, &c. *of the Difference between their common Age and* 86, *will respectively express the Duration required.*

I believe it will not be amiss, in this Place, to obviate a Difficulty that may be formed against some of the foregoing Conclusions; for it may be objected that admitting our Hypothesis to be true, then the Value of an Annuity *for an Age of* 50, *would seem to be equivalent to an* Annuity *certain for the Term of* 18 *Years; now it appears from the* 1st Problem, *wherein this Hypothesis has been assumed, that an* Annuity *for an* Age *of* 50, *is worth only* 10.34 *Years Purchase, which being the present Value of an* Annuity *certain for the Term of* 15 *Years or thereabouts; it might from thence be infer'd that the same Principle leads to Two contradictory Conclusions.*

IN Answer to this, I desire it may be considered that the Value of an Annuity *is partly regulated by the Interest which the Purchaser makes of his Money, and partly by the Chance of* Life; *that the fixing the Value of* 10.34 *Years Purchase to a* Life *of* 50 *is accidental, being derived from an implyed Supposition, that the Interest allowed to the Purchaser is at the Rate of* 5 per Cent. *that, as the Interest sinks, the Value of the* Annuity *rises and* vice versa; *and that in the Estimations made of the* Expectations *of* Life, *there is no Regard to be had to the Rate of Interest, the Years remote from the Age given, being as valuable in Point of Duration as those that are next to it, and consequently that no just Estimation can be made of the* Expectation *of* Life, *but as it is compared with an* Annuity *of which the Purchase admits of no Discount, and to which there is a Payment due, even to the last Moment of* Life.

IT may perhaps seem somewhat strange that the Speculation concerning Survivorship *should be postponed to the Rules given for Settling the Values of* Reversions ; *when those Values seem to suppose that the Chance of* Survivorship *is already known.*

BUT it will not be difficult to account for the Steps taken in this Matter, for although the Notion of Survivorship *may successfully be employed in determining the Values of* Reversions, *yet it will be found that the common* Cases *belonging to that Subject, are so easily derived from a proper Combination of* single *and of* Joint Lives, *that any other Consideration would have been entirely superfluous.*

NEVERTHELESS, the Probability of Survivorship *may be useful in resolving some extraordinary Cases relating to* Reversions, *viz. when it so happens that the Right of* Reversion *does not necessarily descend to the* Life *in Expectation, after the previous Demise of the* Life *in Possession ; for a* Life *may intervene between the present Possessor and the Expectant, to which the Right of* Reversion *is immediately devolved, upon its surviving the* Life *in Possession, by Means whereof the Expectant is for ever excluded the Right of* Reversion, *although he should survive the Person interposed between him and the present Possessor; in this and other Cases of the like Nature, the Chance of* Survivorship *regulates the Value of the Expectation, of which it has been thought sufficient to give one single Instance, which may be seen in my* XXVII. Problem.

THE Rules delivered in this Tract requiring all along that the Extent of Life *should be considered as confined, I have thought it convenient to fix the utmost Limit of it in the 86th Year, whereby I have nearly conformed my self to the Table of Observations ; but as some exceptionable Consequences might perhaps flow from too rigid an Application of that Principle to those Years of* Life *that border upon its Extremity ; it will not be improper to declare, that my Meaning, in fixing that Term, imports no more than this,* viz. *that the Time of contracting for* Annuities *being commonly very remote from the* 86th *Year of the* Life *purchased, it is not likely that any Consideration will then be given for the Chance of receiving the Rent of that Year, which will produce the very same Conclusions in* Theory, *as if the Extremity of that Year were never attainable.*

Page 13. Line 13. for 10.15 read 10.34
Page 56. last Line. for B. read C.

OF THE VALUATION OF ANNUITIES FOR LIFE.

IN eſtimating the Values of ANNUITIES upon LIVES, Regard muſt be had to the Intereſt which Money bears, and to the Probability of the Lives continuing a longer or ſhorter Time.

THE Rate of Intereſt is generally regulated by Law, but the greater or leſs Probability of the Duration of Life muſt be deduced from Obſervation.

THE TABLE publiſhed by Dr. HALLEY for eſtimating the Probabilities of Life being very artificially contrived, and grounded on ſuch Obſervations, as one may reaſonably ſuppoſe have been made with all the Exactneſs poſſible, we have annex'd it to this Treatiſe, in order to make uſe of it as Occaſion ſhall require.

IT exhibits at one View the Probability that a Perſon of any Age propoſed, may live any given Number of Years.

IT is diſtiſtinguiſhed into ſeveral *Columns*, ſhewing alternately the Age, and the Number of Perſons living of that Age, both which are always written over-againſt one another.

SUPPOSE that by the help of this TABLE we would know what the reſpective Probabilities are for a Man of Thirty, to live 1, 2, 3, 4, 5, *&c.* Years.

LOOK for the Number 30, in one of the *Columns* of Age, under which Number you will find 31, 32, 33, 34, *&c.* over-againſt the ſaid Number 30 in the next adjacent *Column* on the Right Hand, you find 531, under which are written 523, 515, 507, 499, *&c.* each reſpectively correſponding in order to the Numbers written in the *Column* of Age; the meaning of which is, that out of 531 Perſons living of the Age of 30, there remain but 523, 515, 507, 499, *&c.* that attain to the reſpective Ages of 31, 32, 33, 34, *&c.* and who conſequently do from that Term of 30, live 1, 2, 3, 4, *&c.* Years reſpectively.

NOW if out of the 531 Perſons living of the Age of Thirty, there remain but 523 after one Year expired, it follows that the Number of Perſons dead in that Time is the Difference between 531 and 523, *viz.* 8, and conſequently the Number of Chances that a Perſon of that Age has to live one Year, is to the Number of Chances he has to die within that Year, as 523 to 8.

BUT if we make a *Fraction* whose *Numerator* shall be the Number of Chances for living, and the *Denominator* the Number of Chances both for living and dying, that *Fraction* will be the Measure of the Probability of Life's continuance.

WHEREFORE, if the Numbers 523, 515, 507, 499, *&c.* answering to the respective Ages, 31, 32, 33, 34, *&c.* be written as *Numerators* of so many *Fractions*, whereof the common *Denominator* be 531, answering to the Number 30, which is the Term from which we begin to reckon; these *Fractions* $\frac{523}{531}$, $\frac{515}{531}$, $\frac{507}{531}$, $\frac{499}{531}$, *&c.* will express the Probabilities of a Man's of 30, living to the respective Ages of 31, 32, 33, 34, *&c.* that is living 1, 2, 3, 4, *&c.* Years computed from the Term 30.

THIS being admitted, suppose it be required to find the Value of an ANNUITY for LIFE, for a Person of 30 Years of Age.

LET the ANNUITY be 100 *l.* and the Rate of Interest 5 *per Cent.*

SINCE the preſent Value of an ANNUITY of 100 *l.* to be receiv-ed a Year hence (Diſcount being made at 5 *per Cent.*) is 95.23 it follows that ſuch would be the Value of the firſt Year's Rent, were the Purchaſer ſure to live one Year; but his living one Year, being only probable according to that Degree of Probability which is meaſured by the *Fraction* $\frac{523}{531}$, we muſt conclude that the foregoing Sum of 95.23 ought to be diminiſhed in the Proportion of 523 to 531, or, in other Words, that it ought to be mul-tiplied by the *Fraction* $\frac{523}{531}$, which will reduce it to 93.80, and this will be the Value of the firſt Year's Rent.

IN the ſame manner may the ſecond Year's Rent be calculated; for were it certain that this Rent would be received, the preſent Value of it would be found to be 90.70; now its being receiv-ed is only probable according to that Degree of Probability which is mea-ſured by the *Fraction* $\frac{515}{531}$; wherefore the Sum 90.70 being multiplied by the ſaid *Fraction*, the Product will be

87.90, which will be the preſent Value of the the ſecond Year's Rent.

AND by the like Proceſs, the preſent Values of the 3*d*, 4*th*, 5*th*, &c. Years Rents to the utmoſt extent of Life, may be calculated, and all theſe ſeveral Values being added together, the Sum will be the preſent Value of an ANNUITY upon a Life of Thirty, which will be found to be about 1300 *l*.

ALTHOUGH the Number of *Operations* that are to be made in order to eſtimate one ſingle LIFE be very numerous, yet that being once determined, the Value of the next younger Life may eaſily be obtained,

THUS ſuppoſe it were required to determine the Value of a Life of Nine and Twenty, from the given Value of a Life of Thirty, we may argue thus,

THE preſent Value of the firſt Year's Rent, upon a Certainty of its being received, would be 95.23; but its being received is only probable according to that Degree of Probability which is meaſured by the *Fraction* $\frac{531}{539}$, wherefore the preſent Value of that Rent upon the Contingency of the Life's failing in the first Year, is the Product of 95.23 by $\frac{531}{539}$, that is 93.82.

LIKEWISE, the present Values of all the succeeding Rents will be 1300, when once the Age of Thirty is attained, as we have seen before.

BUT it being uncertain whither that Age will be attained to, that Value ought to be diminished in the Proportion of 531 to 539, which will reduce it to 1280.7, and this Sum the Purchaser might engage should be paid after the Expiration of one Year whether he lived or not, for the Expectation of enjoying the ANNUITY after the Age of Thirty.

BUT if the Sum of 1280.7, which is payable after one Year, be discounted at the Rate of 5 *per Cent.* its present Value will be reduced to 1219.7, which being added with the present Value of the first Year's Rent, *viz.* 93.82, the Sum will be 1313.52, which will be the Value of an ANNUITY for a Life of Nine and Twenty.

BY help of the Method hitherto explained, those that will take the Pains may, if they think fit, compose TABLES of the several Values of those ANNUITIES for any Age proposed, and for any *Rate* of *Interest* that shall be fixed upon.

BUT 'till that be done, it will be convenient to try whether there be not some easy practical Method, whereby the Values of those ANNUITIES may be determined very near as accurately as if they had been deduced Year by Year from the *Tables* of *Observation*.

THIS may be so much the more readily undertaken, that any small Difference that may arise from the two Methods of Calculation, is not to be regarded in a Subject of this Nature.

IN order to it, we may consider that whatever be that Law which is observed by Nature in the perpetual Decrements of human Life, that Law must, conformably to all the other Laws of Nature, be such as to proceed regularly, at least for some short Intervals of Time.

WHEREFORE if we examin Dr. HALLEY's Tables with a View of diſcovering what Regularity there may be in the perpetual Decrement of Lives, and how far that Regularity is extended, we ſhall find that out of 646 Perſons of twelve Years of Age, there remain 640 after one Year, 634 after two, 628, 622, 616, 610, 604, 598, 592, 586, after 3, 4, 5, 6, 7, 8, 9, 10 Years reſpectively.

FROM whence we may conclude, that for a Space of ten Years, there is a Decrement of the Probabilities of Life, according to the Order of an Arithmetic Progreſſion, theſe Probabilities being $\frac{634}{640}$, $\frac{628}{640}$, $\frac{622}{640}$, &c.

IT is carefully to be obſerved that the Decrement of theſe Probobilities is here conſidered as beginning from the ſame Term, and that as the firſt *Fraction* above written, repreſents the Probability of living from Twelve to Thirteen, ſo the next repreſents the Probability of living from Twelve to Fourteen, the next to this, the Probability of living from Twelve to Fifteen, &c.

IN the ſame Manner, if we take the Term 42, we ſhall find that for 8 Years together, the Probabilities of living to 42, 43, 44, 45, &c. are reſpectively repreſented by the *Fractions* $\frac{417}{427}$, $\frac{407}{427}$, $\frac{397}{427}$, $\frac{387}{427}$, &c. which decreaſe in *Arithmetic Progreſſion.*

AND in taking greater *Intervals*, we find that out of 531 Perſons of Thirty Years of Age, there are but 262 remaining after Twenty Eight Years; and again that all thoſe who are then remaining are very near extinct after Twenty Eight Years more, *viz.* in the 86*th* Year, which we may well ſuppoſe without any conſiderable Error to be the utmoſt Term of human Life.

NOW ſince thoſe that are living of Thirty Years of Age are reduced to about one Half in Twenty Eight Years, and that in Twenty Eight Years more, the remaining Half is very near extinct; we may ſuppoſe that, during the Interval of Fifty Six Years, the Decrements of Life conſidered from the Term of Thirty, are conſtantly equal.

LET us therefore consider, 1° what would be the result of an *Hypothesis* that makes the Probabilities of Life to decrease in *Arithmetic Progression* : 2° how far the Calculations deduced from it agree with the Tables : 3° what Corrections are necessary to be made to it where it varies from the Tables.

PROBLEM I.

SUPPOSING the Probabilities of Life to decrease in Arithmetic Progression, *to find the Value of an Annuity upon such a Life.*

SOLUTION.

LET 1, be the Rent ; *r*, the *Rate of Interest*, that is the Interest of one Pound joined with its Principal ; *n*, the Number of Years comprehended between the Term given, and the last Term in which the Probability of Life is supposed to be extinguished : Let also *P* be the present Value of an *Annuity* certain for the given Number of Years.

THIS being supposed, the Value of an *Annuity* upon such a Life will be $\frac{1-\frac{r}{n}P}{r-1}$, which may be thus expressed in Words at Length.

TAKE the Value of an *Annuity* certain, for so many Years as are intercepted between the Age given, and the utmost Term of Life supposed to be at Eighty Six compleat; multiply this Value by the *Rate of Interest*, and divide the Product by the Number of Years belonging to the *Annuity*; let the Quotient be subtracted from Unity, and let the Remainder be divided by the Interest of one Pound: This last Quotient will express the Value of an *Annuity* for the Life given.

THUS, suppose it were required to find the present Value of an *Annuity* of one Pound for a Life of Fifty, Interest being at 5 *per Cent.*

THE Number of Years intercepted between Fifty and Eighty Six, is Thirty Six; therefore let the Value of an *Annuity* certain for Thirty Six Years be taken out of the *Tables* of

Annuities; this Value will be found to be 16.5468.

LET this be multiplied by 1.05 *Rate of Interest*, the Product will be 17.3741.

LET this Product be divided by the Number of Years, *viz.* by 36; the Quotient will be 0.4826.

SUBTRACT this Quotient from 1, the Remainder will be 0.5174.

LASTLY, divide this Quotient by the Interest of one Pound, *viz.* by 0.05, and the new Quotient, *viz.* 10.35 will be the Value of an *Annuity* of one Pound for a Life of Fifty.

DEMONSTRATION.

SINCE, by Hypothesis, the Probabilities of Life decrease in *Arithmetic Progression*, it follows that they may be represented by the following Series,

$\frac{n-1}{n}, \frac{n-2}{n}, \frac{n-3}{n}, \frac{n-4}{n}, \ldots \frac{n-n}{n},$

whose Terms being severally divided by the Terms of the *Geometric Progression*, r, rr, r^3, r^4, &c. the new Series

reſulting from theſe Diviſions, *viz.*
$\frac{n-1}{nr}$, $\frac{n-2}{nrr}$, $\frac{n-3}{nr^3}$, $\frac{n-4}{nr^4}$, ... $\frac{n-n}{nr^n}$
will expreſs the Value of all the Rents to be received yearly, and eſtimated in preſent Money; and conſequently the Sum of the Terms of this Series is the preſent Value of the *Annuity* required.

BUT in order to find the Sum of all theſe Terms, it is to be obſerved that the Series which they compoſe may be divided into two other Series, *viz.*

$$\frac{1}{r} + \frac{1}{rr} + \frac{1}{r^3} + \frac{1}{r^4} \ldots\ldots + \frac{1}{r^n}$$
$$\frac{1}{nr} + \frac{2}{nrr} + \frac{3}{nr^3} + \frac{4}{nr^4} \ldots\ldots + \frac{n}{nr^n}$$

whereof the Second is to be ſubtracted from the Firſt.

THE Sum of the firſt Series may be look'd upon as given, being an *Annuity* certain for a Number of Years expreſſed by *n*, and may either be derived from Tables exhibiting the Values of *Annuities* for any Term of Years, and a given Intereſt, or be readily calculated by the known Method of ſumming up the Terms of a *Geometric Progreſſion*; this Sum being contained in the ſhort Expreſſion $\frac{1-\frac{1}{r^n}}{r-1}$, which we may ſuppoſe equal to P.

THE Method of calculating the Sum of the ſecond Series is not ſo vulgarly known, but it may be deriv-ed from a general *Theorem* in the *Doctrine of Chances*, *pag.* 132, which ſhews it to be $P+\frac{\frac{r}{n}P-1}{r-1}$. Wherefore, we may conclude that the preſent Value of the *Annuity* required is $\frac{1-\frac{r}{n}P}{r-1}$.

IN order to compare this, with the Value deduced from Dr. HALLEY'S Tables, Let us ſuppoſe firſt, the Age for which the *Annuity* is to be calculated to be Thirty; in this Caſe, $n=56$, let the *Rate of Intereſt* be $=1.06=r$; then P will be $=15.524$; from which *Suppoſitions*, the Value of the *Annuity* required will be found to be 11.61, which differs from that given by Dr. HALLEY, *viz.* 11.72, by very little more than $\frac{1}{10}$ of a Year's Purchaſe.

LET us now suppose the Age required to be Forty, then the Value required will be found to be 10.70, which exceeds that given by Dr. HALLEY, *viz.* 10.57 only by the small *Fraction* 0.13.

IF the Age be Fifty, then the Value required will be found to be 9.49, which differs in Excess from the Value of the Tables by 0.28.

IF the Age be Sixty, the difference in excess will be 0.23.

IF the Age be Seventy, the difference in excess will be 0.18.

FROM whence we may conclude, that let the *Rate of Interest* be what it will, the Value of an *Annuity* for an Age not less than Thirty, will by help of our Canon, be found nearly the same as the Values deduced from the Tables.

BUT if we try by our Canon what will be the Value of an *Annuity* for an Age less than Thirty, suppose Twenty, we shall find that this Value will be 12.30; whereas the Value found by the Tables is 12.78; therefore the difference .058 now lies on the contrary *Side* of what it did after Twenty.

AND if we try what will be the Value of an *Annuity* for an Age of Ten, we ſhall find this Value to be 12.84, which is deficient from the Value found by the Tables, *viz.* 13.44 by 0.60.

LASTLY, if we calculate what would be the Value of an *Annuity* for an Infant One Year old, we ſhall find this Value to be 12.57, which differs in Exceſs from the Value found by the Tables, *viz.* 10.28 by 2.29.

The Reaſon of which Variations may eaſily be aſſigned; for the Decrements of Life towards old Age are ſomething quicker in the Tables, than the Decrements ſuppoſed in our Hypotheſis, for which Reaſon the Values of *Annuities* deduced from the Tables are a little below thoſe that are deduced from our Canon.

BUT towards the Beginning of Life, *viz.* from the Age of Ten and upwards, the Derements of the Tables are ſomething ſlower than in our Hypotheſis; for Inſtance, if we examin the Numbers ſet down in the Tables over-againſt 20 and 21 we find 598, 592, and conſequently the firſt Decrement after the Age of Twenty, being 6 in 598, it follows that if the ſucceeding Decrements were to continue in that Uniformity, a Life of Twenty could not be ſuppoſed to be neceſſarily extinguiſhed 'till 100 Years after, which might make it reach to 120, and this Difference between the Decrements of the Tables, and thoſe of our Hypotheſis, are the Occaſion of the ſecond Variation obſerved in the *Eſtimation of Annuities.*

THE third Variation, which is the moſt conſiderable, is occaſioned by the Increments of *Life*, from Year to Year, between the firſt Year and the Twelfth; for according to the Tables, the Probabilities of living One, Two, Three, Four, *&c.* Years, all to begin from the Firſt, are reſpectively $\frac{855}{1000}$, $\frac{798}{1000}$, $\frac{760}{1000}$, $\frac{732}{1000}$, *&c.* from whence it follows, that the Probability of living from the Second to the Third, is greater than the Probability of living from the Firſt to the Second, and that the Probability of living from the Third to the Fourth, is greater than the Probability of living from the Second to the Third, and ſo on; theſe Probabilities written in their natural Order being expreſſible by the *Fractions* $\frac{855}{1000}$, $\frac{798}{855}$, $\frac{760}{798}$, $\frac{732}{760}$, *&c.* of which every One is greater than that which preceds it, 'till we come to the greateſt of all, *viz.* $\frac{640}{646}$, which expreſſes the Probability of living from the Twelfth to the Thirteenth Year, after which there is a perpetual Decreaſe to the End of Life.

NOW in the Hypotheſis of a perpetual and equable Decrement of the Probabilities of Life, to begin from a Term given, there is alſo a perpetual, though not equable Decrement of the Probabilities of Life when eſtimated from Year to Year, which makes it that ſuch an Hypotheſis muſt differ the moſt from the Tables of Obſervations for the Twelve firſt Years of Life.

BUT although the Notion of an equable Decrement of Life to begin from the Age of Twelve, and to continue throughout the whole Extent of Life, do not exactly agree with the *Tables*; yet that Notion may successfully be employed in constructing a *Table* of the Values of *Annuities* for *Ages* not inferiour to Twelve, as will appear by the Consequences deduced from the following *Problem*.

PROBLEM II.

TO find the Value of an Annuity *for a limited Interval of Time, during which the Decrements of Life may be considered as equal.*

SOLUTION.

LET *a* and *b* represent the Number of People respectively living in the Beginning and End of the given Interval of Years, which Interval we will suppose $= n$; Let *P* be the Value of an *Annuity* certain for that Number of Years; make $\frac{1 - \frac{r}{n} P}{r - 1} = Q$, then will the Value of an *Annuity* granted for that Interval of Life be $= Q + \frac{b}{a} \times \overline{P - Q}$, which may be thus expreſſed.

1° Take by the preceding *Problem* the Value of an *Annuity* for a Life ſuppoſed neceſſarily terminated in the given Interval of Time.

2° Subtract this Value from the Value of an *Annuity* certain, to continue ſo many Years, as are contained in the given Interval.

3° Multiply the Remainder by the Number, which in the *Tables* terminates the given Interval, and divide the Product by the other Number, which anſwers to the Age given.

4° To this *Quotient* add the Value firſt found, and the *Quotient* will be the Value required.

THUS, ſuppoſe we would find the Value of an *Annuity* for an Age of Twelve, to continue Ten Years and no longer, and to ceaſe from the

Time that the Life may happen to fail within the Interval given: *Interest at 5 per Cent.*

THE Value of an *Annuity* for a Life, ſuppoſed to be neceſſarily extinguiſhed in Ten Years is by the preceding *Problem*, 3.7843.

THIS being ſubtracted from the Value of an *Annuity* certain for Ten Years, *viz.* 7.7217, the *Remainder* will be 3.9374.

THIS *Remainder* being multiplied by the Number 628, which in the *Tables* anſwers to Twenty Two, terminating the given Interval, and divided by the Number 646, which in the *Tables* anſwers to Twelve, the Age given, the *Quotient* will be 3.8277.

THIS *Quotient* added with 3.7843, Value found by the firſt Article, the Sum will be 7.6120, which will be the Value of the *Annuity* required, and is juſt the ſame as if it had been deduced Year by Year from the *Tables.*

DEMONSTRATION.

SINCE the whole Interval between a and b is filled up with *Arithmetic Means*, it follows that the Number of People living in the Beginning and End of every Year of the Time given, will respectively be represented by the following *Series*, viz.

$$a,\ \frac{na-a+b}{n},\ \frac{na-2a+2b}{n}\ \ldots\ldots\ b.$$

and consequently, the Probabilities of living 1, 2, 3, 4, &c. Years, to begin from the Term given, will be represented by the *Series*.

$$\frac{na-a+b}{na},\ \frac{na-2a+2b}{na}\ \ldots\ldots\ \frac{b}{a}.$$

WHEREFORE the Value of an *Annuity*, granted for the limited Time comprehended within the given Interval of Years, will be expressed by the *Series*,

$$\frac{na-a+b}{nar}+\frac{na-2a+2b}{narr}\ \ldots\ldots\ \frac{+b}{ar^{n}}$$

which *Series* is divisible into two others, *viz.*

$$\frac{n-1}{nr}+\frac{n-2}{nrr}+\frac{n-3}{nr^3}\ldots\ldots+\frac{n-n}{nr^n}$$

$$\frac{b}{a}\times\overline{\frac{1}{nr}+\frac{2}{nrr}+\frac{3}{nr^3}\ldots\ldots+\frac{n}{nr^n}}$$

BUT the Value of the firſt *Series* $= Q$ by the firſt *Problem*, and the Value of the ſecond is by the ſame $\frac{b}{a}\times\frac{\overline{P+\frac{r}{n}P-1}}{r-1}$ or $\frac{b}{a}\times\overline{P-Q}$; Therefore the Value required is $Q+\frac{b}{a}\times\overline{P-Q}$.

COROLLARY.

SINCE the Decrements of Life may without any ſenſible Error be ſuppoſed equal, for any ſhort Interval of Time; it follows that if the whole Extent of Life be divided into ſeveral ſhorter Intervals, whether equal or unequal; the Values of *Annuities* for Life to be eſtimated from the Beginning of each of theſe Periods, may eaſily be calculated from the preceding *Theorem*, conformably to any *Tables of Obſervations*, and for any *Rate of Intereſt*.

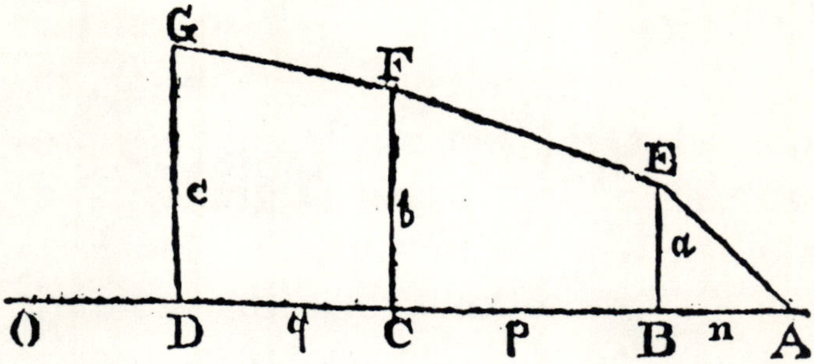

LET OA represent the whole Interval of Life, intercepted between the first Instant of Birth at O, to the Extremity of old Age at A.

LET that *Interval* OA be divided into smaller Intervals of Time, AB, BC, CD, *&c.* respectively equal to *n*, *p*, *q*, &c. during the Continuance of which, the Decrements of Life considered from the respective Terms B, C, D, *&c.* may be supposed to be equal; Let BE, CF, DG, *&c.* respectively equal to *a*, *b*, *c*, &c. represent the Number of Persons living in the Beginning of each of these Periods of Time.

THE Value of an *Annuity* for the Interval AB is given by the first *Problem*; Let it be called *A*.

THIS same Value estimated from the Term C, would be, according to the Rules of *Discount*, $\frac{A}{rp}$ if it was ſure the Life would continue during the Interval CB; but this being only probable according to that Degree of Probability, which is meaſured by the *Fraction* $\frac{a}{b}$, it follows that the abſolute Value of an *Annuity* to continne for the Time AB, and to be eſtimated from the Term C, is $\frac{a}{b} \times \frac{A}{rp}$; Now this Value being added to the Value of an *Annuity*, to continue during the Interval CB (which may be obtained by our ſecond *Problem*) the Sum will be the Value of an *Annuity* for the Interval CA.

IN the ſame Manner, this laſt Value, which we may call *B*, being eſtimated from the Term C, will be reduced to $\frac{b}{c} \times \frac{B}{rq}$; and this being added to the Value of an *Annuity* to continue during the Interval DC, the Sum will be the Value of an *Annuity* for the Interval DA.

AND by the ſame Method, the Value of *Annuities* may by Retrogreſſion be found for any Age not inferiour to Twelve.

AS for the firſt Twelve Years, the Proceſs may be as follows.

LET the Number ſet down in the *Tables*, over-againſt the 2*d*, 7*th*, and 12*th* Year, be ſeverally divided by the Number ſet down over-againg the firſt, and let the *Quotients* be ſeverally divided by r, r^6, r^{11}, which may be readily perform'd by *Logarithms*; Let the new Quotients be reſpectively called E, F, G, and let the Interval between the firſt and twelfth Year, *viz*. 11 be called q; then will the Value of an *Annuity* granted for that Interval of *Life* which begins at 1, and terminates at 12, be very near equal to

$$\frac{q+1}{3q} \times \overline{\tfrac{1}{2}q+1 \times E+G+2q-2 \times F}.$$

UPON the Principles hitherto explained, I have calculated the Values of *Annuities* for every 10th Year for an *Intereſt* of 5 *per Cent*. which are as follows,

Age.	Yrs. Purch.	Age.	Yrs. Purch.
76	3.78	36	12.20
66	6.46	26	13.60
56	8.88	16	14.84
46	10.62	6	15.21
		1	11.70

Of the Valuation of Annuities *upon ſeveral* Lives.

PROBLEM III.

SUPPOSING *a Fictitious* Life, *of which the Number of Chances to continue yearly, be conſtantly equal to* a, *and the Number of Chances to fail, conſtantly equal to* b; *ſo that the Odds of its continuing, during the Space of any one Year, be to its failing in that ſame Interval of Time as* a *to* b; *to find the Value of an* Annuity *upon ſuch a* Life.

SOLUTION.

LET 1 be the *Annuity*, *r* the *Rate of Intereſt*; make $a+b=s$.

IT is plain from what has been ſhewn already, that the preſent Value of the firſt Year's Rent is $\frac{a}{rs}$; of the Second $\frac{aa}{rrss}$, of the Third $\frac{a^3}{r^3s^3}$, *&c.* and ſo on; which Terms conſtituting a *Geometric Progreſſion*, the Sum of it, is $\frac{a}{rs-a}$.

THEREFORE 1° take the Number of Chances which the *Life* given has for its continuing one Year, and let that be made the *Numerator* of a *Fraction*.

2° MULTIPLY the Number of all the Chances both for the *Life*'s continuing and failing, by the *Rate of Interest*, and from the *Product* subtract the Number of Chances for its continuing, and let the *Remainder* be made the *Denominator* of the same *Fraction*.

3° DIVIDE the *Numerator* by the *Denominator*, and the *Quotient* will express the Value of an *Annuity*.

THUS if there was a *Life* so constituted as that the Chances of its continuing any one Year, were to the Chances of its failing in that Year, constantly as 21 to 1, the Value of an *Annuity* upon such a *Life* would be worth exactly 10 Years Purchase; *Interest* being supposed at 5 *per Cent.* as appears from the following Operation.

21 Number of Chances for continuing One Year, Numerator of the Fraction.

1 Chance for failing in that Year.

22 *Sum* of all the Chances, which multiply'd

by 1.05 *Rate* of *Interest*.

Product 23.1 from which subtract

21. Number of Chances for continuing

Remain[r.] 2.1 *Denominator* of the *Fraction*.

Fraction $\frac{21}{2.1}$ = 10 Years Purchase.

COROLLARY. I.

AN *Annuity* upon a fictitious *Life* being given, the Probability of its continuing any one Year is also given, for let the Value of such a *Life* be $= M$, then $\frac{a}{r-a} = M$, Therefore $\frac{a}{r} = \frac{Mr}{M+1}$, that is

IF the Value of the *Life* be multiply'd by the *Rate* of *Interest*, and the Product be divided by the Value of the *Life* increased by *Unity*, the Quotient will express the Probability of the *Life's* continuing one Year, or thus

1° MULTIPLY the Value of the *Life* by the *Rate* of *Interest*.

2° FROM the Value of the *Life* increased by *Unity* subtract the preceding Product.

THEN the Proportion of the Product to the Remainder, will express the Proportion of the Chances which the *Life* has for continuing one Year, to the Chances it has for failing in that Year.

COROLLARY II.

IF a real *Life*, whose Value as deduced from the *Tables* of *Observations*, be worth 10 Years Purchase; then such a Life is equivalent to a Fictitious *Life*, whose Chances for continuing one Year, are to the Chances of its failing in that Year, as 21 to 1.

COROLLARY III.

WHEREFORE, having calculated a *Life* from the *Tables* of *Observations*, and having obtained the true Value of it, we may transfer the Value of that *Life* to that of a Fictitious *Life*, and find the Number of Chances it would have to continue or to fail yearly.

COROLLARY IV.

AND the Combination of two or more *real Lives*, will be very near the same as the Combination of so many corresponding *fictitious Lives*, and therefore an *Annuity* granted upon two or more *real Lives*, will be very near the same as an *Annuity* granted upon so many corresponding *fictitious Lives*, and the Values of the Reversions granted upon the *real Lives*, will be very near the same as those granted upon the *fictitious Lives*.

PROBLEM IV.

THE *Values of two single* Lives *being given to find the Value of an* Annuity *granted for the Time of their Joint Continuance.*

SOLUTION.

LET the Values be respectively M and P, r the *Rate of Interest*; then the Value of an *Annuity* upon the two joint *Lives*, will be

$$\frac{MPr}{\overline{M+1}\times\overline{P+1}-MPr}$$; which may be thus expressed.

1° MULTIPLY together the Values of the Lives and the *Product* again by the *Rate of Interest*, and let the new *Product* be made the *Numerator* of a *Fraction*.

2° ADD *Unity* to each of the single Values, and let these two Values thus increased by *Unity* be multiplied together, and from the *Product* subtracting the *Numerator* before found, let the *Remainder* be made the *Denominator* of the said *Fraction*.

3° DIVIDE the *Numerator* by the *Denominator*, and the *Quotient* will be the Value of an *Annuity* to continue so long as both the *Lives* together are in being.

THUS it will be found that if the two *Lives* singly taken, be respectively worth 8 and 10 Years Purchase, the Value of an *Annuity* upon the two joint *Lives* will be worth 5.6 Years Purchase, as will appear by the following *Operation.*

8 Value of the first *Life.*
10 Value of the second

Product 80 which multiplied by the *Rate* of
Interest 1.05

84.0 new *Product*, *Numerator* of the *Fraction.*

9 first Value increased by 1
11 second Value increased by 1

Product 99
subtract 84. *Numerator* first found

Remain[r] 15 *Denominator* of the *Fraction.*

Fraction $\frac{84}{15}$

15) 84 (5.8 Value of the two *joint Lives.*

IN the same manner, it will be found that if the Values of the *single Lives* were respectively 10 and 12 Years

Purchase, the Value of an *Annuity* upon the two *joint Lives* would be 7.412 Years Purchase.

AND that if the Values upon the *single Lives* were respectively 8 and 12, the Values of an *Annuity* upon the two *joint Lives* would be 6.222 Years Purchase.

DEMONSTRATION.

LET x and y represent the respective Probabilities of the *Lives* continuing One Year, then the *Product* xy will express the Probability of their Joint continuance for One Year; and $xxyy$, the Probability of their Joint continuance for Two Years; and x^3y^3 the Probability of their Joint continuance for Three Years, and so on: Wherefore the Value of an *Annuity* granted for all the Time of their Joint continuance will be expressible by the following *Geometric Progression*, viz. $\frac{xy}{r} + \frac{xxyy}{rr} + \frac{x^3y^3}{r^3} + \frac{x^4y^4}{r^4}$ &c. whose Sum is $\frac{xy}{r-xy}$, but by the First *Corol-*

lary of the Third *Problem*, $x = \frac{Mr}{M+1}$, and by the same *Corollary*, $y = \frac{Pr}{P+1}$; Wherefore the Values of the two *joint Lives* is $\frac{MPr}{\overline{M+1} \times \overline{P+1} - MPr}$ as had been determined.

PROBLEM V.

THE Values of two *single Lives* being given, to find the Value of an *Annuity* upon the *longest* of them; that is to continue so long as either of them is in being.

SOLUTION.

FROM the Sum of the Values of the *single Lives*, subtract the Values of the two *joint Lives* found by the preceding *Problem*, the *Remainder* will be the Value of the *Annuity* required.

THUS if the two *Lives* singly taken be respectively worth 8 and 10 Years

Purchaſe, the two *joint Lives* by the preceding *Problem* will be worth 5.6; Therefore

From 18 Sum of the Values of the *ſingle Lives*
ſubtract 5.6 Value of the two *joint Lives.*

remains 12.4 Value of an *Annuity* upon the longeſt of them.

DEMONSTRATION.

LET x and y be the reſpective Probabilities of the *Lives* continuing One Year; then the Probability of their reſpective failing in that Year, are $1-x$, and $1-y$, which multiplied together, the *Product viz.* $1-x-y+xy$ exhibits the Probability of their both failing in that Year, and this ſubtracted from Unity, the *Remainder*, viz. $x+y-xy$, expreſſes the Probability of one of them at leaſt ſurviving the Year, and for the ſame Reaſon, the Terms $xx+yy-xxyy$ expreſs the Probability of One of them at leaſt ſurviving Two Years, and ſo on:

From whence ariſe the following *Geometric Progreſſions*, expreſſing the Value of an *Annuity* upon the *longeſt* of the two *Lives*, viz.

$$\frac{x}{r}+\frac{xx}{rr}+\frac{x^3}{r^3}+\frac{x^4}{r^4}+\frac{x^5}{r^5}\ \&c.$$

$$+\frac{y}{r}+\frac{yy}{rr}+\frac{y^3}{r^3}+\frac{y^4}{r^4}+\frac{y^5}{r^5}\ \&c.$$

$$-\frac{xy}{r}-\frac{xxyy}{rr}-\frac{x^3y^3}{r^3}-\frac{x^4y^4}{r^4}-\frac{x^5y^5}{r^5}\ \&c.$$

of which the firſt is the Value of the firſt *Life* ſingly taken; the ſecond is the Value of the ſecond *Life* ſingly taken; and the third is the Value of an *Annuity* upon the two *joint* Lives, and therefore the Value of an *Annuity* upon the *longeſt* of two *Lives*, is the Sum of the Values of the two *Lives* leſſened by the Values of the two *joint Lives*.

PROBLEM VI.

THE *Values of three ſingle* Lives *being given to find the Value of an* Annuity *granted for the Time of their Joint Continuance*.

SOLUTION.

LET the ſingle Values be reſpectively *M*, *P*, *Q*; *r* the *Rate* of *Intereſt*; then the Value of an *Annuity* upon the three *joint Lives* will be

$$\frac{MPQrr}{\overline{M+1}\times\overline{P+1}\times\overline{Q+1}-MPQrr}$$

which may be expreſſed as follows.

1° MULTIPLY the Values of all the ſingle Lives together, and the Product again by the Square of the *Rate* of *Intereſt*, and let the Product be made the Numerator of a Fraction.

2° ADD Unity to each of the ſingle Lives, and let all the Values thus increaſed by Unity be multiplied together; and from the *Product* ſubtracting the *Numerator* before found, let the *Remainder* be made the *Denominator* of the ſame *Fraction*.

3° DIVIDE the *Numerator* by the *Denominator*, and the *Quotient* will be the Value of an *Annuity* upon the three *joint Lives*.

THUS it will be found, that if the three Lives singly taken, be respectively worth 8, 10 and 12 Years Purchase, the Value of an *Annuity* upon the three *joint* Lives will be 4.630 as will appear by the following *Operation*.

8 Value of the first *Life*.
10 Value of the second.
12 Value of the third.

960 Product of the three Values, which multiplied
by 1.1025 Square of the *Rate* of *Interest*.
New *Product* 1058.4 *Numerator* of the *Fraction*.

9 Value of the first Life increased by 1.
11 Value of the second increased by 1.
13 Value of the third increased by 1.

Product 1287 from which subtracting
1058.4 *Numerator* before found.

remains 228.6, *Demominator*.

Fraction $\frac{1058.4}{228.6}$

228.6) 1058.4 (4.630 Value of the three *joint Lives*.

DEMONSTRATION.

LET x, y, z, represent the respective Probabilities of the *Lives* continuing one Year; then the *Product* xyz will express the Probability of their joint Continuance for one Year; and $xxyyzz$ the Probability of their joint Continuance for two Years; and $x^3 y^3 z^3$, the Probability of their joint Continuance for three Years, and so on. Wherefore the Value of an *Annuity* granted for the whole Time of their joint Continuance will be expressible by the following *Geometric Progression*, viz.

$$\frac{xyz}{r} + \frac{x^2 y^2 z^2}{rr} + \frac{x^3 y^3 z^3}{r^3} + \frac{x^4 y^4 z^4}{r^4} \ \&c.$$

the Sum of whose Terms is $\frac{xyz}{r - xyz}$; but by the First *Corollary* of the Third *Problem* $x = \frac{Mr}{M+1}$, $y = \frac{Pr}{P+1}$, $z = \frac{Qr}{Q+1}$. Wherefore the Value of the three *joint Lives* is

$$\frac{MPQrr}{\overline{M+1}\times\overline{P+1}\times\overline{Q+1}-MPQrr}$$

as had been determined.

PROBLEM VII.

THE *Values of three single* Lives *being given to find the Value of an* Annuity *upon the longest of them.*

SOLUTION.

FROM the Sum of the Values of the *single Lives*, subtract the Sum of the Values of all the *joint Lives* combined Two and Two; to the *Remainder* add the Value of the three *joint Lives*, the Sum will be the Value of an *Annuity* upon the longest of them.

THUS, if the three *Lives* singly taken be respectively worth 8, 10 and 12 Years Purchase, it will be found that the Value of an *Annuity* upon the longest of them will be worth 15.396 Years Purchase, as will appear by the following *Operation.*

8 Value of the firſt *Life.*
10 Value of the ſecond.
12 Value of the third.

30 Sum of all the ſingle Values.

5.6 Value of the firſt and ſecond jointly taken, as may be deduced from the Fourth *Problem.*

6.222 Value of the firſt and third.

7.412 Value of the ſecond and third.

19.234 Sum of all the Values combined Two and Two; which being ſubtracted from 30 Sum of all the ſingle Values.

remains 10.766 to which adding
4.630 Value of the three joint *Lives.*

Sum 15.396 Value of the *Annuity* upon the longeſt *Life.*

DEMONSTRATION.

LET x, y, z, represent the respective Probabilities of the *Lives* continuing one Year; then the Probabilities of their respective failing in that Year are $1 - x$, $1 - y$, $1 - z$; which being multiplied together the *Product*, viz. $1 - x - y - z + xy + xz + yz - xyz$, will express the Probability of their all failing in that Year, and this subtracted from *Unity*, the *Remainder*, viz. $x + y + z - xy - xz - yz + xyz$ will express the Probability of their not all failing in that Year, ; otherwise, the Probability of one of the *Lives* at least surviving the Year, from whence, by following the *Step* of the Fifth *Problem*, may be deduced the Rule delivered in this *Problem*.

COROLLARY I.

AND by the same way of arguing, will be easily found the Value of an *Annuity* upon as many *Lives* as may be aſſigned; for if from the Sum of the Values of all the *Lives* be ſubtracted the Sum of the Values of all the *joint Lives* combined Two and Two, and to the *Remainder* be added the Sum of the Values of all the *joint Lives* combined Three and Three; and from this laſt Sum be ſubtracted the Sum of the Values of all the *joint Lives* combined Four and Four, and ſo on, (adding and ſubtracting alternately) the laſt Reſult will exhibit the Value of an *Annuity* upon the laſt of the *given Lives*.

AND as the Method taken in the *Solution* of the Fourth and Sixth *Problems*, for finding the Values of Two and Three *joint Lives* may, by bare Inſpection, be carried on for finding the Values of as many *joint Lives* as may be aſſigned, ſo it appears that there remains no Difficulty in the *Solution* of the Caſe propoſed in the preſent *Corollary*.

COROLLARY II.

IF all the *Lives* be equal, the *Operations* neceſſary to the *Solution* of the *Problem* will conſiderably be ſhortened, for let M', M'', M''', M'''' be the reſpective Values of one *ſingle Life*, two, three, and Four *joint Lives*; then the Value of an *Annuity* upon the longeſt of the four *Lives* will be
$4M' - 6M'' + 4M''' - M''''$; in which the Numerical Quantities are the Coefficients of a Binomial, whoſe Index is equal to the Number of the *Lives* given.

REMARK.

TO the End that the *Readers* may be freed from any Scruple they may entertain, that the converting *real Lives* into *fictitious* ones, and then combining them together, from thence to deduce the Values of *Annuities* upon the *real Lives*, may perhaps not be altogether to be truſted to; I ſhall here annex a Calculation of an *Annuity* upon two *Lives* whose Decrements are in *Arithmetic Progression*; which consequently very nearly agree with the Values as deduced from the *Tables*; and then compare the Result with the Value of an *Annuity* upon the two *Lives* considered as *fictitious*.

LET the Difference between the first Age and 86 be supposed $= n$, and the Difference between the second and 86 $= p$; let the Value of an *Annuity* certain for the Number of Years n be supposed $= N$, and the Value of an *Annuity* certain for the Number of Years p $= P$; then the Value of an *Annuity* upon the two *Lives* will be

$$\frac{1 - \frac{r}{n}\overline{N+P}}{r-1} + \frac{2rp - Prr - Pr}{\overline{r-1}^{2}}.$$

SUPPOSING now $n = 50$, $p = 40$, and $r = 1.05$, the Value of an *Annuity* upon the two *Lives* will be found to be 14.53, as may easily be derived from the foregoing *Cannon*.

AGAIN, if n be $= 50$, and $p = 40$, then by the first *Problem* the Value of an *Annuity* upon the first *Life* will be 12.332, and the Value of an *Annuity* upon the ſecond will be 10.191; let theſe two *Lives* be conſidered as *fictitious*, then by the Fifth *Problem* the Value of an *Annuity* upon both will be found to be 14.55; which differs from the preceding Value only by 0.02.

IF any Perſon has the Curioſity of calculating the Value of an *Annuity* upon two or three *Lives*, as it may be deduced from the *Tables*, the eaſieſt way of doing it will be firſt to calculate the Values of the *ſingle* and of the *joint Lives*, and then to combine them in the ſame manner as has been done for the *fictitious Lives*; we have ſhewn already how to compute the Values of the *ſingle Lives*, as deduced from the *Tables*; now in order to eſtimate in the ſame manner the Values of the *joint Lives*, nothing more is requiſite than to follow the *Steps* of the Method employed in eſtimating the Values of the *joint Lives* conſidered as *fictitious*; with this Difference, that inſtead of the Quantity x, there ought to be written a *Fraction*, whoſe *Numerator* be the Number in the *Tables*, anſwering to the next Year above the Age given, and the *Denominator* the Number anſwering to the Age given; and inſtead of $x\,x$ ought to be written a *Fraction*, whoſe *Numerator* be the Number in the *Tables*, anſwering to the ſecond Year above the Age given, and the *Denominater* ſtill the Number anſwering to the Age given, and ſo on; the like being alſo to be done for z and y, then inſtead of the Terms of *Geometric Progreſſion*, there will be a *finite* Number of Terms to be ſummed up by vulgar Addition.

Of *REVERSIONS.*

PROBLEM VII.

TO *find the Value of the Reverſion of one* Life *after another.*

SOLUTION.

FROM the Value of the two *Lives*, ſubtract the Value of that *Life* which is in Poſſeſſion, there will remain the Value of the *Life* in Reversion; thus if the Value of the *Life* in Possession be worth Ten Years Purchase, and the Value of the other *Life* be worth 8 Years Purchase, then by *Problem* V. the Value of the two *Lives*, (by which is meant the Value of an *Annuity* upon the longest of the two *Lives*) will be 12.4, from which subtracting the Value of the *Life* in Possession, *viz.* 10, there will remain 2.4 for the Value of the Reversion, but if the second *Life* be in Possession, then the Reversion will be worth 4.4.

PROBLEM VIII.

To find the Value of the Reversion of one Life *after two.*

SOLUTION.

FROM the Value of the three *Lives*, subtract the Value of the two *Lives* in Possession, there will remain the Value of the *Life* in Reversion; thus if the three *Lives* be worth 12, 10 and 8 Years Purchase, and the first *Life* be in Reversion, then from the Value of the three *Lives*, *viz.* 15.396 subtracting the Value of the two *Lives* in Possession, *viz.* 12.4 the Remainder, *viz.* 2.996 will be the Value of the first *Life* in Reversion; but if the second *Life* be in Reversion, it will be found to be 1.618, and if the third be in Reversion, it will be but 0.808.

PROBLEM IX.

T*O find the Value of the Reversion of two* Lives *after one.*

SOLUTION.

FROM the Value of the three *Lives*, subtract the Value of the *Live* in Possession, there will remain the Value of the two *Lives* in Reversion; thus if the three *Lives* be respectively 12, 10 and 8 Years Purchase, the Value of the three *Lives* will be 15.396 from which ſubtracting ſeverally the three *Lives* 12, 10 and 8, the three Remainders, *viz.* 3.396, 5.396, 7.396 will expreſs the reſpective Values of the ſecond and third after the firſt, of the firſt and third after the ſecond, and of the firſt and ſecond after the third.

PROBLEM X.

TO *find the Value of the Reverſion of one* Life, *after two* joint Lives.

SOLUTION.

FROM the Value of *Life* in Expectation, ſubtract the Value of the two *joint Lives* in Poſſeſſion, there remains the Value of the Reverſion.

PROBLEM XI.

TO *find the Value of the Reverſion of two* joint Lives *after one.*

SOLUTION.

FROM the Value of the two *joint Lives* in Expectation, ſubtract the Value of the three *joint Lives*, there remains the Value required.

THUS, ſuppoſe three Perſons, A, B, C; that C is in Poſſeſſion, and that A expects the Reverſion of an *Annuity*, after the *Life* of C, to be by him enjoyed no longer than whilſt he and B continue in being; then the Value of ſuch Reverſion to A, will be the Value of the *joint Lives* of himſelf and B, leſſened by the Value of the three *joint Lives*, and that Reverſion to B, would be of the ſame Value as it is to A.

PROBLEM XII.

IF A, B, C *agree amongſt themſelves to buy an* Annuity *to be by them equally divided, whilſt they live together, then to be divided equally between the two next*

Survivours, then to belong intirely to the last Survivour for Life, *to find what each of them ought to contribute towards the Purchase.*

SOLUTION.

LET the whole *Annuity* be 1 *l.* then,

1° A expects an *Annuity* of $\frac{1}{3}$*l.* upon the three *joint Lives* of himself, B and C; the Value of which Expectation is to be found by *Problem* V.

2° HE expects the Reversion of $\frac{1}{2}$*l.* a Year after the *Life* of C, so long as he and B are in being; the Value of which is to be found by *Problem* XI.

3° HE expects the Reversion of $\frac{1}{2}$ *l.* a Year after the *Life* of B, to be by him enjoyed so long as he and C are in being; the Value of which is found also by *Problem* XI.

4° HE expects the Reversion of 1 *l.* a Year, to be by him enjoyed for his *Life*, after the *Lives* of B and C; the Value of which Expectation, may be determined by *Problem* VIII.

WHEREFORE adding all these Expectations together, the Sum will be the Share which A, ought to contribute towards the Purchase.

AND in the like Manner, may the Shares of B and C be determined.

BUT all the preceding *Operations* may be contracted into a narrower Compass, as follows:

FROM *Unity* subtract $\frac{1}{2}$ the Sum of the Values of the *single Lives* of B and C; and to Remainder add $\frac{1}{3}$ of the Value of their *joint Lives*, the Sum multiplied by the Value of the *Life* of A, the *Product* will be the Share which A ought to contribute,

And the like may be done for B and C.

PROBLEM XIII.

IF B *and* C, *expect the Reversion of an* Annuity *after the* Life *of* A, *and this* Annuity *is to be by them equally enjoyed so long as they both continue in being, then entirely to belong to the last Survivour for*

Life; *to find what Proportion of the Purchase both* B *and* C *ought to contribute.*

SOLUTION.

LET the whole *Annuity* be 1.

1° B expects after the *Life* of A, the Reversion of an *Annuity* to be by him enjoyed as long as he and C both continue in being; the Value of which Expectation is to be found by *Probelm* XI.

2° HE expects after the *Lives* of A and C, the Reversion of an *Annuity* of 1*l.* for his *Life*, the Value of which Expectation is found by *Problem* VIII.

WHEREFORE adding these two Expectations together, the Sum will be the Share which B ought to contribute, towards the Purchase of the Reversion.

AND in the like Manner may the Share of C be determined.

THE Contractions that may be made in these *Operations* are so inconsiderable that they are not worth mentioning.

OF

SUCCESSIVE LIVES.

PROBLEM XIV.

If A *enjoys an* Annuity *for his* Life, *and at his Decease has the Nomination of a Successor who is likewise to enjoy the* Annuity *for his* Life; *to find the Value of the two* Successive Lives.

SOLUTION.

LET the Values of the *Lives* considered separately be respectively M and P; *r* the Rate of Interest, and *a* the Interest of One Pound; then the Value of the two *Successive Lives* will be $\frac{r - \overline{1 - aM} \times \overline{1 - aP}}{ra}$; which may be thus expressed.

MULTIPLY each given *Life* by the Intereſt of One Pound, and ſubtract each *Product* from *Unity*; let the two *Remainders* be multiplied together, and the *Product* ſubtracted from the *Rate* of *Intereſt*; then the *Remainder* being divided by the *Rate* of *Intereſt* multiplyed by the *Intereſt* of One Pound, the *Quotient* will give the Value of the two *Succeſſive Lives*.

PROBLEM XV.

THREE *Lives* M, P, Q, *being given in Succeſſion, to find their Value.*

SOLUTION.

LET r and a ſtand for the ſame Quantities as in the preceding *Problem*; then the Value ſought will be $\frac{rr - \overline{1 - aM} \times \overline{1 - aP} \times \overline{1 - aQ}}{rra}$; which may be thus expreſſed.

MULTIPLY each given *Life* by the Intereſt of One Pound, and ſubtract the ſeveral *Products* from Unity; let the three *Remainders* be multiplied together, and the *Product* ſubtracted from the Square of the Rate of Intereſt, then the *Remainder* being divided by the Square of the Rate of Intereſt multiplyed by the Intereſt of One Pound, the *Quotient* will be the Value ſought.

AND the ſame Rule may be extended to four, five or as many *Lives* as may be aſſigned; the *Diviſor* for four *Lives* being to be the *Product* of the Cube of the Rate of Intereſt, by the Intereſt of One Pound, and ſo on.

PROBLEM XVI.

IF there be three equal Lives, *and* A *or his Heirs are to have the Sum* ſ *paid them upon the Vacancy of any of thoſe* Lives, *what is the Expectation of* A *worth in preſent Money.*

SOLUTION.

1° LET the Value of one *Life* increaſed by Unity be raiſed to its Cube.

2° MULTIPLY the Value of one *Life* by the Rate of Intereſt, and let the *Product* be raiſed to its Cube.

3° FROM the firſt Cube ſubtract the ſecond, and keep the *Remainder.*

4° MULTIPLY the firſt Cube by the Rate of Intereſt, and from the *Product* ſubtract the ſecond Cube, then keep the *Remainder.*

5° MULTIPLY the firſt *Remainder* by the Sum to be paid, and divide the Product by the ſecond *Remainder*; then the Quotient will expreſs the preſent Value of the Expectation required.

THUS ſuppoſe that each *Life* is worth Ten Years Purchaſe, and that 100 *l.* is to be paid upon the Vacancy of any one of the *Lives*; to find the Value of that Sum in preſent Money.

11. Value of one *Life* increaſed by Unity.

Its Cube 1331.

10. Value of one *Life.*

multiply by 1.05 Rate of Intereſt.

Product	10.5	
its Cube	1157.625	which subtracted from the preceding Cube
First *Remain*^{r}.	173.375	
First *Cube*	1331.	
Rate of Int.	1.05	
Product	1397.55	
subtract	1157.625	second Cube.
2d *Remaind.*	239.925	
1st *Remaind.*	173.375	
Multiply by	100.	Sum to be paid.
Product	17337.5	

239.925) 17337.500 (74. present Value of the Expectation.

DEMONSTRATION.

LET x be the Probability that any one of the *Lives* may continue one Year.

THEN, the Probability that all the *Lives* may continue one Year is x^3, therefore the Probability that some of them may fail the first Year is $1 - x^3$,

THE Probability that all the *Lives* may continue one Year, and then that some of them may fail the next Year is $x^3 \times \overline{1 - x^3}$.

THE Probability that all the *Lives* may continue two Years, and then that some of them may fail on the third Year is $x^6 \times \overline{1 - x^3}$.

WHEREFORE the Value of A's Expectation is $\overline{\frac{1}{r} + \frac{x^3}{rr} + \frac{x^6}{r^3} + \frac{x^9}{r^4}}$, &c. $\times \overline{1 - x^3} \times f$ the Sum of which is $\frac{f}{r - x^3} \times \overline{1 - x^3}$; but $x = \frac{Mr}{M+1}$, therefore the Value of A's Expectation is $\frac{\overline{M+1}|^3 - M^3 r^3}{\overline{M+1}|^3 \times r - M^3 r^3} \times f$.

PROBLEM XVII.

IF A *buys an* Annuity *upon three equal* Lives, *and he obliges himself that in Case one* Life *becomes vacant he shall renew it for the Sum* a; *in Case two* Lives *become vacant in the same Year, he shall renew them both for the Sum* b; *and in Case they all become vacant in the same Year, he shall renew them all three for the Sum* c; *to find how much it is that the whole Purchase is estimated.*

Solution *of the first* Case.

1° FROM the Value of one *Life* increased by Unity, subtract the Product of the Value of one *Life* by the Rate of Interest.

2° MULTIPLY the Remainder by three times the Square of that Product, and let the new Product be made the Numerator of a Fraction.

3° LET the Value of one *Life* increased by Unity, be raised to its Cube, and multiply that Cube by the Interest of one Pound, then let the Product be made the Denominator of that Fraction.

4° THIS Fraction being multiplyed by the Sum agreed to be given for the renewing of one *Life*, the Product will be the present Value of all the Renewals of one *Life*, that may be made for ever.

Solution *of the ſecond* Caſe.

1° FROM the Value of one *Life* increaſed by Unity, ſubtract the Product of the Value of one *Life* by the Rate of Intereſt.

2° LET the Remainder be raiſed to its Square, and let that Square be multiplyed by three Times the Product abovementioned, and let the new Product be made the Numerator of a Fraction.

3° LET the Value of one *Life* increaſed by Unity be raiſed to its Cube, and multiply that Cube by the Intereſt of one Pound, then let the Product be made Denominator of the *Fraction* abovementioned.

4° THIS *Fraction* being multiplyed by the Sum agreed to be given for the renewing of two *Lives*, the Product will be the preſent Value of all the Renewals of two *Lives* that may be made in the ſame Year for ever.

Solution *of the third* Case.

1° FROM the Value of One *Life* increased by Unity, subtract the Product of the Value of one *Life* by the *Rate* of *Interest*.

2° LET the Remainder be raised to its Cube, and let that Cube be made Numerator of a Fraction.

3° LET the Denominator of that Fraction be the same as the Denominators of the Two preceding Cases.

4° THE Fraction being multiply'd by the Sum agreed to be given for the renewing of Three *Lives*, the Product will be the present Value of all the Renewals of three *Lives* that may be made in the same Year for ever.

AND the Three several Sums resulting from the *Solution* of these Three *Cases*, being added with the present Value of the Three *Lives*, the Sum of the whole will be the Value of the whole Purchase.

DEMONSTRATION.

LET x represent the Probability of each *Life*'s continuing one Year, M the Value of one *Life* and r the Rate of Intereſt.

THE Probability that Two of the Three *Lives* may continue one Year, and the third become vacant, is $3xx \times \overline{1-x}$.

WHEREFORE the Sum, which A may happen to give at the Year's end for renewing one *Life* eſtimated in preſent Money is $\frac{3xx \times \overline{1-x}}{r} a$.

SUPPOSE that *Live* renewed, then the Probability that one of the Three *Lives* may become vacant the next Year is again $3xx \times \overline{1-x}$.

WHEREFORE the Sum which A may happen to give at the End of the ſecond Year, for renewing one *Life* eſtimated in preſent Money, is $\frac{3xx \times \overline{1-x}}{rr} a$.

IN the like Manner, the Sum which *A* may happen to give at the End of the third Year estimated in present Money, is $\frac{3xx\times\overline{1-x}}{r^3}$.

FROM whence it follows, that all the Sums which *A* may happen to give from Time to Time for the renewing of one Life estimated in present Money, are

$$\frac{3xx\times\overline{1-x}}{r-1}a=\frac{3MMrr\times\overline{M+1-Mr}}{\overline{M+1}^3\times\overline{r-1}}a.$$

THE probability that one of the Three Lives may continue one Year, and the other two become vacant, is $3x\times\overline{1-x}^2$.

WHEREFORE the Sum which *A* may happen to give at the Year's End for the renewing of two Lives, estimated in present Money, is worth $\frac{3x\times\overline{1-x}^2}{r}b$

AND for the same Reason, the Sum which he may happen to give at the end of two Years for the renewing of Two Lives, estimated in present Money, is $\frac{3x\times\overline{1-x}^2}{rr}b$, and so on.

From whence it follows, that all the Sums which *A* may happen to give from Time to Time, for the renewing of Two Lives, eſtimated in preſent Money, are

$$\frac{3x \times \overline{1-x}}{r-1}\, b = 3Mr \times \frac{\overline{M+1-Mr}^3}{\overline{M+1}^3 \times \overline{r-1}}\, b.$$

The Probability that the Three *Lives* may be vacant the firſt Year, is $\overline{1-x}^3$.

From whence it follows that all the Sums which *A* may happen to give from Time to Time for the renewing of Three Lives, eſtimated in preſent Money, are $\frac{\overline{M+1-Mr}^3}{\overline{M+1}^3 \times \overline{r-1}}\, c.$

REMARK.

If one Life be eſtimated at Nine Years Purchaſe; then the Value of two equal *Lives* is 12.3111, and the Value of three equal *Lives* is 14.0281: Wherefore what *A* ought in Juſtice to give for the renewing of One *Life* is 1.7170, what he ought to give for the renewing of Two is 5.0281; and what he ought to give for the renewing of Three is 14.0281 if he loſes the laſt Year's Rent; or 15.0281 if he receives it. Let us therefore ſuppoſe that in the foregoing *Problem*, $a = 1.7170$, $b = 5.0281$, $c = 15.0281$; then what *A* ought in Juſtice to give in preſent Money for the renewing of One *Life* for ever, is 5.0600; what he ought to give for the renewing of Two for ever, is 0.8624; and what he ought to give for the renewing of Three for ever is, 0.0500, the Sum of all which, *viz.* 5.9724 being added to 14.0281 Value of the three *Lives*, the Sum is 20, which makes up the whole Purchaſe of an *Annuity* bought for ever, *Intereſt* being ſuppoſed at 5 *per Cent.*

SUPPOSING now that one *Life* being eſtimated at Nine Years Purchaſe as before, what is given for the renewing One, Two and Three *Lives* ſhould be reſpectively 3, 5 and 15.0281 Years Purchaſe, or that inſtead of renewing the Three *Lives*, whenever they happen to be vacant in the ſame Year, the right of the *Annuity* ſhould return to the firſt Proprietor; then it will be found by the Rules above delivered that the whole Purchase is estimated at 24.1197 Years Purchase.

PROBLEM XVIII.

THE *same Things being given as in the preceding* Problem, *suppose it be agreed that instead of renewing One* Life *for the Sum* a, *whenever it happens to be vacant, the Purchaser shall constantly pay that same Sum* a *at a Certainty, at equal Intervals of Time; to find at what Intervals it ought to be paid.*

SOLUTION.

1° FROM the Value of One *Life* increased by Unity, subtract the Product of the Value of one *Life* multiplyed by the Rate of Interest.

2° MULTIPLY the *Remainder* by three Times the Square of that Product, and let the new Product be made the Numerator of a Fraction.

3° LET the Value of One *Life* increased by Unity be raised to its Cube, and let that Cube be made the Denominator of the Fraction.

4° TO the Quotient of the Numerator divided by the Denominator, add the Intereſt of One Pound, then find the Logarithm of that Sum.

5° FROM that Logarithm ſubtract the Logarithm of the Fraction before-mentioned, and let the Remainder be divided by the Logarithm of the Rate of Intereſt; the Quotient will be the Number of Years ſought.

DEMONSTRATION.

THE firſt Renewal of One *Life* may happen to be at the End of the firſt Year, whereof the Probability is $3xx \times \overline{1-x}$; let that Quantity for Brevity's Sake be called S; therefore the preſent Value of the Renewal of one *Life* ariſing from the Expectation of its happening in the firſt Year, is $\frac{S}{r}\ a$.

THE Probability of the firſt Renewal's being in the ſecond Year, is $S \times \overline{1-S}$; wherefore the preſent Value of the firſt Renewal ariſing from the Expectation of its happening in the ſecond Year is $\frac{S \times \overline{1-S}}{rr}\,a$.

AND for the ſame Reaſon, the preſent Value of the firſt Renewal ariſing from the Expectation of its happening in the third Year is $\frac{S \times \overline{1-S}^2}{r^3}\,a$, and ſo on.

FROM whence it follows, that the preſent Value of the firſt Renewal ariſing from the Expectation of its happening at any Time is expreſſible by the following *Geometric Progreſſion*, viz.

$$\frac{S}{r}a + \frac{S + \overline{1-S}}{rr}a + \frac{S \times \overline{1-S}^2}{r^3}a$$

$+ \frac{S \times \overline{1-S}^3}{r^4}a$, &c. whoſe Sum is $\frac{S}{r-1+S}a$.

LET now, n be the Number of Years ſuppoſed to be intercepted between the the preſent Time, and the Time of the firſt Renewal; then the

Quantity $\frac{S}{r-1+S}a$ before found being put out at Interest for that Number of Years n, ought to produce the Sum a; then according to the Rules of *Compound Interest*, $\frac{S}{r-1+S}ar^n = a$ or $\frac{S}{r-1+S}r^n = 1$. Wherefore $n = \frac{Log.\overline{r-1+S}-Log.S}{Log.r}$; then instead of S, writing its Value $3xx \times \overline{1-x}$, and instead of x writing its Value $\frac{Mr}{M+1}$, the Reason of the Rule given in Words at length, will evidently appear.

COROLLARY I.

THE present Value of the first Renewal of one *Life* being $\frac{a}{r^n}$, the present Value of the Second will be $\frac{a}{r^{2n}}$; of the Third $\frac{a}{r^{3n}}$, &c. Wherefore the present Value of all the Renewals for ever is $\frac{a}{r^n-1}$, and in the room of r^n, substituting its Value $\frac{r-1+S}{S}a$, the preſent Value of all the Renewals of one *Life*, will be $\frac{S}{r-1}a = \frac{3xx \times \overline{1-x}}{r-1}a$, which is the ſame Concluſion that was drawn in the *Solution* of the preceding *Problem* by a Method different from this.

COROLLARY II.

IN the ſame manner may the renewing of Two or Three *Lives* be compounded for by equal Payments made at equal Intervals of Time.

COROLLARY III.

AND theſe Three Setts of Intervals may be reduced to One ſingle Interval, of which the Duration may be determined.

Of the Expectation of Life *and the Probability of Survivourſhip.*

THE Queſtions that may be formed about the Expectation of *Life*, and the Probability of Survivourſhip being independent from the Conſideration of the *Rate* of *Intereſt*, we have thought fit to treat this Subject by it ſelf, and ſhew how to make a very near Eſtimation of both by Dr. HALLEY's *Tables*, or any other *Tables* that may happen to be conſtructed from Obſervations.

BUT becauſe, as I have already obſerved ſomewhere elſe, the Decrements of *Life* are for any ſmall Interval of Time nearly in *Arithmetic Progreſſion*, it will not be improper to conſider what would be the Conſequence of an Hypotheſis that ſhould make the Decrements of *Life*, throughout the whole extent of it, to be in *Arithmetic Progreſſion*, and then ſhew how ſuch an Hypotheſis ought to be corrected from the *Tables* of *Obſervations*.

DEFINITION.

I Call that the Complement of *Life*, which is the Time comprehended between an Age given, and the Extremity of Old Age.

THUS if the Age be 50, and the Extremity of Old Age be 86, the Complement of *Life* is 36.

HYPOTHESIS.

A B C D E F G ——————— S

LET it be ſuppoſed that the Complement of *Life* A S being divided into an infinite Number of equal Parts, repreſenting Moments; the Probabilities of living from A to B, from A to C, from A to D, *&c.* are reſpectively proportional to the ſeveral Complements S B, S C, S D; in ſo much that theſe Probabilities may reſpectively be repreſented by the *Fractions*, $\frac{SB}{SA}$, $\frac{SC}{SA}$, $\frac{SD}{SA}$, &c. This Hypotheſis being admitted, the following *Corollaries* may be deduced from it.

COROLLARY I.

THE Probability of *Life*'s failing in any Interval of Time A F, is meaſured by the *Fraction* $\frac{FA}{SA}$.

COROLLARY II.

WHEN the Interval AF is once paſt, the Probability of *Life's* continuing from F to G is $\frac{SG}{SF}$ (for at F, the Complement of *Life* is SF) and the Probability of its failing in the Interval FG is $\frac{FG}{SF}$.

COROLLARY III.

THE Probability of *Life's* continuing from A to F, and then failing from F to G is $\frac{SF}{SA} \times \frac{FG}{SF} = \frac{FG}{AS}$.

COROLLARY IV.

THE Probabilities of *Life's* failing in any Two or more equal Intervals of Time aſſigned between A and S are exactly the ſame, the Eſtimation being made at A, conſidered as the preſent Time.

PROBLEM XIX.

To find how long it may be expected that a Life of a given Age may continue in Being.

SOLUTION.

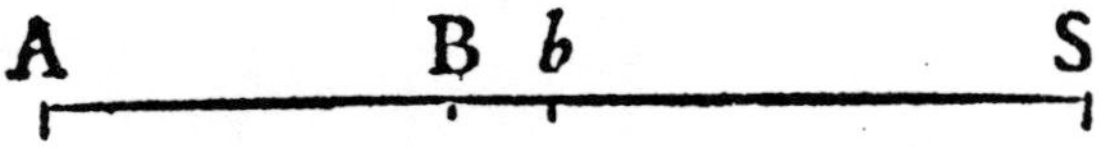

IN the Interval AS take any Term B at Pleasure, and next to it another Term b, so that the Distance Bb may represent a Moment of Time; let the whole Interval AS be called n, the Interval AB, z, and the Moment Bb, o.

WHEN the *Life* given has continued from A to B, the Thing immediately expected is the Moment Bb, but the Probability of its continuing from A to B is $\frac{n-z}{n}$ by Hypothesis, and the Moment expected is o.

THEREFORE the Value of the Expectation of the Moment o is $\frac{n-z}{n} \times o$: Consider now $\frac{n-z}{n}$ as the Ordinate of a Curve raised perpetually upon the Abcine z; then the Area of that Curve, *viz.* $\frac{nz - \frac{1}{2}zz}{n}$ will express the Right or Expectation of the *Life* given upon the Interval AB: Let now n be written instead of z, and the Value of the *Fraction* will become $\frac{1}{2}n$.

WHEREFORE the Number of Years that a *Life* given may expect to continue in Being is equal to the Number of Years contained in half the Complement of the said *Life*; that if the Age given be 40, and the Extremity of Old Age be supposed at 86, the Complement of the *Life* is 46 whereof the Half 23 is the Number of Years it may be expected to continue after 40.

BUT if that *Life* once reaches 63, then it may expect 11 $\frac{1}{2}$ Years more;

and if it reach 74 $\frac{1}{2}$, then may expect 5 $\frac{3}{4}$ more, and so on.

COROLLARY I.

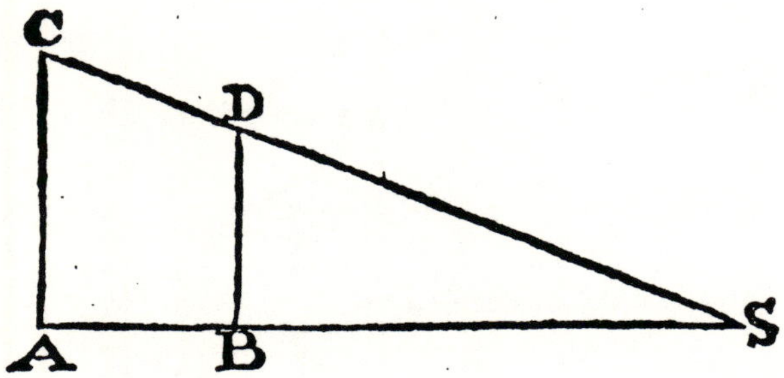

SUPPOSE the Parallels AC and BD terminated in C and D to represent the Number of Persons of two different Ages according to the *Table of Observations*, and AB the Number of Years between those Ages; draw the Line CD 'till it meet the Line AB in S, let AS be supposed $= n$, AB $= z$, AC $= a$, BD $= b$: now since the Triangles CAS, DBS are similar, it follows that

AC — BD, AB : : AC, AS, that is,
$a - b, \quad z \quad : : \quad a, \quad n$

THEREFORE $n = \frac{az}{a-b}$. But the Expectation of the *Life* at A upon the Interval AB has been found to be $\frac{nz - \frac{1}{2}zz}{n}$; Wherefore writing $\frac{az}{a-b}$ in the room of n, that Expectation will be found to be $\frac{\frac{1}{2}a + \frac{1}{2}b}{a}z$.

COROLLARY II.

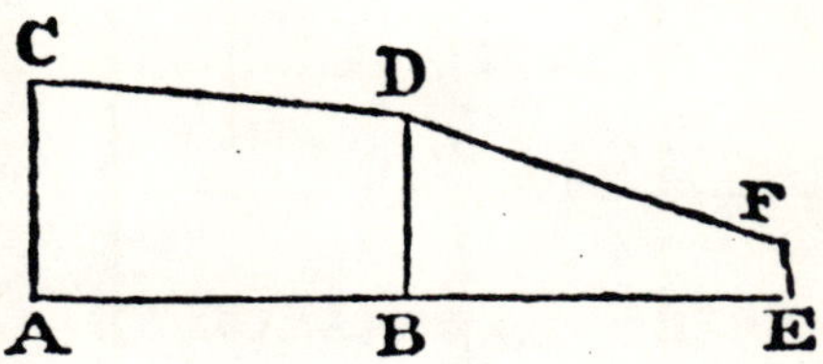

LET also AC, BD, EF; the the Number of Persons of three different Ages as taken from the *Tables* of *Observations*, which Numbers we suppose respectively denominated by a, b, c; let AB, BE represent Two equal Intervals of Time, intercepted between those Ages, which Interval we suppose denominated by z.

THIS being ſuppoſed, the Expectation of the *Life* at A upon the Interval AB is $\frac{\frac{1}{2}a+\frac{1}{2}b}{a}z$, by the preceding *Corollary*; the Expectation of the ſame *Life* upon the next Interval BE, will be $\frac{\frac{1}{2}b+\frac{1}{2}c}{b}z$, when once the Extremity of the Interval AB is attained; but the Probability of attaining it, is meaſured by the *Fraction* $\frac{b}{a}$; wherefore the Expectation of the *Life* at A upon the Interval BE is

$$=\frac{\frac{1}{2}b+\frac{1}{2}c}{b}z\times\frac{b}{a}=\frac{\frac{1}{2}b+\frac{1}{2}c}{a}z,$$ and therefore the Expectation of the *Life* at A upon the whole Interval AE

$$=\frac{\frac{1}{2}a+b+\frac{1}{2}c}{a}z.$$

COROLLARY III.

AND therefore if the Complement of *Life* be divided into equal Intervals, and we take out of the *Table* of *Obſervations* the Numbers terminating thoſe Intervals, and from the

Sum of all those Numbers, we subtract one Half of the First, and then multiply the *Remainder* by One of the equal Parts, and lastly divide the *Product* by the Number answering to the Beginning of the First Interval; the *Quotient* will express the Number of Years which compose the Expectation of the *Life* given.

THUS if we consider a *Life* of 50, and divide its Complement, or Difference between 50 and 86, into several equal Intervals of Six Years each; then the Numbers terminating those Intervals will be

Years.	Persons.
50	346
56	282
62	222
68	162
74	98
80	41
86	0

1151 Sum

From which subtract 173 one Half of the first.

Remainder 978
Multiply by 6 One of the equal Parts.

Product 5868

which *Product* being divided by 346 Number anſwering to the Beginning of the firſt Interval; then the *Quotient* 16.95 or 17 nearly will expreſs the Number of Years which a *Life* of 50 may reaſonably expect.

COROLLARY IV.

BUT if the Age be ſuch, that having divided the Complement of *Life* belonging to it, into any Number of Parts taken at Pleaſure, as many of them as poſſible containing the ſame Number of Years, ſuch as 6, it ſhould happen that the laſt of the equal *Diviſions* could not be terminated by 86, as will happen for a *Life* of 40.

THEN having added together all the Numbers terminating the equal Intervals; from the Sum of the whole, ſubtract the half Sum of the greateſt and leaſt of them, then multiply the *Product* by one of the equal Parts, and to the *Product* add another *Product* made of one Half the Number terminating the laſt of the equal Intervals, by the laſt odd Interval; then the Sum being divided by the Number anſwering to the Beginning of the firſt Interval, the *Quotient* will expreſs the Number of Years which the *Life* given may expect.

THUS ſuppoſing a *Life* of 40, the *Operation* will be as follows,

Years.	Perſons.	
40	455	
46	387	
52	324	
58	262	
64	202	
70	142	
76	78	
82	28	
86	0	
	1868	Sum
ſubtract	236	half Sum of 445 and 28.

Remainder 1632
which multiplied by 6 one of equal Parts.

Product 9792
to which add 56 *Product* of the Number 28 by the last Interval 4.

Sum 9848

Divide this Sum by 445 Number answering to 40 beginning of the first Interval; the *Quotient*, viz. 22.13 will express the Number of Years due to a *Life* of 40.

PROBLEM XX.

TWO Lives *being given, whether equal or unequal; To find how many Years they may be expected to continue together.*

SOLUTION.

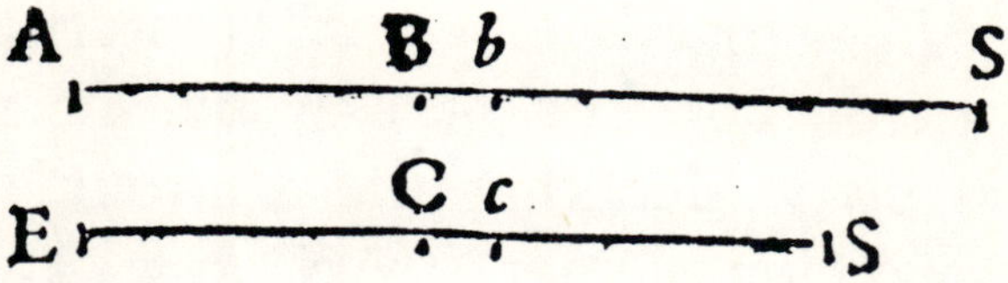

LET the Complements, of the *Lives*, AS, ES be reſpectively ſuppoſed equal to *n* and *p*; take upon AS and ES Two equal Intervals AB, EC.

THE Probability of the firſt *Life*'s continuing from A to B is $\frac{n-z}{n}$; the Probability of the ſecond *Life*'s continuing from E to C, is $\frac{p-z}{p}$; wherefore the Probability of their both continuing during the Interval AB or EC is meaſured by the Product of thoſe Two Fractions, *viz.* $\frac{np-nz-pz+zz}{np}$. Let this *Product* be conſidered as the Ordinate of a Curve whoſe Abciſſe is *z*, then the Area of that Curve, *viz.*

$\frac{npz - \frac{1}{2}nzz - \frac{1}{2}pzz + \frac{1}{3}z^3}{np}$ will express the Right or Expectation of the Two *Lives* together upon the Interval AB or EC; Let now z be interpreted by p, denoting the shortest of the Two Complements AS, ES, and then the Expectation of both *Lives* together upon the shortest Interval AS will be measured by the *Fraction* $\frac{npp - \frac{1}{2}npp - \frac{1}{2}p^3 + \frac{1}{3}p^3}{np}$ $= \frac{1}{2}p - \frac{\frac{1}{6}pp}{n}$; which may be express'd as follows.

TAKE the Square of the shortest Complement, and divide it by the greatest, the sixth Part of the *Quotient* being subtracted from one Half of the shortest Complement, the *Remainder* will express the Number of Years sought.

THUS supposing a *Life* of 40, and another of 50, the shortest Complement will be 36; the greatest, 46; the Square of the shortest Complement will be 1296; which being divided by the greatest 46, the *Quotient* will be

28.175, whereof the 6th Part, *viz.* 4.69 being ſubtracted from half the ſhorteſt, *viz.* 18, the Remainder 13.31 will expreſs the Number of Years due to the two *joint Lives*.

COROLLARY.

IF the two *Lives* be equal, the Number of Years due to their joint Continuance, is expreſſible by the Third Part of their common Complement.

THUS ſuppoſing each *Life* to be 50, the Number of Years due to the two *joint Lives* is 12.

PROBLEM XXI.

ANY Number of Lives *being given whether equal or unequal, to find how many Years they may be expected to continue together.*

SOLUTION.

1° TAKE $\frac{1}{2}$ the ſhorteſt Complement.

2° TAKE $\frac{1}{2}$ Part of the Square of the ſhorteſt, which divide ſucceſſively by all the other Complements; then add all the *Quotients* together.

3° TAKE $\frac{1}{12}$ Part of the Cube of the ſhorteſt Complement, which divide ſucceſſively by the Products of all the other Complements taken Two and Two.

4° TAKE $\frac{1}{20}$ Part of the Biquadrate of the ſhorteſt Complement, which divide ſucceſſively by the *Products* of all the other Complements taken Three and Three, and ſo on.

5° THEN from the Reſult of the firſt *Operation*, ſubtract the Reſult of the ſecond, to the Remainder add the Reſult of the Third; from the Sum ſubtract the Reſult of the fourth, and ſo on.

6° THE laſt Quantity remaining after theſe alternate Subtractions and Additions will be the Thing required.

N. B. THE Diviſors 2, 6, 12, 20, *&c.* are the Products of 1 by 2; of 2 by 3; of 3 by 4; of 4 by 5; *&c.*

COROLLARY.

IF all the *Lives* be equal, add Unity to the Number of *Lives*, and divide their common Complement by that Number thus increaſed by Unity, and the Quotient will always expreſs the Time due to their joint Continuance.

PROBLEM XXII.

TWO Lives *being given, to find the Number of Years due to the longeſt.*

SOLUTION.

FROM the Sum of the Years due to each *Life*, ſubtract the Number of Years due to their joint Continuance, the *Remainder* will be the Number of Years due to the longeſt.

THUS ſuppoſing a *Life* of 40, and another of 50; the Number of Years due to the *Life* of 40, is 23; the Number of Years due to the *Life* of 50, is 18; from the Sum of 23 and 18, *viz.*

41, subtract 13.31 due to their joint Continuance; the *Remainder* 27.69 will be the Time due to the longest.

COROLLARY.

BUT if the *Lives* be equal, then $\frac{2}{3}$ of their common Complement will be the Number of Years due to the longest.

THUS supposing Two *Lives* of 50, it may be expected that the longest of the Two will continue 24 Years.

PROBLEM XXIII.

THREE Lives *being given, to find the Number of Years due to the longest.*

SOLUTION.

FROM the Sum of the Years due to the single *Lives* subtract the Sum of the Years due to all the *joint Lives* combined Two and Two; then to the *Remainder* add the Number of Years due to the three *joint Lives*; and this last Sum will be the Number of Years due to the longest of the Three *Lives*.

COROLLARY.

BUT if all the *Lives* be equal, then $\frac{3}{4}$ of their common Complement will be the Number of Years due to the longest.

AND Universally, supposing any Number of equal *Lives*; take such Part of their common Complement as may be exprest by a *Fraction* whose *Numerator* be equal to the Number of *Lives*, and *Denominator*, the same Number increased by Unity, and that Part thus taken will answer the Number of Years due to the longest.

PROBLEM XXIV.

TWO Lives *being given, to find the Probability of one of them, fixt upon, surviving the other.*

SOLUTION.

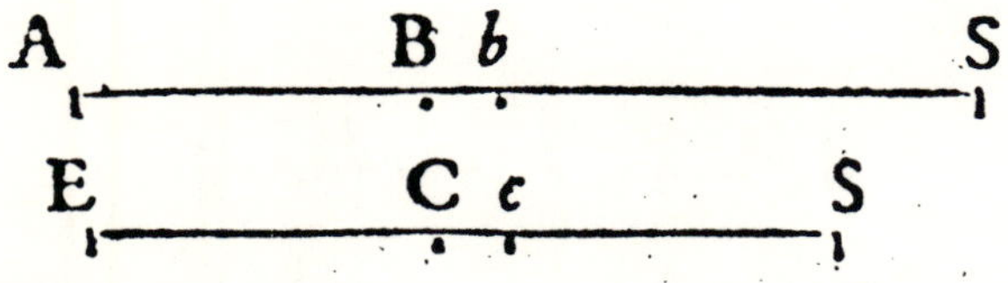

LET the Complements of the Two *Lives* be respectively AS and ES, upon which take Two equal Intervals AB, EC $= z$; as also Two Moments Bb, Cc $=$ o.

THE Probability of the first *Life's* continuing from A to B or beyond it, is measured by the *Fraction* $\frac{n-z}{n}$; the Probability of the Second's continuing from E to C and then failing in the Interval Cc, is measured by the *Product* of the Two *Fractions* $\frac{p-z}{p}$ and $\frac{o}{p-z}$, that is by $\frac{o}{p}$; therefore the Probability of the first *Life's* continuing during the Time AB or beyond it, and of the Second's failing just at the End of that Time, is $\frac{n-z}{n} \times \frac{o}{p}$: Let the Quantity $\frac{n-z}{np}$

be conſidered as the Ordinate of a Curve whoſe Abciſſe is z; then the Area of it, *viz.* $\frac{nz - \frac{1}{2}zz}{np}$ will expreſs the Probability of the firſt *Life*'s continuing during any Interval of Time z or beyond it, and of the ſecond's failing any Time before or preciſely at the attaining the End of that Interval. Let now p be written inſtead of z, and then the Probability of the firſt *Life*'s ſurviving, the ſecond will be

$$\frac{np - \frac{1}{2}pp}{np} = 1 - \frac{\frac{1}{2}p}{n}.$$

FROM the foregoing Concluſion we may immediately infer that the Probability of the ſecond *Life*'s ſurviving the firſt will be $\frac{\frac{1}{2}p}{n}$, which may alſo be proved thus.

THE Probability of the ſecond *Life*'s continuing during any Interval of Time z or beyond it, and of the firſt's failing any Time before or at the attaining that Interval is $\frac{pz - \frac{1}{2}zz}{pn}$; let now p be written inſtead of z, then the

Probability of the ſecond *Life's* ſurviving the firſt will be $\frac{pp - \frac{1}{2}pp}{np} = \frac{\frac{1}{2}p}{n}$ as before.

FROM whence the following Rule may be derived.

FROM the greater Complement ſubtract Half of the leaſt; then the Propoſition of the *Remainder* to Half the leaſt Complement, will expreſs the Propoſition of the Chances which the youngeſt *Life* has to ſurvive the oldeſt, and which the oldeſt has to ſurvive the youngeſt.

THUS ſuppoſing Two *Lives*, viz. of 50 and 62 the Chances of Survivourſhip are reſpectively as 24 to 12, or as 2 to 1.

TO adapt this Rule to the *Table* of *Obſervations*, we may proceed as follows.

1° DIVIDE the Complement of the oldeſt *Life* into any Number of Intervals, whether equal or unequal.

2° DIVIDE alſo the Complement of the youngeſt *Life* into the like Number of Intervals each reſpectively equal to the Intervals belonging to the oldeſt *Life*, neglecting the Overplus.

3° TAKE out of the *Tables* the Numbers terminating the Intervals given, and that for both the given *Lives*.

4° MULTIPLY the Sum of the Two Numbers terminating the firſt Interval belonging to the oldeſt *Life* by the Difference of the Two Numbers terminating the firſt Interval belonging to the youngeſt *Life*.

5° MULTIPLY the Sum of the Two Numbers terminating the ſecond Interval belonging to the oldeſt *Life*, by the Difference of the Two Numbers terminating the ſecond Interval belonging to the youngeſt *Life*, and ſo on.

6° THE Sum of the foregoing *Product* being divided by twice the *Product* of the Two Numbers terminating the Beginning of the Two Sets of Intervals, the *Quotient* will expreſs the Probability of the oldeſt *Life* ſurviving the youngeſt.

AND therefore this *Quotient* being ſubtracted from Unity, the *Remainder* will expreſs the Probability of the youngeſt *Life* ſurviving the oldeſt.

THUS ſuppoſe a *Life* of 62, and one of 50, let the Difference between 62 and 86 be divided into ſeveral parts at Pleaſure ; let, for Inſtance, the four firſt contain each an Interval of 5 Years, and the laſt an Interval of 4.

TAKE out of the *Tables* the Numbers anſwering to

	62,	67,	72,	77,	82,	86.
viz.	222,	172,	120,	68,	28,	0.

TAKE alſo out of the *Tables* the Numbers anſwering to

	50,	55,	60,	65,	70,	74.
viz.	346,	292,	242,	192,	142,	98.

THE Sum of the Numbers terminating the firſt Interval belonging to the oldeſt *Life* is 394.

THE Difference of the Numbers terminating the firſt Interval belonging to the youngeſt *Life* is 54.

WHEREFORE Multiplying 394 by 54, the *Product* will be 21276.

THEN taking in the like Manner the other ſucceſſive *Products*, we ſhall have 14600, 9400, 4800, 1232, which *Products* being added with the firſt before found, *viz.* 21276, the Sum of all will be 51308, and this being divided by 152514 which is twice the *Product* of 222 and 346, Numbers terminating the Beginning of each Set of Intervals, the *Fraction* resulting from that Division, *viz.* $\frac{51308}{152514}$ will express the Probability of the oldest *Life* surviving the youngest; and this subtracted from Unity, the *Remainder*, viz. $\frac{101206}{152514}$ will express the Probability of the youngest *Life* surviving the oldest; and consequently the Odds of the youngest *Life* surviving the oldest, are as 101206 to 51308, that is very near in the Proportion of 2 to 1, as it had been found from the *Hypothesis* of an equable Decrement of *Life*.

PROBLEM XXV.

THREE Lives *being given, to find the Probability of One of them fixed upon, surviving the other Two.*

SOLUTION.

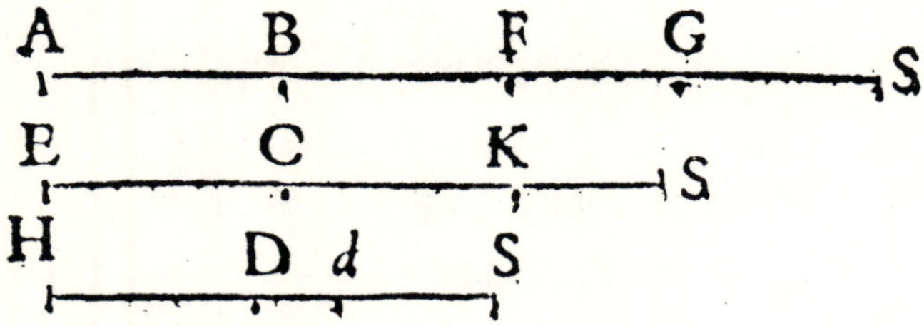

LET the Complements of the Ages, *viz.* AS, ES, HS be respectively called n, p, q.

1° LET us find the Probability of the first *Life*'s surviving the other Two; in order to which, let AG be taken equal to ES, and both AF and EK equal to HS; let there also be taken three equal Distances AB, EC, HD at the End of which the first *Life* may be look'd upon as having survived the other Two, that is, the second *Life* any Time before it reached the Point C, and the third *Life* just at its reaching the corresponding Point D, or immediately after; then there are three Circumstances to be expressed, *viz.* that of the first *Life*'s reaching the Point B, that of the second's failing any Time before it comes to the Points C, and that of the third's failing just at its reaching the Point D, or immediately after; all which Circumstances may be represented by the *Product* $\frac{n-z}{n} \times \frac{z}{p} \times \frac{o}{q}$; let therefore $\frac{nz-zz}{npq}$ be considered as the Ordinate of a Curve whose Absciße is z, then the Area of it, *viz.* $\frac{\frac{1}{2}nzz-\frac{1}{3}z^3}{npq}$ will expreß the Probability of all those Circumstances having happened in some Moment of Time or other comprehended within any indeterminate Space supposed equal to z.

AGAIN, the first *Life* at its reaching the Point B, may be look'd upon as having survived the third *Life* any Time before it reached the Point D, and the second *Life* immediately after its reaching the corresponding Point C, all which Circumstances may be represented by the *Product* $\frac{n-z}{n} \times \frac{z}{q} \times \frac{o}{p}$, and therefore $\frac{\frac{1}{2}nzz-\frac{1}{3}z^3}{npq}$ is once more the meaſure of the Probability of all thoſe Circumſtances having happened in ſome Moment of Time or other comprehended within the Space z.

AND therefore $\frac{nzz - \frac{2}{3}z^3}{npq}$ is the Meaſure of the Probability of the firſt *Life*'s having ſurvived the other Two within a Space of Time equal to z.

LET now q be written inſtead of z, then $\frac{np - \frac{2}{3}qq}{np}$ will repreſent the Probability of the firſt *Life*'s having ſurvived the other Two within an Interval of Time equal to the ſhorteſt of the Three AS, ES, HS.

LET us now inquire what the Probability is of the firſt and ſecond *Lives* continuing together during a Time equal to the ſhorteſt Interval HS, and then of the firſt's ſurviving the ſecond.

THE Probability of the firſt *Life*'s continuing during the Interval AG, and of the ſecond's failing before that Time be expired, is by the preceding *Problem* $1 - \frac{\frac{1}{2}p}{n} = \frac{np - \frac{1}{2}pp}{np}$.

THE Probability of the first *Life's* continuing during the Space AF, and of the second's failing before the Expiration of that Time, is $\frac{nq - \frac{1}{2}qq}{np}$.

WHEREFORE, subtracting the second Probability from the First, there will remain $\frac{np - \frac{1}{2}pp - nq + \frac{1}{2}qq}{np}$ expressing the Probability of the First *Life's* having survived the other Two, but not before the End of the shortest Complement be attained.

LET us now add together the Probabilities of the First *Life's* having survived the other Two, both before and after the End of the shortest Complement is attained, and the Sum of those Two Probabilities, *viz.* $1 - \frac{\frac{1}{2}p}{n} - \frac{\frac{1}{6}qq}{np}$ will be the Probability of the First *Life's* surviving the other Two.

2° IN the same Manner it will be found that the Probability of the second *Life's* surviving the other Two is $\frac{\frac{1}{2}p}{n} - \frac{\frac{1}{6}qq}{np}$.

3° AND that the Probability of the the third *Life*'s surviving the other Two is $\frac{\frac{1}{3}qq}{np}$.

ALL which may be expressed as follows.

1° TAKE $\frac{1}{2}$ the Square of the mean Complement, and to it add $\frac{1}{6}$ Part of the Square of the shortest; then let the Sum be subtracted from the *Product* of the greater and mean Complements multiplied together.

2° FROM $\frac{1}{2}$ the Square of the mean Complement, subtract $\frac{1}{6}$ Part of the Square of the shortest.

3° TAKE $\frac{1}{3}$ Part of the Square of the shortest.

THEN the several Numbers arising from the several Results of these *Operations* will be proportional to the respective Chances which each *Life* taken in Order, *viz.* the youngest, middlemost, and oldest have, each of them, of surviving the other Two.

THUS supposing three *Lives*, viz. of 40, 50 and 60, the longest, mean, and shortest Complements, will respectively be 46, 36, 26, by help of which Numbers, the three Numbers arising from the *Operations* here prescribed, will be found $895\frac{1}{3}$, $535\frac{1}{3}$, $225\frac{1}{3}$ which are nearly in the Proportion of 13, 8, and 3; and these Numbers will respectively be proportional to the Chances which each *Life* has of surviving the other Two.

PROBLEM XXVI.

THREE Lives *being given, to find the Probability of any Two of them fixed upon outliving the third.*

SOLUTION.

1° TAKE the *Product* of the longest and mean Complements, from which subtract half the *Product* of the longest and shortest, and from the *Remainder* subtract again half the *Product* of the mean and shortest, then to this last *Remainder* add one third of the Square of the shortest Complement.

2° FROM half the *Product* of the longeſt and mean Complements ſubtract one ſixth Part of the Square of the ſhorteſt.

3° FROM half the *Product* of the longeſt and ſhorteſt Complements ſubtract one ſixth Part of the Square of the ſhorteſt.

THEN the Numbers ariſing from the Reſults of theſe ſeveral *Operations* will be reſpectively proportional to the ſeveral Chances which the youngeſt and middlemoſt *Life*, the youngeſt and oldeſt, the middlemoſt and oldeſt reſpectively have of outliving the third remaining *Life*.

PROBLEM XXVII.

SUPPOSING *Three Perſons* A, B, C, *whereof the Firſt* A *is in Poſſeſſion of an* Annuity *for his* Life; *the ſecond* B *to ſtand next in Reverſion excluſive of* C, *and* C *to have the Expectation of the Reverſion for him and his Heirs for ever, in Caſe* A *ſurvives* B, *to find the Value of the Expectation of* C.

SOLUTION.

1° LET us consider what the Value of the Reversion would be to the Expectant *C* were that Reversion absolute, that is, were there no *Life* intercepted between him and *A*; now by the VIIth *Problem* it appears, that if from the Value of the Two *Lives* of *A* and *C*, the *Life* of *A* be subtracted, there will remain the Value of the Reversion. Let us suppose that the *Life* in Possession be worth 11 Years Purchase; it will follow therefore that the Reversion will be worth 9 Years Purchase; for *C* being to have the *Annuity* for him and his Heirs for ever after the *Life* of *A*, the Two *Lives* of *A* and *C* together are worth 20 Years Purchase, since the *Life* of *C* is to be perpetuated by his Heirs.

2° 9 Years Purchase being the Value of the Reversion to *C*, upon Supposition of an absolute Right, let us consider what Diminution this Value will suffer from the Interposition of the

Life of *B*, for which let us suppose that the Probability of *A*'s surviving *B* is expressible by the *Fraction* $\frac{2}{3}$, therefore by the first Principle laid down in the *Doctrine* of *Chances*, the Value of the Contingent Reversion is $\frac{2}{3}$ of 9, that is 6 Years Purchase.

AND by the same Principle, if there were ever so many *Lives* intervening between the present Possessor *A* and the Expectant *C*, the Value of the Reversion might be determined by previously knowing the Probabilities of Survivorship.

Dr. HALLEY's TABLE *of Observations, exhibiting the Probabilities of* LIFE.

Age.	Persons.	Age.	Perso.	Age.	Perso.	Age.	Perso.	Age	Perso	Age.	Perso.
1	1000	8	680	15	628	22	586	29	539	36	481
2	855	9	670	16	622	23	579	30	531	37	472
3	798	10	661	17	616	24	573	31	523	38	463
4	760	11	653	18	610	25	567	32	515	39	454
5	732	12	646	19	604	26	560	33	507	40	445
6	710	13	640	20	598	27	553	34	499	41	436
7	692	14	634	21	592	28	546	35	490	42	427
Age.	Persons	Age.	Perso.	Age.	Perso.	Age.	Perso.	Age.	Perso.	Age.	Perso.
43	417	50	346	57	272	64	202	71	131	78	58
44	407	51	335	58	262	65	192	72	120	79	49
45	397	52	324	59	252	66	182	73	109	80	41
46	387	53	313	60	242	67	172	74	98	81	34
47	377	54	302	61	232	68	162	75	88	82	28
48	367	55	292	62	222	69	152	76	78	83	23
49	357	56	282	63	212	70	142	77	68	84	20

The present Value of an ANNUITY *of One Pound, for any Number of Years not exceeding* 100, Intereſt *at* 5 per Cent.

Years	*Values.*	*Years*	*Values.*	*Years*	*Values*	*Years*	*Values.*
1	0.9523	26	14.3758	51	18.3389	76	19.5094
2	1.8594	27	14.6430	52	18.4180	77	19.5328
3	2.7232	28	14.8981	53	18.4934	78	19.5550
4	3.5459	29	15.1410	54	18.5651	79	19.5762
5	4.3294	30	15.3724	55	18.6334	80	19.5964
6	5.0756	31	15.5928	56	18.6985	81	19.6156
7	5.7863	32	15.8026	57	18.7605	82	19.6339
8	6.4632	33	16.0025	58	18.8195	83	19.6514
9	7.1078	34	16.1929	59	18.8757	84	19.6680
10	7.7217	35	16.3741	60	18.9292	85	19.6838
11	8.3064	36	16.5468	61	18.9802	86	19.6988
12	8.8632	37	16.7112	62	19.0288	87	19.7132
13	9.3935	38	16.8678	63	19.0750	88	19.7268
14	9.8986	39	17.0170	64	19.1191	89	19.7398
15	10.3796	40	17.1590	65	19.1610	90	19.7522
16	10.8377	41	17.2943	66	19.2010	91	19.7640
17	11.2740	42	17.4232	67	19.2390	92	19.7752
18	11.6895	43	17.5459	68	19.2753	93	19.7859
19	12.0853	44	17.6627	69	19.3098	94	19.7961
20	12.4622	45	17.7740	70	19.3426	95	19.8058
21	12.8211	46	17.8800	71	19.3739	96	19.8151
22	13.1630	47	17.9810	72	19.4037	97	19.8239
23	13.4885	48	18.0771	73	19.4321	98	19.8323
24	13.7986	49	18.1687	74	19.4592	99	19.8403
25	14.0939	50	18.2559	75	19.4849	100	19.8479

F I N I S.

Besides the Faults of the Press, taken Notice of at the Bottom of the *Preface*, it has been found upon an exact Revisal of the Sheets, that the following are also to be corrected.

Page 5. Line next but Two to the last. read $\frac{515}{531}$.
Pag. 22. Lin. 13. for 628 read 616.
Ibid. Lin. 16. for 616 read 628.
Pag. 27. Lin. 15. for $\overline{E + F}$ read $\overline{E + G}$.
Pag. 35. Lin. next to the last. for x^4 read x^4y^4.
Pag. 73. Lin. 7. for $Log.\ r - 1 + S$. read $Log.\ \overline{r - 1 + S}$.
Pag. 79. Lin. 5. read Abcisse.
Pag. 87. Lin. next last. read Abcisse.
Pag. 94. Lin. 16. for $\frac{1}{p-x}$, read $\frac{0}{p-x}$.
Pag. 96. for *Proposition* read *Proportion*.
Ibid. Lin. 10. for *Proposition* read *Proportion*.

Richard Hayes, *A New Method for Valuing of Annuities upon Lives*, London, R. Hayes, J. Bowles and W. Meadows (1727), pp. 6–9.

Richard Hayes was an accountant, a teacher and publisher of mercantile tables and other mercantile works. In this work Hayes offers no original insights of his own. However, the example selected is from a number of examples described by him as 'according to the Proposals and Practices of some Companies and Corporations in and about the City of London'. The problem is basically one of a person making an annual payment in return for a lump sum on death so that a family can be provided for. This is the idea of whole of life assurance beginning to emerge and Hayes is the first to report it. In addition, this is the first book devoted solely to tables of annuities on lives. Hayes's 'new method' is derived from Halley's mortality table at 5% p.a. interest and tables at other rates of interest are calculated by a crude approximate method.

Hayes also published *An Estimate of Places for Life* (1728), which is an extensive practical application of using annuities for valuing incomes.

A NEW METHOD FOR VALUING OF *ANNUITIES* upon *LIVES*.

Shewing at Sight as ſollows:

I. How many Years, Months, *&c.* Purchaſe an Annuity upon Life, for any Age, from 30 to 73 Years, is worth, when Money yields 4, 5, 6, 7, or 8 *per Cent.* Intereſt.

II. How much a Year 100 *l.* is worth upon Life for any of the aboveſaid Ages, *&c.*

III. How many Years an Annuitant muſt live to receive the Value of the Money ſunk.

IV. The Value of the Buyers and Sellers Chances.

V. The preſent Value of any Annuity upon Life, from 1000 *l.* a Year, to one Pound a Year, for any Age from 30 to 73 Years, when Money is worth 4, 5, 6, 7, or 8 *per Cent.*

VI. How many Years, Months, *&c.* Purchaſe, Leaſeholds are worth for any certain Number of Years under 100, at 3, 4, 5, 6, 7, 8, 9, and 10 *per Cent. per Ann.*

VII. The Annuity that 100 *l.* is worth, if laid out upon Leaſeholds; very uſeful for valuing of Buildings and Fines.

VIII. The Increaſe of 100 *l.* at 3, 4, 5, 6, 7, 8, 9, 10, 11, 12 *per Cent. per Ann.*

IX. The Decreaſe of 100 *l.* at 4, 5, 6 and 7 *per Cent. per Annum*; very uſeful for valuing of Fines, payable at certain Terms of Years in Leaſe.

X. The Amount of 100 *l.* a Year, if the Payment is forborn for any Number of Years, under 31, at 5 and 6 *per Cent.* very uſeful in ſettling of Accounts between Executors and Orphans.

Together

With many uſeful Examples and Inſtructions for valuing of ſingle Lives, two or more Lives; Lives taken in with other Lives; Reverſion of Lives; Annuities in Expectation; an Inſtance in the Mercers Company; Eſtates for any certain Term of Years, as Freeholds, Leaſeholds and Reverſions, without any Decimals, *&c.* The whole being made eaſy to a common Capacity.

By *RICHARD HAYES*, Teacher of Merchants Accounts, in that Part of *Cannon Street*, called *Eaſtcheap*. He alſo teaches ſuch Perſons as are of a proper Age or Capacity to be made fit for Buſineſs, Writing and Arithmetick.

LONDON,

Printed for R. HAYES, *and Sold by him*; *and by* J. BOWLES, *Print and Map Seller, at* Mercers Chapel, Cheapſide; *and by* W. MEADOWS, *Bookſeller, at the* Angel, *and* H. WHITRIDGE, *at the Corner of* Caſtle-Alley, *in* Cornhill. 1727.

A Table ſhewing the Annuitant, according to the foregoing Calculations, how many Years he muſt live before he can receive his Principal again, if he receives 6, 7, 8, 9, 10, 11, or 12 *l. a Year for* 100 *l. ſunk upon his own Life, diſcounting his Money at* 4, 5, 6, 7, 8, *and* 10 ℔ Cent. ℔ Annum *Intereſt upon Intereſt.*

£ a Year.	Diſcount at 4 per Cent.		Diſcount at 5 per Cent		Diſcount at 6 per Cent.		Diſcount at 7 per Cent.		Diſcount at 8 per Cent.		Diſcount at 10 per Cent.	
	Years	*Months*	*Years*	*Months*	*Years*	*Months*	*Years*	*Months*	*Years*	*Months*	*Years*	*Months*
6	28	0	36	0	*ſee*	0	0	0	0	0	0	0
7	22	0	26	0	33	0	*ſee*	0	0	0	0	0
8	17	0	20	0	24	0	30	0	*ſee*	0	0	0
9	15	0	16	0	19	0	22	0	28	0	0	0
10	13	0	14	0	16	0	18	0	21	0	*ſee*	0
11	11	0	12	6	13	2	15	0	17	0	25	0
12	10	6	11	0	12	0	13	0	14	9	19	0

The foregoing Table explained.

An Annuitant receiving 8 *l.* a Year during his own natural Life, for 100 *l.* ſunk, he valuing his Money at 5 ℔ *Cent.* being the preſent legal Rate of Intereſt, would know for how many Years he muſt receive the ſaid Annuity to have the Value of his 100 *l.* again?

He looks in the foregoing Table for the Annuity he receives, *viz.* 8 *l.* a Year; and upon the ſame Line towards his right Hand, in the Column at 5 ℔ *Cent.* being the Rate of Intereſt he values his Money at; and there he ſinds 20 Years, which is the Number of Years he muſt enjoy this Annuity of 8 *l.* a Year, before he can receive the Value of his 100 *l* ſunk at 5 ⅌ *Cent.*

Some other Specimens, valuing the principal Money at 4 and 5 ⅌ *Cent.* according to the Intereſt made by the publick Stocks, when the Prices are high and the Dividends low, as may be ſeen at one View, in my Purchaſers Pocket Companion.

If the Annuitant receives 6 *l.* a Year, it will be 28 Years before the Value of the Principal 100 *l.* is received, at 4 ⅌ *Cent.* and 36 Years at 5 ⅌ *Cent.*

If 7 *l.* a Year,	22 Years at	4 ⅌ *Cent.* and	26 Years at	5 ⅌ *Cent.*
8	17	4	20	
9	15	4	16	
10	13	4	14	
11	11	4	12 Years ½ at 5 ⅌ *Cent.*	
12	10 Years ½ at 4		11 Years at 5 ⅌ *Cent.*	

To provide for a Family.

A Clergyman, or *Layman*, aged 47 Years, holding a Benefice or Place during Life, and having a Family, would willingly make ſome certain Proviſion for them; but finding that his Income will let him lay up about 46 *l.* a Year, and that upon no better Security than his own uncertain Life, therefore chuſes rather to ſell the Surpluſage of his Income. The Queſtion is, What Proviſion the ſaid 46 *l.* a Year will make for his Family, admitting the Money is valued at the common legal Rate of 5 ⅌ *Cent.* Intereſt.

To reſolve this Queſtion, I ſhall firſt value the Annuity, eſtimating the Chance according to the Probability of the Sellers living to the Extremity of the oldeſt Age of Life.

And laſtly, by the Practices of ſome in the City of *London.*

Firſt, The Value of this Annuity to the Chance of Age 47, is worth upon that Life at 5 ℔ *Cent.* as may be ſeen in the Tables at the latter Part of this Book, ſhewing the Value of Annuities upon Life, as follows:

		l.	*s.*	*d.*	
	40 *l.* a Year is worth	418	0	11	added.
	6 ——— ——— ———	62	14	1	
Shews	46 *l.* a Year is worth	480	15	0	certain for his Family.

Which Sum of Money put out at Intereſt, will be doubled and quadrupled, at the following Times, at the Rates undermentioned:

At 5 ℔ *Cent.* it will be doubled in 16 Years, to 961 *l.* 10 *s.* and in 32 Years ¼ to 1923 *l.*

At 6 ℔ *Cent.* in 12 or 13 Years, it will double it ſelf to the firſt Sum, or in twenty five Years, be quadrupled to the laſt.

At 7 ℔ *Cent.* it is doubled in 11 Years ½, or quadrupled in 23 Years.

The ſame Queſtion valued another Way.

Laſtly, Suppoſing the Seller would value his Annuity according to the Practices of ſome in *London*, the Securities being the ſame, and ſhould allow but 9 *l.* a Year to the Buyer for his 100 *l.* valuing the Purchaſe Money at the Rate of 5 ℔ *Cent.* to know what Proviſion it will make for his Family. Do as follows:

	l.		
Multiply the Annuity, *viz.*	46	0	a Year
By the Value of the Purchase	11	1/9	Years Purchase
	506	0	
	5	1/9	
Shews 46 *l.* a Year is worth	511	1/9	certain for his Fam.

And this 511 *l.* 1/9 if let to lay out upon Interest, will increase to an incredible Sum, as may be seen in the two following Tables.

100 *l.* increases to *l.*	*A Table shewing the Increase of* 100 *l.* *at* 3, 4, 5, 6, *and* 7 ℔ Cent. ℔ Ann. *Interest upon Interest.*														
	At 3 *per Cent.*			At 4 *per Cent.*			At 5 *per Cent.*			At 6 *per Cent.*			At 7 *per C.*		
	In Yrs.	*Months*	*qrs.*	*In Yrs.*	*Months*	*qrs.*	*In Yrs.*	*Months*	*qrs.*	*In Yrs.*	*Months*	*qrs.*	*In Yrs.*	*Months*	*qrs.*
200	25	5	1	19	7	0	16	2	0	12	10	3	11	6	1
400	50	10	2	39	2	0	32	4	0	25	9	2	23	0	2
800	76	3	3	58	9	0	48	6	0	38	8	1	34	6	3
1600	101	9	0	78	4	0	64	8	0	51	7	0	46	1	0
3200	127	2	1	97	11	0	80	10	0	64	5	3	57	7	1
6400	152	7	2	117	6	0	97	0	0	77	4	2	69	1	2
12800	178	0	3	137	1	0	113	2	0	90	3	1	80	7	3
25600	203	6	0	156	8	0	129	4	0	103	2	0	92	2	0

THE

DOCTRINE

OF

CHANCES:

OR,

A METHOD of Calculating the Probabilities of Events in PLAY.

THE SECOND EDITION,

Fuller, Clearer, and more Correct than the First.

BY A. DE MOIVRE,

Fellow of the ROYAL SOCIETY, *and Member of the* ROYAL ACADEMY OF SCIENCES *of* Berlin.

LONDON:

Printed for the AUTHOR, by H. WOODFALL, without *Temple-Bar.*

M.DCC.XXXVIII.

Abraham de Moivre, *The Doctrine of Chances: or, a Method of Calculating the Probabilities of Events in Play*, 2nd edition, London, printed for the author by H. Woodfall (1738), pp. 211–13.

This work, which is mainly known for its high standard of mathematics and its important binomial approximation to the normal curve, contains a number of problems in life contingencies in addition to the many worked examples of problems in probability. The life assurance single premium in respect of a term of 10 years echoes Edmund Halley's remark in 1693 (*Philosophical Transactions*, Vol. XVII, p. 602) that 'by what has been said' (i.e. using the life table), 'the price of insurance upon Lives ought to be regulated'. Despite de Moivre showing how this was done, the market continued to offer one year policies at a single premium not related to age, often 5%, until the Equitable introduced one year temporary assurances on an age related scale in 1762.

Of Annuities on Lives.

The Table publiſhed by Dr. *Halley* for eſtimating the Probabilities of Life being very artificially contrived, and grounded on ſuch Obſervations as one may reaſonably ſuppoſe have been made with all the exactneſs poſſible, I have annex'd it to this Tract, in order to make uſe of it as occaſion ſhall require.

It is diſtinguiſhed into ſeveral Columns ſhewing alternately the age, and the number of perſons living of that age, both which are written over-againſt one another.

Suppoſe that by help of this Table we would know what the reſpective Probabilities are for a Man of 30 to live 1, 2, 3, 4, 5, &c. years. Look for the number 30 in one of the Columns of Age, under which number you will find 31, 32, 33, 34, 35, &c. then over-againſt the ſaid number 30, in the next adjacent Column on the right hand you find 531, under which are written 523, 515, 507, 499, &c. each reſpectively correſponding in order to the numbers written in the Column of Age; the meaning of which is, that out of 531 perſons living of the Age of 30, there remain but 523, 515, 507, 499, &c. that attain the reſpective Ages of 31, 32, 33, 34, &c. and who conſequently do from that Term of 30 live 1, 2, 3, 4, &c. years reſpectively.

Now in order to eſtabliſh a computation for finding the Value of an Annuity upon a Life of a given Age, let the general quantities A, B, C, D, E, F, &c. repreſent reſpectively the perſons living at the Age given, and the ſubſequent years.

Now it is very obvious that there being A persons of the Age given, and one year after B persons remaining, that the Probability which the person of the given Age has to continue in Life, for one year at least, is measured by the Fraction $\frac{B}{A}$, and that the Probability which it has to continue in Life for two years at least is measured by the Fraction $\frac{C}{A}$, and so on; and that therefore if Money bore no Interest, it would be sufficient to multiply those Probabilities by the Sum to be received Annually, which we suppose here to be $= 1$, and the Sum of the Products would express the present Value of the Annuity. But as Money bears interest, let r represent the Amount of 1 *L.* joined with its Interest at the year's end, then it is well known that the present Values of the Sums to be received Annually would be respectively $\frac{1}{r}$, $\frac{1}{rr}$, $\frac{1}{r^3}$, $\frac{1}{r^4}$, &c. And therefore multiplying actually those Sums by the Probabilities of obtaining them, we shall have the Value of the Annuity expressed by the Series

$$\frac{A}{r} + \frac{B}{rr} + \frac{C}{r^3} + \frac{D}{r^4} + \frac{E}{r^5} + \frac{F}{r^6} + \frac{G}{r^7}, \text{ \&c.}$$

which must be continued to the end of the Tables.

But let us suppose, that instead of an Annuity upon a Life whose Age is given, there should be the Expectation of a Sum (which we may call 1) payable once for all whenever it happens that the Life ceases within a limited time. It is plain that the Probability of the Life's ceasing after one year is $\frac{A-B}{A}$, and that the Probability of its continuing one year and dropping the next will be $\frac{B}{A} \times \frac{B-C}{B}$, or barely $\frac{B-C}{A}$, and that again the Probability of its continuing two years and dropping the third will be $\frac{C-D}{A}$, and so on; and that therefore the Value of the Expectation founded on the Contingency of the Life's failing within a limited time would be

$$\frac{A-B}{Ar} + \frac{B-C}{Arr} + \frac{C-D}{Ar^3} + \frac{D-E}{Ar^4} + \frac{E-F}{Ar^5}, \text{ \&c.}$$

Let us now suppose for instance, that the Party on whose Life this Expectation depends is 10 years of Age, and that the Age limited as a Condition of obtaining the Sum 1, is 21; hence it is plain that the difference between 21 and 10 being 11, we ought to limit ourselves to 11 Terms of the foregoing Series, and then consulting Dr. *Halley*'s Table we shall find the numbers A, B, C, D, E, &c. to be respectively 661, 653, 646, 640, 634, &c. and that therefore A — B, B — C, C — D, D — E, E — F, &c. will respectively be 8, 7, 6, 6, 6, &c. and that consequently the present Value of the Expectation will be

$$\frac{8}{661r} + \frac{7}{661rr} + \frac{6}{661r^3} + \frac{6}{661r^4} + \frac{6}{661r^5} + \frac{6}{661r^6} + \frac{6}{661r^7} + \frac{6}{661r^8} + \frac{6}{661r^9} + \frac{6}{661r^{10}} + \frac{6}{661r^{11}}.$$

Let us farther suppose that this Expectation is not given, but sold to a Purchaser who intends to make 5 *per Cent.* of his Money, then r stands for 1.05, and therefore the Sum which the Purchasers ought in justice to pay for their Expectation, is the Sum of the numbers here annexed, which is about $\frac{2}{25}$, and therefore if the Sum, called 1 before, stands for an Estate whose present real Value is 20 years purchase, the Adventurer ought to pay no more for the consideration of his Chance than $1\frac{3}{5}$ year's Purchase.

0.0115260 —	1
0.0096054 —	2
0.0078412 —	3
0.0074678 —	4
0.0071122 —	5
0.0067735 —	6
0.0064510 —	7
0.0061438 —	8
0.0058512 —	9
0.0055726 —	10
0.0053072 —	11
0.0796599	

I do not design here to calculate other intervening Chances which might defeat this Expectation, such as that of an Heir-Male which might live to the Age of 21; for there being not any Table of Observations concerning a Man's marrying and getting an Heir-Male between 16 and 21, what I could add on this Subject would be barely conjectural, which would not be of a piece with the other parts of this Tract; however it is easy to conceive that this must considerably diminish the Value of the Expectation.

Thomas Simpson, *The Doctrine of Annuities and Reversions, etc.*, London, J. Nourse (1742), pp. 76–81.

Thomas Simpson was a thoroughly competent mathematician who, in this book, borrowed freely from de Moivre but nevertheless added original work of his own. This work, with its copious tables, was very useful to many as they could look up the information they sought instead of having to make mathematical calculations to obtain annuity values. The two results presented here are Simpson's work, although the method of calculating $A = 1 - ia$, given here for three lives, is already clearly discernible in de Moivre's *The Doctrine of Chances*, 2nd edition (1738), pp. 228–9. Note that this formula pays the sum due at the beginning of the year in which death occurs. Multiplying by v gives the usual form of $A_x = 1 - d\ddot{a}_x$.

Simpson's second result is that 0.25 has to be added to the value of an annuity of 1 p.a. in order to make it payable half-yearly and 0.375 for quarterly 'very nearly' – pp. 78–81.

Additionally, this work included the first published tables of joint life annuities based on John Smart's table of mortality from the London Bills of Mortality, which Simpson modified for ages under 25, for two and for three lives and also similar tables of annuities payable until the last death, pp. 40–7. John Richard's 'The Gentleman's Steward and Tenants of Manors Instructed', John Senex (1730) includes a broadly similar range of tables based upon de Moivre's hypothesis. Although the method of calculating multiple life functions had been known since Halley's 1693 paper, the large amount of work involved in producing tables was tackled infrequently.

De Moivre accused Simpson of plagiarism, but did not reply in the face of a vigorous response. Simpson had an unconventional early life and has been regarded as controversial. A colourful account of Simpson's is given in *The History of Statistics in the 17th and 18th Centuries,* editor E. S. Pearson, London, Charles Griffin (1978), pp. 166–76.

THE
DOCTRINE
OF
ANNUITIES and REVERSIONS,

Deduced from

GENERAL and EVIDENT PRINCIPLES:

WITH USEFUL

TABLES,

Shewing the VALUES of

SINGLE and JOINT LIVES, &c.

At different

RATES of INTEREST.

To which is added,

A METHOD of investigating the Value of ANNUITIES by Approximation, without the help of TABLES.

The Whole explain'd in a plain and simple Manner, and illustrated by great variety of Examples.

By *THOMAS SIMPSON.*

LONDON:
Printed for J. NOURSE, at the *Lamb*, without *Temple-Bar*.
M.DCC.XLII.

PROBLEM XXI.

Supposing any given number of lives P, Q, R, *and that* A, *or his Heirs, are to receive the sum* S *upon the first vacancy of any of these lives: To find the value of* A's *expectation in present money.*

SOLUTION.

Multiply the given sum by the value of an annuity for the joint lives P, Q, R, and divide the product by the value of the same annuity for ever; subtract the quotient from the given sum, and there will remain the value sought.

DEMONSTRATION.

Let E be the value of an annuity for ever (*i. e.* the number of years purchase it is worth) and P the value of an annuity for the proposed joint lives; therefore, seeing the value of the reversion for ever, after the joint lives P, Q, R, to be received as soon as one of those lives becomes extinct, is to the sum (S) to be received at the same time, as E to S, the present value of that reversion, must, consequently, be to the present value of this sum, in the same ratio of E to S; but the present value of the reversion is known to be E—P, therefore that of the sum S will be $\frac{E-P}{E} \times S = S - \frac{PS}{E}$. Q. E. D.

EXAMPLE.

Let the number of lives be 3, their ages each 27 years, the rate of interest 4 *per cent.* and the proposed sum 100*l.* then the value of an annuity for the joint lives being (by the table) 8 years purchase, and the value of an annuity for ever 25 years purchase, we shall, by multiplying 100*l.* by 8, and dividing the product by 25, have 32*l.* which subtracted from 100*l.* will leave 68*l.* for the present value of 100*l.* to be received at the first vacancy of the three proposed lives.

PROBLEM XXII.

Supposing a given sum S *to be depending, so as not to become due till the lives* P, Q, R, &c. *are all extinct; 'tis required to find the value of that sum in present money.*

SOLUTION.

Multiply the given ſum by the value of an annuity for the longeſt of the propoſed lives, and divide the product by the perpetuity; ſubtract the quotient from the given ſum, and there will remain the value required.

The reaſons of this Solution will appear evident from the method laid down in the laſt Problem.

REMARK.

In what has been hitherto laid down, we have had regard to ſuch annuities as are paid yearly, but if the payments are to be made every half year, which is moſt commonly the caſe, the true value at which the purchaſe is to be eſtimated, ought to be a little increaſed; and therefore it may not be improper to conſider here, how much that increaſe will be. In order to which, let E denote the perpetuity, or the value of an annuity for ever, and P the value of the ſame annuity for any number of lives; then, ſince that life, upon whoſe failing the annuity ceaſes, has the ſame chance very nearly, to drop in the laſt as in the firſt half of the year, it is manifeſt that the purchaſer has, in this caſe, an equal chance to receive half a year's rent more than when the annuity is paid yearly; and therefore the ſum that ought to be allow'd as an equivalent, for this, to be paid upon ceaſing of the annuity, will be $\frac{1}{4}$ of a year's purchaſe, or $\frac{1}{4}$ L, of which ſum, the preſent value will, by the laſt Prob. be $\frac{E-P}{4E}$; but this is not the only advantage the purchaſer has in this caſe; for, beſides this, he has the uſe of the 1ſt, 3d, 5th, *&c.* half years rents each half a year; the value of which conſideration, ſince the intereſt of $\frac{1}{2}$ L, for half a year, is to 1 L, the whole ſum received in that year, in the conſtant proportion of 1 to 4 E, will, it is manifeſt, be to the preſent value (P) of all the ſums that may be received from time to time, in the ſame conſtant proportion; and therefore is equal to $\frac{P}{4E}$, which added to $\frac{E-P}{4E}$, above found, gives $\frac{1}{4}$ L for the whole value required. Hence it appears, that be the rate of intereſt and the number of lives what they will, the difference of the values of two equal annuities, ariſing from the rents of one being paid yearly, and the other half yearly, will in all cases be $\frac{1}{4}$ of a year's purchase; and in like manner, it will be found, that the difference of the values of two annuities, upon account of the rents of the one being paid yearly, and the other quarterly, will, in all cases be $\frac{3}{8}$ of a year's purchase very nearly.

From the same method of proceeding, may the difference between the value of an annuity payable in money, and the value of an estate in land, where the purchaser enjoys it, by an actual possession, to the last moments of life, be determined; for, since it is an equal chance whether the life on which the estate last depends, drops in the former or latter half of the year, the purchaser may be supposed, in this case, to enjoy an annuity half a year longer, than he who is paid in money yearly, and intirely loses the last payment, if he dies but one day before it becomes due; and therefore the present value of this consideration, by the last Prob. will be $\frac{E-P}{E} \times \frac{1}{2}$; whence it appears, that if from the perpetuity you subtract the value of an annuity payable in money, and divide the remainder by double the perpetuity, the result will be the parts of a year's purchase, expressing the difference of values required.

This is true, when the value of the estate is to be estimated from the yearly rent it would produce, or when the possession for one whole year is exactly equivalent to 1 L, to be received at the end of that year; but if the estate, when let, will bring in $\frac{1}{2}$ L every half year, then there being the advantage of the interest of the 1st, 3d, 5th, &c. payments, for half a year each, the value $\frac{E-P}{2E}$, above found, ought to be increased by $\frac{P}{4E}$, which will bring it to $\frac{1}{2} - \frac{P}{4E}$, for the difference required here, which in most real cases will be $= \frac{3}{8}$ of a year's purchase very near. Hence we may conclude, that if to the value of the annuity, as found in the tables, be added $\frac{1}{4}$ of a year's purchase, when the rents are to be paid half-yearly, or $\frac{3}{8}$ of a year's purchase when they are to be paid quarterly, or the purchase is in land; the sum will give the value of the annuity in those cases respectively.

Thomas Simpson, *Select Exercises for Young Proficients in the Mathematicks*, Part VI: 'Treating of The Valuation of Annuities, for single and joint Lives', London, J. Nourse (1752), pp. 260–3, 284 & 323–4.

In the extract, Thomas Simpson calculates the single premium for a deferred annuity without return of premiums in the event of death in the deferred period. Although this calculation may seem to be simple in comparison with other calculations made by Simpson and his contemporaries, it is, nevertheless, the first time it appears in the literature of actuarial science.

Problem I on page 323 is the important first calculation of the value of a continuous life annuity. De Moivre, 1725, used the calculus to determine expectation of life and Simpson has extended de Moivre. The notation is Newtonian.

SELECT EXERCISES FOR Young Proficients IN THE MATHEMATICKS.

Containing,

I. A large Variety of Algebraical Problems with their Solutions.

II. A choice Number of Geometrical Problems with their Solutions both Algebraical and Geometrical.

III. The Theory of Gunnery, independent of the Conic Sections.

IV. A new and very comprehenſive Method for finding the Roots of Equations in Numbers.

V. A ſhort Account of the Nature and firſt Principles of Fluxions.

VI. The Valuation of Annuities for ſingle and joint Lives, with a Set of new Tables, far more extenſive than any extant.

By THOMAS SIMPSON, F. R. S.

LONDON:
Printed for J. Nourse, oppoſite *Katharine-Street* in the *Strand*. M.DCC.LII.

TABLE V.

For the Valuation of Annuities upon one LIFE.

Age.	Year's Purch. at 5 *per cent.*	Year's Purch. at 4 *per cent.*	Year's Purch. at 3 *per cent.*	Age.	Year's Purch. at 5 *per cent.*	Year's Purch. at 4 *per cent.*	Year's Purch. at 3 *per cent.*
6	14.1	16.2	18.8	21	12.9	14.7	17.0
7	14.2	16.3	18.9	22	12.7	14.5	16.8
8	14.3	16.4	19.0	23	12.6	14.3	16.5
9	14.3	16.4	19.0	24	12.4	14.1	16.3
10	14.3	16.4	19.0	25	12.3	14.0	16.1
11	14.3	16.4	19.0	26	12.1	13.8	15.9
12	14.2	16.3	18.9	27	12.0	13.6	15.6
13	14.1	16.2	18.7	28	11.8	13.4	15.4
14	14.0	16.0	18.5	29	11.7	13.2	15.2
15	13.9	15.8	18.3	30	11.6	13.1	15.0
16	13.7	15.6	18.1	31	11.4	12.9	14.8
17	13.5	15.4	17.9	32	11.3	12.7	14.6
18	13.4	15.2	17.6	33	11.2	12.6	14.4
19	13.2	15.0	17.4	34	11.0	12.4	14.2
20	13.0	14.8	17.2	35	10.9	12.3	14.1

Age.	Year's Purch. at 5 *per cent.*	Year's Purch. at 4 *per cent.*	Year's Purch. at 3 *per cent.*	Age.	Year's Purch at 5 *per cent.*	Year's Purch. at 4 *per cent.*	Year's Purch at 3 *per cent.*
36	10.8	12.1	13.9	56	8.4	9.1	10.1
37	10.6	11.9	13.7	57	8.2	8.9	9.9
38	10.5	11.8	13.5	58	8.1	8.7	9.6
39	10.4	11.6	13.3	59	8.0	8.6	9.4
40	10.3	11.5	13.2	60	7.9	8.4	9.2
41	10.2	11.4	13.0	61	7.7	8.2	8.9
42	10.1	11.2	12.8	62	7.6	8.1	8.7
43	10.0	11.1	12.6	63	7.4	7.9	8.5
44	9.9	11.0	12.5	64	7.3	7.7	8.3
45	9.8	10.8	12.3	65	7.1	7.5	8.0
46	9.7	10.7	12.1	66	6.9	7.3	7.8
47	9.5	10.5	11.9	67	6.7	7.1	7.6
48	9.4	10.4	11.8	68	6.6	6.9	7.4
49	9.3	10.2	11.6	69	6.4	6.7	7.1
50	9.2	10.1	11.4	70	6.2	6.5	6.9
51	9.0	9.9	11.2	71	6.0	6.3	6.7
52	8.9	9.8	11.0	72	5 8	6.1	6.5
53	8.8	9.6	10.7	73	5.6	5.9	6.2
54	8.6	9.4	10.5	74	5.4	5.6	5 9
55	8.5	9.3	10.3	75	5.2	5.4	5.6

TABLE VI.

Exhibiting the Value of an Annuity for a given Term of Years, on the Contingency of its ceasing upon the Extinction of an assigned Life.

Given Age.	N. Years.	Val. at 5 per Cent.	Val. at 4 p. Cent.	Val. at 3 per Cent.
5	5	4.0	4.1	4.2
	10	7.0	7.3	7.7
	15	9.1	9.8	10.5
	20	10.7	11.7	12.8
	25	11.8	13.0	14.5
	30	12.6	14.1	15.8
	35	13.2	14.9	16.8
	40	13.6	15.4	17.5
	45	13.8	15.7	18.0
	50	13.9	15.9	18.3
10	5	4.1	4.2	4.3
	10	7.2	7.6	8.0
	15	9.4	10.1	10.8
	20	11.0	12.0	13.1
	25	12.1	13.4	14.8
	30	12.8	14.4	16.2
	35	13.3	15.1	17.1
	40	13.7	15.5	17.7
	45	13.9	15.8	18.2
	50	14.0	16.0	18.5

Given Age.	N. Years	Val. at 5 per Cent.	Val. at 4 per Cent.	Val at 3 per Cent.
15	5	4.1	4.2	4.4
	10	7.1	7.5	7.9
	15	9.3	10.0	10.7
	20	10.8	11.8	12.9
	25	11.8	13.1	14.5
	30	12.5	14.0	15.7
	35	13.0	14.6	16.6
	40	13.3	15.0	17.2
	45	13.5	15.3	17.6
	50	13.6	15.5	17.9
20	5	4.1	4.2	4.3
	10	7.0	7.4	7.8
	15	9.1	9.7	10.5
	20	10.5	11.4	12.5
	25	11.4	12.6	13.9
	30	12.0	13.4	15.0
	35	12.5	13.9	15.7
	40	12.7	14.3	16.3
	45	12.8	14.5	16.6
	50	12.9	14.6	16.8

Given age.	N. Years.	Val. at 5 per Cent.	Val. at 4 per Cent.	Val. at 3 per Cent.
25	5	4.1	4.2	4.3
	10	6.9	7.3	7.6
	15	8.9	9.5	10.1
	20	10.2	11.0	12.0
	25	11.0	12.1	13.4
	30	11.5	12.8	14.3
	35	11.8	13.2	15.0
	40	12.0	13.5	15.4
	45	12.1	13.7	15.6
30	5	4.0	4.1	4.2
	10	6.8	7.1	7.5
	15	8.6	9.2	9.8
	20	9.8	10.6	11.5
	25	10.6	11.6	12,7
	30	11.0	12.2	13.5
	35	11.2	12.6	4 0
	40	11.4	12.8	14.4
35	5	4.0	4.1	4.2
	10	6.6	6.9	7.3
	15	8.3	8.9	9.5
	20	9.4	10.2	11.1
	25	10.1	11.1	12.2
	30	10.5	11.6	13.0
	35	10.7	11.9	13.5
40	5	3.9	4.0	4.1
	10	6.4	6.8	7.1
	15	8.0	8.6	9.2
	20	9.1	9.8	10.6
	25	9.7	10.6	11.6
	30	10.0	11.0	12.2

Given Age.	N. Years.	Val. at 5 per Cent.	Val. at 4 per Cent.	Val. at 3 per Cent.
45	5	3.9	4.0	4.1
	10	6.3	6.7	7.0
	15	7.9	8.4	9.0
	20	8.8	9.5	10.3
	25	9.4	10.2	11.2
	30	9.6	10.6	11.7
50	5	3.8	3.9	4.0
	10	6.2	6.5	6.8
	15	7.6	8.2	8.8
	20	8.5	9.1	9.9
	25	8.9	9.7	10.6
55	5	3.8	3.9	4.0
	10	6.1	6.4	6.7
	15	7.4	7.9	8.4
	20	8.0	8.7	9.4
	25	8.3	9.0	9.9
60	5	3.7	3.8	3.9
	10	5.8	6.1	6.4
	15	7.0	7.4	7.9
	20	7.5	8.0	8.7
65	5	3.6	3.7	3.8
	10	5.4	5.7	6.0
	15	6.4	6.8	7.2
70	5	3.4	3.5	3.6
	10	5.0	5.2	5.4

Of REVERSIONS.

PROBLEM XIII.

To find the Value of the Reversion of an assigned Life after a given Term of Years.

Solution.

* From the Value of the proposed Life, subtract the Value of an Annuity for the given Term of Years, on the Contingency of its ceasing upon the Extinction of the foresaid Life; the Remainder will be the Answer.

Example.

A, aged 15 Years, expects to enter upon an Estate of 500 *l. per Annum*, after the Expiration of 10 Years; which he is to hold thence-forward, during Life; what is the present Value of his Expectation, reckoning Interest of Money at 4 *per Cent.*

Here the Answer will be 8.3 Years-Purchase, or 4150*l.* For the Value of the whole Life A being 15.8 *(by Tab.* V), and That of the first 10 Years 7.5 *(by Tab.* VI), the Difference will be 8.3, *as above.*

PROBLEM XIV.

To find the Value of the Reversion of an Annuity, for the Remainder of a given Term of Years, after an assigned Life.

Solution.

* From the Value of an Annuity certain for the given Term, subtract the Value of the Annuity for the said Term, on the Contingency of its ceasing upon the Failing of the proposed Life; the Remainder will be the Value of the Reversion.

PROBLEM I.

To determine the present Value of an Estate in Land, for a single Life A, *of a given Age, according to the Hypothesis of an uniform decrease of the Probability of Life.*

Let r denote the Rate, p the Perpetuity, and a the Complement of the proposed Life. Moreover let x (considered as flowing uniformly) be any Time elapsed from his entering into Possession: Then the present Value of the Expectation on the next succeeding Moment $\dot{x}$, will, evidently, be expressed by $\frac{a-x}{a} \times \frac{\dot{x}}{r^x}$, or, its Equal, $\dot{x}q^x - \frac{x\dot{x}q^x}{a}$ (by putting $q = \frac{1}{r}$) whereof the Fluent, when $x = a$, will consequently be the true Value required.

But the Fluent of the first Term $(\dot{x}q^x)$ is found $= \frac{q^x}{m}$; and That of the Second $\left(\frac{x\dot{x}q^x}{a}\right) = \frac{q^x}{ma} \times \overline{x - \frac{1}{m}}$; *by Prob.* 1, *Sect.* 6, *Vol.* 2, *of my Doctrine and Application of Fluxions*: Where m denotes the Hyperbolical Logarithm of q.

These Fluents, corrected by their constant Quantities, become $\frac{q^x - 1}{m}$, and $\frac{q^x}{am} \times x - \frac{1}{m} + \frac{1}{am^2}$: Which, when x is $= a$, are expressed by $\frac{q^a - 1}{m}$, and $\frac{q^a}{m} + \frac{1 - q^a}{am^2}$, respectively. The Difference of which, or $-\frac{1}{m} - \frac{1 - q^a}{am^2}$, is consequently the true Value of the proposed Life.

But $\frac{q^x - 1}{m}$ (the Fluent of $\dot{x} q^x$), when x becomes infinite, will be equal to the Perpetuity, that is $-\frac{1}{m}$ $\left(= \frac{1}{\text{Hyp. Log. } r}\right) = p$: Whence, $-m$ being $= \frac{1}{p}$, the Value found above will, also, be expressed by $p - \overline{1 - q^a} \times \frac{p^2}{a}$, or, its Equal, $p - \frac{pM}{a}$; supposing M to be put for $(\overline{1 - q^a \times p})$ the Value, *certain*, for the Time a.

The Value here brought, it may be observed, exceeds $\left(p - \frac{\overline{p+1} \times M}{a}\right)$ That given in *p*. 316, by $\frac{M}{a}$: Which is owing to the Advantage of enjoying an Estate in Land (by an actual Possession to the last Moments of Life) preferable to an Annuity, where no Regard is had to the Time elapsed from the last Yearly-Payment to the Dropping of the proposed Life.

James Dodson, *The Mathematical Repository*, Vol. 3 (1755), pp. 362–6.

This work is a compendium of problems in several branches of mathematics and was published in three volumes in 1748/53/55. The extract printed includes James Dodson's calculation of a whole life assurance by level annual premiums using de Moivre's methods. The way the algebra works, the sum assured is payable at the beginning of the year in which death occurs. The problem of the increasing cost of risk being spread into level annual payments had not been solved previously. This led directly to the introduction of scientific life assurance with level annual premiums differentiated by age at entry.

The second volume of *The Mathematical Repository* consists mainly of problems relating to probability, lotteries, interest, annuities for lives and their reversions and contains the fullest development of de Moivre's hypothesis. The third volume contains more difficult problems of the same type.

Dodson, having been rejected for life assurance by the Amicable Society because he was over the age of forty-five, was the stimulus to the founding of the Equitable Assurance, but he died before its inception. Dodson published other mathematical works, including *The Anti-Logarithmic Canon* (1742), and *The Calculator* (1747). Dodson was a pupil of de Moivre, a Fellow of the Royal Society and a Master at the Royal Mathematical School in Christ's Hospital.

THE

MATHEMATICAL REPOSITORY.

VOL. III.

CONTAINING

Analytical Solutions

OF

A great Number of the most difficult PROBLEMS,

RELATING TO

ANNUITIES, REVERSIONS, SURVIVORSHIPS, || INSURANCES, and LEASES dependent on Lives;

In which it has been endeavoured to exhaust the SUBJECT.

By JAMES DODSON, F. R. S.
Accomptant and Teacher of the MATHEMATICS.

LONDON,
Printed for JOHN NOURSE, at the *Lamb*, opposite *Katherine Street* in the *Strand*.
MDCCLV.

QUESTION XCVI.

What ſum ought to be paid for inſuring, for one year, a given ſum, s, on a life, whoſe complement is n?

SOLUTION.

Since the probability of the life's failing in that year is $\frac{1}{n}$, and (if that happens) the inſurer is to pay to the inſured, the ſum, s; therefore, the premium, for that inſurance, ſhould be $\frac{s}{n}$.

EXAMPLE.

If the ſum of 100 £. is inſured on a life, aged ſixty ſix years; then $n =$ (86—66=) 20; and ($\frac{100}{20}$ =) 5 £. will be the required premium.

Note. The premium of inſurance is uſually paid down, at the time of inſuring; but the ſum inſured does (in caſe of the death of the perſon whoſe life is inſured) generally remain unpaid, till the end of the year, and ſometimes longer; now (if the computation be made, as above) it is evident, that the premium is but juſt, adequate to the hazard: and conſequently, if the inſurer is to expect any profit, on the tranſaction; the intereſt of the premium (which by the above cuſtom he enjoys) for one year, will be a very moderate one; being (in the above example) but 5 s. if he could make 5 £. per cent. of his money.

QUESTION XCVII.

What conſtant yearly ſum, of which the firſt payment is to be made immediately, ought to be paid, for inſuring the ſum, s, on a life whoſe complement is n?

SOLUTION.

By the last question, the premium for insuring the first year, will be $\frac{s}{n}$; and, when that is elapsed, then, for the second year, $\frac{s}{n-1}$; for the third, $\frac{s}{n-2}$, &c.

But, forasmuch as the premium, for the second, third, &c. year, will not be payable, unless the insured survives the first, second, &c. year; the probabilities of which are $\frac{n-1}{n}$, $\frac{n-2}{n}$, &c. therefore, the premiums for the second, third, &c. year, being estimated at the beginning of the first year, will be $\frac{n-1}{n} \times \frac{s}{n-1}$. $\frac{n-2}{n} \times \frac{s}{n-2}$, &c. or $\frac{s}{n}$, $\frac{s}{n}$, &c.

Again, because the said premiums for the 2d. 3d. &c. year, do not become payable, till the expiration of the 1st. 2d. &c. year; the present worth of them, computed at the beginning of the first year, will be $\frac{s}{nr}$, $\frac{s}{nr^2}$, &c. and, since one payment is to be made immediately, therefore

$$\left(\frac{s}{n} + \frac{s}{nr} + \frac{s}{nr^2}\ (n) =\right) \overline{\frac{s}{n} \times 1 + \frac{1}{r} + \frac{1}{r^2} + \frac{1}{r^3}\ (n)},$$

will be the present worth of all the yearly premiums, that can be received by the insurer; for, by the hypothesis of equal decrements, the life will be necessarily extinct, at the end of the nth year; and consequently, $\frac{s}{nr^{n-1}}$ will be the present worth of the last premium, that he can possibly receive.

Now $1 + \frac{1}{r} + \frac{1}{r^2} (n) = (r \times \frac{1}{r} + \frac{1}{r^2} + \frac{1}{r^3} (n) =)$ $\frac{r}{r-1} \times \overline{1 - \frac{1}{r^n}}$ (by queſt. 15.vol. 2.) therefore (putting $\frac{1}{r-1} = P$, and $\frac{1}{r^n} = p$) $\frac{s}{n} + \frac{s}{nr} + \frac{s}{nr^2} (n)$ the preſent worth of all the unequal premiums, which can be received by the inſurer, will be $\frac{srP}{n} \times \overline{1-p}$.

But the preſent worth of all the conſtant annual ſums, which the inſurer is to receive, for inſuring the life in queſtion, will (if N repreſents the value of a life, not ſecured by land, whoſe complement is n; and a, the yearly ſum, ſo to be received) be ($a + Na$ or) $\overline{1 + N} \times a$; for the ſum, a, is to be immediately received, and the receipt thereof is to be annually continued, during the life, whoſe value is N; alſo, if the life fails, in any part of a year, no ſum is to be received at the end of that year; for then, the ſum inſured is to be paid to the inſured, or his aſſigns.

It follows, therefore, that $\frac{srP}{n} \times \overline{1-p}$, the preſent worth of all the yearly unequal premiums, which the inſurer would receive, if the life was to be annually inſured; will be equal to, $\overline{1+N} \times a$, the preſent worth of all the equal premiums, which he is to receive, if he engages to inſure the life, on the receipt of a conſtant yearly ſum:

That is $\overline{1 + N} \times a = \frac{srP}{n} \times \overline{1-p}$;

Therefore $a = \frac{srP}{n} \times \frac{1-p}{1+N}$.

Example. What conſtant annual premium ſhould be paid, for inſuring 100£. on a life, aged 66, allowing 4 per cent. compound intereſt?

Here $s = 100$; $r = 1{,}04$; $P = 25$; $n = (86 - 66 =)\ 20$; $p = 0{,}4564$; $1 - p = 0{,}5436$; $N = 7{,}333$; and $1 + N = 8{,}333$;

Therefore ($\frac{100 \times 1{,}04 \times 25 \times 0{,}5436}{20 \times 8{,}333}$ =) 8,481 will be the annual premium required.

Scholium. The above question may be, otherwise, solved, in the following manner: the insured purchases the sum s, to be paid to him, or his assigns, on the decease of a life, whose value is N; by the payment of the sum, v, in hand, and by the annual payment of the like sum, a, during the continuance of the said life.

Now (by quest 89. vol, 2.) the present worth of 1£. payable on the failure of the proposed life, is $\frac{\overline{1-p} \times r}{n \times \overline{r-1}}$, or $1 - \overline{r-1} \times N$; and, consequently, the present value of s will be equal to $\frac{\overline{1-p} \times rPs}{n}$ (because $\frac{1}{r-1} = P$), or $\overline{1 - \overline{r-1} \times N} \times s$:

But $\overline{1+N} \times a = \left(\frac{\overline{1-p} \times rPs}{n}\right.$ or) $\overline{1-\overline{r-1} \times N} \times s$;

Therefore $a = \left(\frac{\overline{1-p} \times rPs}{\overline{1+N} \times n}\right.$ or) $\frac{\overline{1-\overline{r-1} \times N} \times s}{1+N}$.

In the above example; $r - 1 = 0{,}04$; $7{,}333 \times 0{,}04 = 0{,}29332$; $1 - 0{,}29332 = 0{,}70668$; and $0{,}70668 \times 100 = 70{,}668$:

Therefore $\left(\frac{70{,}668}{8{,}333} =\right)$ 8,481 will be the annual payment, as before.

QUESTION XCVIII.

A, who has a place, or other annual income for life, would borrow a sum of money of *B*, and (besides a bond, bearing interest) would insure his life, as a collateral security; *B* undertakes to be the insurer, and to remit the payment of the principal, to the heirs of *A*, if he constantly pays the said interest and insurance, during his life to him, *B*, or his heirs; what ſum ought *A* to pay, annually for intereſt and inſurance, for 1£. ſo lent?

SOLUTION.

Let *N* be the value of *A*'s life; then (by the ſcholium to queſt 97.) the annual inſurance of 1£. will be $\frac{1-\overline{r-1}\times N}{1+N}$; to which add, $r-1$, the intereſt of 1£.

And the ſum $\left(\frac{1-\overline{r-1}\times N}{1+N}+\overline{r-1}=\right)\frac{r}{1+N}$ will be the annual payment required.

Example. If *A*, the borrower, be aged 66; and intereſt be computed at 4 per cent; then $r=1{,}04$, and $1+N=8{,}333$:

Whence $\left(\frac{1{,}04}{8{,}333}=\right)$ 0,125 will be the ſum required.

SCHOLIUM.

It is neceſſary, here, to obſerve, that the borrower ought not to receive the full ſum of 1£. (here ſuppoſed to be lent) becauſe he is to pay the firſt year's inſurance down; and, conſequently ſhould receive but

$$\left(1-\frac{1-\overline{r-1}\times N}{1+N}=\frac{1+N-1+\overline{r-1}N}{1+N}\right.$$

$$=\frac{N+\overline{r-1}\times N}{1+N}=\left.\right)\frac{rN}{1+N}:$$ in the above example $\left(\frac{1{\cdot}04\times7{\cdot}333}{8{,}333}=\right)$ 0,915.

This will appear to be true, by conſidering that the ſum, $\frac{rN}{1+N}$ will purchaſe an annuity of, $\frac{r}{1+N}$, for a life whoſe value is *N*; for if $Na=\frac{rN}{1+N}$; then $a=\frac{r}{1+N}$.

OBSERVATIONS

ON

REVERSIONARY PAYMENTS

ON

SCHEMES for providing ANNUITIES for WIDOWS, and for Perſons in OLD AGE;

ON

The METHOD of Calculating the VALUES of ASSURANCES on LIVES;

AND ON

THE NATIONAL DEBT.

To which are added,

FOUR ESSAYS

On different Subjects in the Doctrine of LIFE ANNUITIES and POLITICAL ARITHMETICK.

ALSO,

AN APPENDIX,

Containing a complete Set of TABLES; particularly, Four New Tables, ſhewing the Probabilities of Life in LONDON, NORWICH, and NORTHAMPTON; and the Values of *joint* Lives.

By RICHARD PRICE, D.D. F.R.S.

LONDON:

Printed for T. CADELL, in the Strand.

M.DCC.LXXI.

Richard Price, *Observations on Reversionary Payments; on Schemes for providing Annuities for Widows, and for Persons in Old Age; on the Method of Calculating the Values of Assurances on Lives*, London, T. Cadell, (1771), pp. iii–xv, 1–134 & 222–344 (excludes chapter 3 and essay 1).

This major work contains a number of notable features. These include problems in life contingencies, covering age related single premiums and annual premiums (the first after Dodson in 1755), for assurances and for annuity schemes. Some of the problems are then used to demonstrate the unsoundness of recently founded annuity societies for widows and persons in old age. Price's analysis of how long a marriage would 'probably ... not last longer than' and his attention to other survivorship problems did not bring anything new to the mathematics, but did much to focus the attention of the public at large to the subject. Further features are the first Life Table based on the mortality rates of the parish of All-Saints in the town of Northampton (for the 36 years from 1735 to 1770), remarks on the Society for Equitable Assurances upon Lives and a plan for provision for old age, and in the footnote at the end of section IV of chapter 2 proposals for a Friendly Society providing sickness and pension benefits.

The book eventually ran to seven editions, each larger than before, and was an important source for persons wishing to obtain access to life contingency algebra and the numerous mortality and monetary tables.

Richard Price is best known for his contribution to philosophy and civil liberties. Price supported the American Revolution and the French Revolution, but died in 1791 before some of the worst abuses took place. Price also presented Bayes's theorem to the Royal Society in December 1763, it having been found in Thomas Bayes's papers after Bayes's death.

CONTENTS.

APPENDIX.

INTRODUCTION.

BEFORE the Reader enters upon this Work, it will not be improper to give him the following information concerning it.

A few years ago, many gentlemen, of the first eminence in the law, formed themselves into a *Society*, for providing annuities for the widows of all such persons in judicial offices, barristers, civilians, and sollicitors, as should chuse to become members. A plan was agreed upon and printed; but, some doubts happening to arise with respect to it, the directors resolved to ask the opinion and advice of three gentlemen, well known for their skill in calculation. This occasioned a further reference to me; and the issue was, that the plan being found to be insufficient, the whole design was laid aside.

About the same time, several other societies were formed with the same views; but all on plans alike improper and insufficient.

Finding, therefore, that the public wanted information on this ſubject, I was led to undertake this work; imagining, that it might be ſoon finiſhed, and that all I could ſay might be brought into a very narrow compaſs. But in this I have been much miſtaken. A deſign, which I at firſt thought would give little trouble, has carried me far into a very wide field of enquiry; and engaged me in many calculations that have taken up much time and labour. I ſhall, however, be ſufficiently rewarded for my labour, ſhould it prove the means of preventing any part of that diſtreſs, which is likely to be hereafter produced by the ſocieties now ſubſiſting for the benefit of widows.——I have proved the inadequateneſs of their plans, by undeniable facts and mathematical demonſtration (*a*).— I have, further, given an account of ſome of the beſt plans, that are conſiſtent with a ſufficient probability of permanency and ſucceſs.——Should, therefore, any of theſe ſo-

(*a*) In the note p. 68, I take notice of the five guineas *fine* required by ſome of theſe ſocieties at admiſſion; and mention ſome reaſons for not making any particular allowance for it. But I have ſince learnt, that it is indeed no more, than the firſt of the yearly payments, which I have always ſuppoſed to begin immediately. No allowance, therefore, was neceſſary to be made for it.

cieties determine to reform themſelves; or ſhould any inſtitutions of the ſame kind be hereafter eſtabliſhed, they will here find direction and aſſiſtance (*b*).

In

(*b*) I have lately learnt, that Mr. *Cadell*, the publiſher of this work, and alſo Mr. *Becket*, Bookſeller in the *Strand*, are commiſſioned to deliver in *London*, printed accounts of the ſcheme of a ſociety, eſtabliſhed five years ago at *Amſterdam*, for granting annuities on ſurvivorſhip.——I cannot ſatisfy my own mind without introducing here, though an improper place, the following remarks on this ſcheme.

From the ſolution of Queſtions I and IV. in the Firſt Chapter of the following Work, it may be gathered, that, (reckoning intereſt at $3\frac{1}{2}$ *per cent.* and the probabilities of life as they are in Tables III. IV. and V. in the *Appendix*) the value of an annuity of 1*l.* for life, to be enjoyed by a perſon aged 20, provided he ſurvives another perſon aged 60, is 8*l.* 16*s.* 6*d.* in one preſent payment; and 18*s.* 6*d.* in annual payments, during the two joint lives: the firſt payment to be made immediately. A *ſingle payment*, therefore, of 130 *florins*, entitles to an annuity of 15 *florins*; and an *annual* payment of 110 *florins*, to an annuity of 119 *florins*; and both together, to an annuity of 134 *florins*. If the annual payments are to be made, not during the *joint* lives, but during the whole continuance of the oldeſt *ſingle* life, they will, together with the ſingle payment, entitle to an annuity of 144 *florins*. But this ſociety promiſes, for theſe payments, an annuity of 100 *florins*, if the oldeſt life fails in the firſt year after admiſſion; 200 *florins*, if it fails in the 2d year; 300 *florins*, if it fails in the third; 400 *florins*, if it fails in the 4th; and 500 *florins*, if it fails in the *fifth* year, or at any time afterwards. It is, therefore, evident that the ſcheme of this ſociety is, in this inſtance, groſsly defective. There are other inſtances in which it is even more defective; and the *whole* of it, like the ſchemes of moſt of the *Lon-*

In Queſtion VI. Chap. I. a general method is deſcribed of finding the values, in *ſingle* and *annual* payments, of all life-annuities which are to begin after a given term of years; and, in the 4th Section of the 2d Chapter, the plans of the ſocieties for granting ſuch annuities are particularly conſidered, and proved to be extremely deficient.—— Indeed, the general diſpoſition which has lately ſhewn itſelf to encourage theſe ſocieties, is a matter of the moſt ſerious concern; and ought, I think, to be taken under the notice of the Legiſlature. The leading perſons among the *preſent* members, will be the *firſt*

den ſocieties, appears to have been contrived by perſons who had no principles to go upon. And yet it has been much encouraged. Many have entered themſelves into it from different parts of *Europe*; and the printed plan acquaints us, that it is now in poſſeſſion of an annual income of 200,000 *florins*. What diſappointment then muſt it in time produce?——It is provided by its rules, that the terms of admiſſion ſhall become leſs and leſs advantageous, the longer it has ſubſiſted; juſt as if the value of the annuities it promiſes depended, not on the probabilities of life, and the improvement to be made of money, but on the age of the ſociety.——I have taken notice of a ſimilar abſurdity in the rules of our own ſocieties. But it is eaſy to ſee what is meant by it.

Mr. *Cadell* can procure from his correſpondents in *Holland*, any information for thoſe who may want to know more of this ſociety. But indeed I ſhould be ſorry to find it much enquired after in LONDON.

annuitants; and they are ſure of being gainers: and the more inſufficient the ſcheme is; on which a ſociety is formed, the greater will be the gains of the firſt annuitants. The ſame principle, therefore, that has produced and kept up other *bubbles*, has a tendency to preſerve and promote theſe; and, for this reaſon, it is to be feared, that, in the preſent caſe, no arguments will be attended with any effect (*c*). The conſideration, that "the gain made by ſome in theſe ſocieties, "will be ſo much plunder taken from "others," ought immediately to engage all to withdraw from them, who have any regard to juſtice and humanity; but experience proves, that this argument, when oppoſed to

(*c*) This apprehenſion has been verified by fact.—At the beginning of laſt winter a letter was publiſhed to the *Provident Society*, containing a clear proof of the inſufficiency of the plans of all theſe ſocieties. It was at leaſt to be expected, that ſuch a publication would prevent the riſe of new ſocieties, formed on *more* inadequate plans. But this was ſo far from being the effect, that, ſoon afterwards, a ſociety ſprung up which calls itſelf the *Rational Annuity Society*; and which, though it does not take *half* the values of the annuities it promiſes, has had the ſhameleſſneſs to *aſſure* the public, that it is formed on a plan *inconteſtably durable*. The *Conſolidated*, the *Public Annuitant*, and the *Weſtminſter Union* Societies, are yet *worſe* inſtitutions, which have been ſince formed; and there may, for ought I know, be many more: for, indeed, all LONDON ſeems to be now entering into aſſociations of this kind.

private intereſt, is apt to be too feeble in its influence.

It cannot be ſaid with preciſion, how long theſe ſocieties may continue their payments to annuitants, after beginning them. A continued increaſe, and a great proportion of young members, may ſupport them for a longer time than I can foreſee. But the longer they are ſupported by ſuch means, the more miſchief they muſt occaſion.—So, a tradeſman, who ſells cheaper than he buys, may be kept up many years by increaſing buſineſs and credit; but he will be all the while *accumulating* diſtreſs; and the longer he goes on, the more extenſive ruin he will produce at laſt.

In the latter end of the firſt chapter, I have ſtated very particularly, the method of computing the values of *aſſurances* on lives and ſurvivorſhips, in all caſes where no more than two lives are concerned: and, in the 3d Eſſay, I have pointed out a conſiderable error, into which there is danger of falling in computing ſome of theſe values. The ſocieties and offices for tranſacting buſineſs in this way, are very uſeful; and it is neceſſary that they ſhould go upon the beſt principles, and poſſeſs all the information that can be given them.

But there is no part of this work in which the public is ſo much concerned, as the 3d Chapter. It will be there proved, that had the ſums raiſed for public ſervices ſince the REVOLUTION, been much greater than they have been, the increaſe of the public debts to their preſent ſtate might have been prevented in the eaſieſt manner, and at a trifling expence. A method, likewiſe, of reducing within due bounds theſe debts, heavy as they now are, will be propoſed.——All competent judges will, I believe, ſee, that this method, being founded on the moſt perfect improvement that can be made of money, is the moſt expeditious and effectual that the natures of things admit of. Nor, in my opinion, if the nation is not yet too near the *limit* of its reſources, can there be any *good* reaſon againſt carrying it into execution.——It is well known, to what prodigious ſums, money, improved for ſome time at *compound intereſt*, will increaſe (*a*). A ſtate, if there is no miſ-

(*a*) A *penny*, put out to 5 *per cent.* coumpound intereſt at our Saviour's birth, would, by this time, have increaſed to more money than would be contained in 150 millions of globes, each equal to the earth in magnitude, and all ſolid gold.

application of money, muſt neceſſarily make this improvement of any ſavings, which can be applied to the payment of its debts. It need never, therefore, be under any difficulties; for, with the *ſmalleſt* ſavings, it may, in as little time as its intereſt can require, pay off the *largeſt* debts.——Several of the obſervations I have made on this ſubject, have not, perhaps, been duly conſidered. Could they engage the attention of the managers of our public affairs, they might, I think, be of ſome ſervice. But this, I am ſenſible, I cannot expect. I have, however, in ſome degree, ſatisfied my own mind; and I ſhall always reflect with pleaſure, that, in this part of the following treatiſe, I have endeavoured to convey to the public, an information which is of particular importance to it.

In the *firſt* Eſſay I have made many obſer-ſervations on the expectations of lives, the pernicious influence of great towns on health, and manners, and population; the increaſe of mankind; and other ſubjects in the doctrine of Annuities and Political Arithmetick.—— In the Laſt Eſſay I have ſtated carefully the proper method of forming tables of the probabilities of human life, from given obſervations: And, in the *Appendix*, besides several new Tables, I have thought it necessary to give Mr. *Simpson*'s Tables of the values and expectations of LONDON lives; and all the other Tables which can be wanted in the perusal of this work.——I have also, in the *Appendix*, given the Demonstrations of the Answers to the *Questions* in Chap. I. These Demonstrations I have chosen to keep out of sight in the body of the work, in order to avoid discouraging such readers as may be unacquainted with mathematics.

Upon the whole. A great part of this work is, I believe, new; and I am in hopes also, that it will be found to contain some improvements in those branches of philosophical enquiry, which are the subjects of it.

The Reader is desired to correct the following Error.

In page 148, line 11. *instead of* 11, *read* 9 years purchase; *and in the next line, instead of* $6\frac{1}{2}$, *read* $15\frac{1}{2}$ years purchase.

CHAP. I.

Questions relating to Schemes for granting Reversionary *Annuities, and the Values of Assurances on Lives.*

QUESTION I.

"A Set of married men enter into a "society for securing annuities to "their widows. What sum of "money, in a single present pay-"ment, ought every member to "contribute, in order to entitle his widow "to an annuity of 30*l. per annum* for her life, "estimating interest at 4 *per cent*?"

ANSWER.

It is evident, that the value of such an expectation is different, according to the different ages of the purchasers, and the proportion of the age of the wife to that of the husband. Let us then suppose, that every person in such a society is of the same age with his wife, and that one with another all the members when they enter may be reckoned 40 years of age, as many entering above this age as below it. It has been demonstrated by Mr. *De Moivre* and Mr. *Simpson*, that "the value of an annuity on the *joint continuance* of any two lives, subtracted from "the value of an annuity on the life in expectation," gives the true present value of an annuity on what may happen to remain of the latter of the two lives after the other.

In the present case, the value of an annuity to be enjoyed during the *joint continuance* of two lives, each (*a*) 40, (*b*) is 9.826, accord-

(*a*) See Table VII. Appendix.

(*b*) The values of *joint* lives and reversions, as deduced from the *Breslaw* observations, are not given in any part of this work from Mr. *De Moivre*'s rules in his treatise on annuities on lives. For these rules are approximations, which give results so far from the truth, as to be, not only useless, but dangerous. In the second essay in the Appendix, a particular account of this will be given, and also of the method in which these values have been calculated.

Mr. *De Moivre* has calculated the values of *single* lives, on the supposition of an *equal decrement of life* thro' all its stages till the age of 86, which he considered as the utmost probable extent of life. Thus; let there be 56 persons alive at 30 years of age. It is supposed that one will die every year till, in 56 years, they will be all dead. The same will happen to 46 at 40, in 46 years. To 36 at 50, in 36 years, and so on for all other ages. The number of years which a given life wants of 86, he calls the *complement* of that life. Fifty-six, therefore, is the *complement* of 30; 46 of 40, and 36 of 50.

This hypothesis eases very much the labour of calculating the values of lives; and it is so conformable to Dr. *Halley*'s table of observations, that there is little or no reaing to the probabilities of life in the table of observations formed by Dr. *Halley*, from the bills of mortality of *Breslaw* in *Silesia*. The value of a single life 40 years of age, as given by Mr. *De Moivre*, agreeably to the same table, is 13.20 (*a*); and the former subtracted from the latter, leaves 3.37, or the true number of years purchase, which ought to be paid for any given annuity, to be enjoyed by a

son for distinguishing between the values of lives as deduced from this Table, and the same values deduced from the hypothesis.

In order to avoid putting the reader to trouble, I have given this table at the end of this work. And I have also given two other tables which I have formed from the bills of mortality at *Northampton* and *Norwich*. These last tables answer more nearly to Mr. *De Moivre's* hypothesis than even Dr. *Halley's* table; and the difference between the values of *single* and *joint* lives by the *hypothesis*, and the same values computed strictly from the tables, is generally less in these tables than in Dr. *Halley's*, as will be shewn in the last Essay. When, therefore, in the course of this work the values of *single* and *joint* lives are mentioned, as given agreeably to Dr. *Halley's* table, it must be understood, that they are taken from Tables VI. and VII. in the Appendix, and given in strict agreement only to the *hypothesis*; and that for this reason, they are in reality still more conformable to the *Northampton* and *Norwich* tables.

The inhabitants of *London*, as is well known, not living so long as the rest of mankind; the values of *single* and *joint* lives there, are considerably less than in any other place where observations have been kept. Whenever, therefore, I have had *London* lives in view, I have given particular notice of it, and taken their values from Mr. *Simpson*, who has calculated them with much accuracy from the *London* tables of observation. See Tables X. and XI.

(*a*) See Table VI. Appendix.

person 40 years of age, *provided* he survives another person of the same age, interest being reckoned at 4 *per cent. per annum.* The annuity, therefore, proposed in this question being 30*l.* the present value of it is 30 multiplied by 3.37, or 101*l.* 2*s.*

By calculating from Mr. *Simpson*'s tables (*a*), formed from the bills of mortality of *London*, this value comes out 102*l.*

The difference in the value of the reversion will be inconsiderable, whether the common age is taken a few years more or less than 40. Thus married men of 30 ought not, according to Dr. *Halley*'s table, to give two fifths of a year's purchase more, for any given reversionary annuity for their wives, than married men of 50, provided they are of the same ages with their wives; and one quarter more, according to Mr. *Simpson*'s table. If the wives are younger (as is generally the case) there will indeed be a considerable difference; for the value now determined would be 120*l.* according to the *Breslaw* observations, supposing the two lives to be 40 and 33, or that wives are one with another seven years younger than their husbands; and 118*l.* 10*s.* according to the *London* observations.

(*a*) See Table X. and XI. Appendix.

Question II.

" Supposing such a society as that describ-
" ed in the preceding question, to be limit-
" ted to a certain number of members, and
" constantly kept up to that number, by the
" admission of new members as old ones are
" lost, in consequence of their own deaths,
" and the deaths of their wives: What is the
" number of annuitants which, in some time
" after its establishment, will come to be
" constantly upon it?"

Answer.

Since every marriage produces either a widow or widower; and since all marriages taken together would produce as many widows as widowers, were every man and his wife of the same age, and the chance equal which shall die first; it is evident, that the number of widows that have ever existed in the world would, in this case, be equal to *half* the number of marriages. And what would take place in the world must also, on the same suppositions, take place in this society.——In other words; every *other* person in such a society leaving a widow, there must arise from it a number of widows equal to half its own number.—But this does not determine what number, all living at one and the same time, the society may expect will come to be constantly upon it. For if every widow lived no more than a year, the society would never have more annuitants upon it than came on in a year. And on the contrary, if none ever died, the number of annuitants would go on increasing for ever.—'Tis, therefore, necessary, in order to answer the present enquiry, to determine how long the *duration* of *survivorship* between persons of equal ages will be, compared with the *duration* of *marriage*. And the truth is, that, supposing the probabilities of life to decrease uniformly (*a*), the former is equal to the latter; and consequently, that the number of *survivors*, or (which is the same, supposing no second marriages) of *widows* and *widowers* alive together, which will arise from any given set of such marriages constantly kept up, will be equal to the whole number of marriages; or *half* of them (the number of widows in particular) equal to *half*

(*a*) That is, supposing that out of any given number alive at any age the same number will die every year 'till all are dead. See the preceding note. That on this hypothesis, the duration of survivorship is equal to the duration of marriage, when the ages are equal; or, in other words, that the *expectation* of two joint lives, the ages being equal, is the same with the *expectation* of survivorship, may be learnt from the 18th and 20th problems of Mr. *De Moivre*'s treatise on annuities; and a demonstration of it, together with a particular explanation of this subject, may be found at the beginning of the first Essay to which I must beg the reader to turn, if he is at any loss about the full meaning of what is here said.

the number of marriages.—Now, it appears that the decrease in the probabilities of life, is in fact nearly uniform. According to the *Breslaw*, the *Northampton* and *Norwich* tables of observation, almost the same numbers die every year from 20 years of age to 77 (*a*). After this, indeed, fewer die, and the rate of decrease in the probabilities of life is retarded. But this deviation from the hypothesis is inconsiderable; and its effect, in the present case, is to render the duration of survivorship *longer* than it would otherwise be. According to the *London* table of observations, the numbers dying every year begin to grow less at 50 years of age; and from hence to extreme old age, there is a constant retardation in the decrease of the probabilities of life (*b*). Upon the whole, therefore, it appears in answer to the present question, that "according to the *three* " *former tables* of observations, and suppo- " sing no widows to marry, the number " enquired after is *somewhat greater* than " half the number of the society; but, ac- " cording to the *London table*, a *good deal* " *greater*."

It must be carefully remembered, that this has been determined on the supposition, that

(*a*) See Tables III. IV. and V. Appendix.

(*b*) The reason of this difference between the *London* and other tables, will be given at the end of the fourth Essay.

husbands and their wives are of equal ages, and that in this case it becomes an equal chance which shall die first. In reality neither of these suppositions is just. Husbands in general are older than their wives; and in equal ages the mortality of males has been found to be greater than the mortality of females. For both these reasons, it is much more than an equal chance that the husband will die before his wife, or that the woman shall be the survivor of a marriage, and not the man. This will increase considerably the duration of survivorship on the part of the woman, and consequently the number enquired after in this question. The marriage of widows will also diminish this number, and the operation of these causes will be different in different situations. But it is by no means to be expected (in the situation of the societies I have in view) that the diminution from the latter cause will be considerable enough, to overbalance the operation of all the other causes which have been mentioned, and reduce the number under consideration so low, as half the number of marriages (*a*).

SCHOLIUM.

In *London* it appears, that there is a retardation of the decrease in the probabilities

(*a*) It will be observed hereafter, that this observation has been found to be true in fact.

of life, which renders the duration of ſurvivorſhip between two lives of equal ages, conſiderably longer than their joint continuance. It ſeems worth obſerving, that this is the reaſon why, though the probabilities of life, and therefore the values of ſingle and joint lives, are leſs in *London* than in other places, yet the values of reverſions depending on ſurvivorſhips, are in ſome caſes greater there. It is proper to add, that this likewiſe is the reaſon why, in calculating the values of joint lives and reverſions, the preſent value of an annuity payable yearly to the ſurvivor of two equal lives, may come out equal to, or even greater than, the preſent value of a like annuity for the joint lives. As an annuity, during ſuch ſurvivorſhip, will probably not become payable for ſome years, and therefore the money given for it will have time to accumulate, it is manifeſt, that the value of it could never be equal to the value of an annuity on the joint lives, the payment of which begins immediately, were not the obſervation now made true.

QUESTION III.

"Such a ſociety as that deſcribed in the "preceding queſtions being ſuppoſed, in "what time will the number of annuitants "upon it come to a *maximum*?"

ANSWER.

In order to be more clear in answering this question, I will first suppose the society to comprehend in it from its first establishment, *all* the married persons of *all* ages in any town or country, where the number of people continue constantly the same. In this case, the whole collective body of members will be at their greatest age, at the time of the establishment of the society; and the number of members, together with the number of widows left every year, will, taking one year with another, admit of no increase or diminution. The number of widows in life together, derived from any given number coming on a society every year, will increase continually, till as many die off as are added every year; that is, till they come to die off as fast as possible. But they cannot die off as fast as possible, till the whole collective body of widows are at their greatest age; or, till there is among them the greatest number possible of the oldest widows; and, therefore, not till there has been time for an accession to the oldest widows, from the youngest part of the widows that come on annually.

Let us, for the sake of greater precision, divide the whole medium of widows that come on every year, into different classes according to their different ages, and suppose some to be left at 56 years of age, some at 46, ſome at 36, and ſome at 26. The widows, conſtantly in life together, derived from the firſt claſs, will come to their greateſt age, and to a *maximum*, in 30 years, ſuppoſing with Mr. *De Moivre*, 86 to be the utmoſt extent of life. The ſame will happen to the ſecond claſs in 40 years, and to the third in 50 years (*a*). But the whole body, compoſed of theſe claſſes, will not come to a *maximum*, till the ſame happens to the fourth or youngeſt claſs; that is, not till the end of 60 years. After this, the affairs of the ſociety will become *ſtationary*, and the number of annuitants upon it of all ages will keep always nearly the ſame.

Such is the anſwer to this queſtion, ſuppoſing a ſociety to begin with its complete number of members, conſiſting of married perſons of all ages, in the ſame proportions to one another, with the proportions in which they exiſt in the world.——If it begins with its complete number of members, but at the ſame time admits none above a particular age: If, for inſtance, it begins with 200 members all under 50, and afterwards limits itſelf to this number, and keeps it up by admitting every year, at all ages between 26 and 50, new members as old ones drop off;

(*a*) In the *Appendix*, note (*a*), a rule is given, by which the numbers alive at the end of any particular number of years may be very eaſily determined.

in this caſe, the period neceſſary to bring on the *maximum* of annuitants will be juſt doubled. For, in the firſt place, the whole collective body of members will be 60 years in getting to their greateſt age, as may eaſily appear from what has been juſt ſaid. The annual medium of widows, therefore, that will come on the ſociety will increaſe continually for 60 years, it being evident, that the older any ſet of married men are, taken one with another, the faſter they will leave widows. And after this annual medium is increaſed to a *maximum*, 60 years more will be neceſſary to bring to a *maximum* the number in life together, derived from ſuch a *fixed* annual medium conſtantly coming on.——If ſuch a ſociety is any number of years in gaining its *maximum* of members, the time neceſſary to bring on the *maximum* of annuitants will be ſtill further prolonged, and will be equal to twice 60 years with that number of years added.—Moſt of the ſocieties for granting annuities to widows are of this kind; and, therefore, ſuppoſing them to gain their complete number of members in ten years, and for ever afterwards to preſerve it, the number of annuitants upon them will go on increaſing for 130 years.—It is proper, however, to be remembered, that the increaſe will be quicker at firſt, and afterwards ſlower; and that, within 20 or 30 years of the end of this term, it will be ſo ſlow as ſcarcely to be ſenſible, though ſtill real.

All who will beſtow due attention on this ſubject muſt ſee theſe deciſions to be juſt; and a demonſtration of them might be given, in a form more ſtrictly mathematical, were it neceſſary.

QUESTION IV.

" Suppoſe the members of ſuch a ſociety
" as that deſcribed in the preceding queſti-
" ons, to chuſe making *annual payments during*
" *the continuance of marriage*, in lieu of the
" ſum which the reverſionary annuity for
" their widows is worth in *preſent money*:
" What ought theſe *annual payments* to be,
" eſtimating intereſt at 4 *per cent*?"

ANSWER.

This will be eaſily determined, by finding what annual payments, during two joint lives of given ages, are equivalent to the value of the reverſionary annuity in *preſent money*.— Suppoſe, as in Queſtion I. the two joint lives to be each 40, and the reverſionary annuity 30*l*. *per annum*. An annual payment during the continuance of two ſuch lives is worth, according to Dr. *Halley*'s table of obſervations, 9.82 (*a*) years purchaſe. The annual

(*a*) See Table VII.

payment then ought to be such as being multiplied by 9.82, will produce (*a*) *l.* 101.1, the present value of the annuity in one payment by Question I. Divide then *l.* 101.1 by 9.82, and the *quotient*, or *l.* 10.3 will be the answer.——This is very nearly the annual payment of all the members at an average, supposing equal numbers to offer themselves for admission of every age between 30 and 50. As much as some give less, others ought to give more, according to their excess of age. Thus, the annual payment of a married person, 30 years of age, ought to be *l.* 9.39; and of a person 50 years of age *l.* 11.33.——If the values of joint lives and the reversionary annuity are taken agreeably to the *London* table of observations, these annual payments will be, for 30 years of age (*b*), *l.* 10.9,—for 40, *l.* 12.5,—for 50, *l.* 14.5.

(*a*) Particular notice should be taken of the method of notation here used, because it will be carried through the whole of this work.——The figures on the right hand of the full-point, signify the decimal parts of 1 *l.* Thus; *l.* 101.1, is *l.* 101 and the 10th of 1 *l.* or *l.* 101 and 2 *s.*——*l.* 9.39, is *l.* 9, and 39 hundredths of 1 *l.* or *l.* 9 : 7 *s.* : 10 *d.*——*l.* 11.33, is *l.* 11, and 33 hundredths of 1 *l.* or *l.* 11 : 6 *s.* : 7 *d.*——In general; it should be remembered, that 2 shillings allowed for every unit in the first place of decimals, and two-pence half-penny for every unit in the second place of decimals, will give, nearly enough, the value of the decimal part of every such expression.

(*b*) The value of two joint lives of 30, taken from Table XI. is 9.6. This subtracted from the value of the life in expectation, or from 13.1, by Table X. gives 3.5,

If either the rate of interest is supposed lower, or wives are supposed younger than their husbands, the annual payments will be increased. But there is no occasion for pointing out particularly the difference. It may be easily found in any cases by the directions now given. There is, however, one observation which ought to be here carefully attended to.—This method of calculation supposes, that the first annual payment is not to be made 'till the end of a year. If it is to be made *immediately*, the value of the joint lives will be increased one year's purchase; and, therefore, in order to find in this case the annual payments required, the value in present money found by Quest. I. must be divided by the value of the joint lives increased by unity, and, in this way, the preceding values at 4 *per cent*. according to the *Breslaw* observations, will be found to be *l*.8.62—*l*.9.35—*l*. 10.07.—According to the *London* observations, *l*. 10,—*l*.11.2,—*l*.12.7.

the number of years purchase which an annuity for a life of 30 years of age, *after* another life of the same age, is worth. This remainder, multiplied by 30, gives 105*l*. the value in a single payment, supposing the reversionary annuity to be 30*l*. And 105*l*. divided by 9.6, gives *l*. 10.9, the value of the same annuity in annual payments, during the joint continuance of the two lives, according to the *London* observations.—By similar operations all the other values above given have been found.

Question V.

" A ſociety may chuſe to make abate-
" ments in theſe annual payments, and to re-
" quire the remainder of the value of the
" reverſionary annuity to be given, in fines
" or premiums at the time of admiſſion; it
" may, for inſtance, chuſe to fix the annual
" payments of all the members to 5 guineas.
" What, in this caſe, would be the premium
" due at admiſſion, the annuity being ſup-
" poſed 30*l. per annum*, and intereſt being
" at 4 *per cent*?"

Answer.

From the whole preſent value of the annuity in one payment, ſubtract the value of 5 guineas *per annum*, during the joint lives; and the remainder will be the anſwer.

Suppoſing the joint lives both 40, the whole preſent value of the annuity in one payment is, according to the *Breſlaw* obſervations, *l.* 101.1, by Queſt. I.—The value of 5 guineas *per annum*, or of *l.* 5.25 *per annum*, during two ſuch joint lives, is 5.25, multiplied by the value of the joint lives; that is, 5.25, multiplied by 9.82, or *l.* 51.55; and this ſubtracted from *l.* 101.1, gives *l.* 49.5, the anſwer required for two lives at the age of 40.—The anſwer found in the ſame way for two lives whoſe common age is 30, is *l.* 46.5,—and for two lives at 50, 50*l.*

According to the *London* obſervations, theſe values are, for two lives at 30, *l*.54.6.—At 40, *l*.59.4.—At 50, *l*.63.3.

If the firſt of the annual payments is to be made immediately, the true anſwer will, in every inſtance, be the values found in the manner now directed, diminiſhed by the annual payment; or, in the preſent caſe, 5 guineas leſs than the values ſpecified.

The values, in *premiums* and *annual payments*, of any other reverſionary annuity, will be as much greater or leſs than theſe, as the annuity itſelf is greater or leſs.

QUESTION VI.

"A perſon 35 years of age wants to buy "an annuity, for what may happen to remain of his life after 50 years of age. "What is the value of ſuch an annuity in "*ready money*, and alſo in *annual payments*, "till he attains to the ſaid age; that is, in "annual payments for 15 years, ſubject in "the mean time to failure, ſhould his life "fail?"

ANSWER.

The preſent value of ſuch an annuity is the *preſent* value of a life at 50, in money to be received 15 years hence, and the payment of which depends on the contingency of the continuance of the given life 15 years. That is; it is equal to the value of a life at 50, multiplied by the preſent value of 1 *l.* to be received at the end of 15 years, and alſo by the probability that the given life will continue ſo long.—A life at 50, according to Mr. *De Moivre*'s valuation of lives, and reckoning intereſt at 4 *per cent.* is worth 11, 34 year's purchaſe. The preſent value of 1 *l.* to be received at the end of 15 years, is, by Table I, 0.5553. And the probability that a life at 35, will continue 15 years, is, according to the *Breſlaw* obſervations $\frac{346}{490}$ (*a*). And theſe three values, multiplied by one another, give *l.* 4.44, or the number of years purchaſe that ought to be given for the annuity.—The annuity then being ſuppoſed 50 *l.* its value in preſent money is 222 *l.*

(*a*) The probability that a given life ſhall continue any number of years, or attain to a *given age*, is (as is well known) the fraction, whoſe *numerator* is the number of the living in any table of obſervations oppoſite to the *given age*, and *denominator*, the number oppoſite to the preſent age of the given life.—Thus, in the preſent inſtance; 346 is the number in Dr. *Halley*'s table oppoſite to 50, and 490 the number oppoſite to 35.—$\frac{346}{490}$, (or the odds of 17 to 7) is, therefore, the probability that a perſon whoſe age is 35 ſhall attain to 50, or live 15 years. In the ſame manner it will appear, that, according to the ſame table, the probability that a perſon at this age ſhall live 25 years, is $\frac{243}{490}$; or nearly an even chance.

At *Northampton* and *Norwich* a perſon at the ſame age, has an even chance of living 26 years; but in *London*, ſcarcely 20 years. See Tables III, IV, V, and VIII. Appendix. I will add, though foreign to my preſent purpoſe, that a perſon at the ſame age has in theſe towns a better chance of living one year, than in *London*, in the proportion of 3 to 2.

In order to find this value in *annual payments*, while the given life is attaining to 50, it is necessary to find the value of an annuity for 15 years, subject to failure on the extinction of the given life. And the value of such an annuity is, evidently, the last value subtracted from the value of the given life; or, in the present instance, *l*. 4.44, subtracted from *l*. 13.97. (See Table VI, Appendix) that is, *l*. 9.53,—222*l*. then, being the present value of an annuity of 50*l*. for the remainder of a life now 35, after attaining to 50; and 9.53 being the number of years purchase, which ought to be given for an annual payment to last 15 years, if a life now 35 lasts so long, it follows, that the value of the same annuity in annual payments till this life attains to 50, is 222*l*. divided by 9.53; or *l*. 23.3.

This calculation supposes, that the first of the annual payments is not to be made till the end of a year. If the first payment is made immediately, the value will be, the *single payment* divided by the value of the life for the given term increased by unity; that is, in the present case, 222*l*. divided by 10.53; or *l*. 21.08.

If the value of the annuity is required in a single payment, over and above any given annual payment; deduct the value of the annual payment from the whole value in a single present payment, and the remainder will be the anſwer.—Thus; let 5 guineas, in the preſent inſtance, be the given annual payment for the aſſigned term; and let the enquiry be, how much more in preſent money the ſuppoſed annuity is worth. By what has been juſt ſaid, 9.53, multiplied by 5 guineas, that is, 50*l.* is the value of the annual payment; and this ſum deducted from 222*l.* leaves 172*l.* the anſwer.

If the annual payment begins immediately, its value is 10.53, multiplied by 5 guineas, and the anſwer comes out *l.* 166.75.

In this way may be found the value, in ſingle and annual payments, of any other annuity, payable to an aſſigned life, after a given term of years, taking any valuation of lives or intereſt of money. But care muſt be taken to remember, that it is the title to the annuity that will commence at the end of the given term, and that the firſt payment is not to be made 'till a year afterwards; that is, in the caſe here ſpecified, not 'till the end of 16 years.

SCHOLIUM.

The value of the *remainder* of two joint lives, after a given term of years, is likewiſe the value of 1 *l.* due at the end of the given term, multiplied by the value of two joint lives, each older by the given term than the given lives; and this product, multiplied by the probability, that the given joint lives ſhall not fail in the given term; or (which is the ſame) by the product of the two probabilities, that the ſingle lives ſhall each continue the given term. And the value of an annuity, on any given joint lives for a term of years beginning now, is this laſt value, ſubtracted from the whole preſent value of the joint lives. Thus; the value of two joint lives, one 40 years of age, and the other 50, (ſee Table VII.) is 8.91; which, multiplied by 0.6755, the value of 1 *l.* due 10 years hence, and by $\frac{445}{531}$, (the probability that a life at 30 ſhall continue 10 years) and alſo by $\frac{346}{445}$, (the probability that a life at 40 ſhall continue 10 years) gives 3.92, the preſent value of the remainder of two joint lives, aged 30 and 40, after 10 years; and this value, ſubtracted from 10.43 (the value in Table VII. of two joint lives, aged 30 and 40) leaves 6.51, their value for 10 years.

As the value of the longeſt of two lives is always the value of the *joint* lives, ſubtracted from the ſum of the values of the two *ſingle* lives; their value alſo for any *given term*, is the value of the *joint* lives for the given term, ſubtracted from the ſum of the values of the *ſingle* lives for the given term.

The truth of theſe rules may eaſily appear without particular proof. I have, however, pointed out the method of demonſtrating them in a note (*a*) at the end of this work.

(*a*) See note (B) in the Appendix.

By ſimilar operations, may be found the values of 3 or more *joint* lives, or the longeſt of *three* or more lives, for a given term of years, or of what ſhall remain of them after a given term of years.

QUESTION VII.

" The preſent value is required of an an-
" nuity to be enjoyed by one life, for what
" may happen to remain of it beyond ano-
" ther life, after a given term; that is, pro-
" vided *both* lives continue, from the pre-
" ſent time, to the end of a given term of
" years?"

ANSWER.

Find the value of the annuity for two lives greater, by the given term of years, than the given lives. Diſcount this value for the given term; and then, multiply by the probability, that the two given lives ſhall *both* continue the given term; and the product will be the anſwer.

EXAMPLE.

Let the two lives be each 30. The term ſeven years. The annuity, 10*l*. Intereſt, 4 *per cent.*——The given lives, increaſed by 7 years, become each 37. The value of two joint lives each 37, is (by Table VII) 10.25.

The value of a ſingle life at 37, is (by Table VI) 13.67. The former, ſubtracted from the latter, is 3.42, or the value of an annuity for the life of a perſon 37 years of age, after another of the ſame age, by Queſt. I.—3.42 diſcounted for 7 years, (that is, multiplied by 0.76, the value of 1 *l.* due at the end of ſeven years, by Table I.) is 2.6.—The probability that a ſingle life at 30 ſhall continue 7 years, is (by the hypotheſis explained page 2.) $\frac{49}{56}$ (*a*). The probability, therefore, that two

(*a*) In this caſe, it is on ſome accounts beſt, as well as eaſieſt, to take the probabilities of life from the hypotheſis, rather than immediately from the Tables.—Fifty-ſix perſons being ſuppoſed alive at 30, one will die every year, according to the hypotheſis. At the end of ſeven years then, the number of the living will be 49, and $\frac{49}{56}$, or the odds of 7 to 1, is, by note p. 18. the probability, that a life, aged 30, will continue 7 years; and this fraction, multiplied by itſelf, is the probability, that two lives of this age, ſhall *both* continue 7 years. In general, it muſt be remembered, that the probability, that any two or more events ſhall *all* happen, is the product ariſing from multiplying by one another, the probabilities of all the events taken ſeparately. The probability, therefore, that any number of perſons will *all* live any given time, is rightly found by multiplying into one another the probabilities that each of them will live that time.—It may further be of uſe to ſome, that I ſhould obſerve here, that the difference between unity and the fraction expreſſing the probability, that an event will happen, gives the probability that it will *not* happen. Thus; the probability, that a perſon 40 years of age will live 11 years, is by the *Breſlaw* Table $\frac{335}{445}$. The probability, therefore, that he will *not* live 11 years, is $\frac{335}{445}$, ſubtracted

ſuch lives ſhall both continue 7 years, is $\frac{2401}{3136}$, or, in decimals 0.765. And 2.6 multiplied by 0.765, is 1.989, the number of years purchaſe which ought to be given for an annuity, to be enjoyed by a life now 30 years of age, after a life of the ſame age, provided both continue 7 years. The annuity then being 10*l.* its preſent value is *l.* 19.89.

By ſimilar operations, it may be found, that ſuppoſing the term one year, and the ages and the rate of intereſt the ſame, the preſent value of the ſame reverſionary annuity is *l.* 32.4; and that if the term is 15 years, the value is *l.* 9.7.

For two lives each 40, theſe values are *l.* 30.33.—*l.* 17.44.—*l.* 7.3. the term being 1, 7, or 15 years.

For two lives each 50, the ſame values for the ſame terms, are *l.* 28.2,—*l.* 13.86,—*l.* 4.34 (*a*).

Theſe values, according to the *London* obſervations and Mr. *Simpſon*'s Tables of the values of ſingle and joint lives, are,

from unity or $\frac{110}{443}$.—In like manner: The probability that two perſons aged 30, ſhall *both* live 7 years, being 0.765, the probability that they will *not* both live ſo long, or that *one or other* uf them will die in 7 years, is 0.765 ſubtracted from unity, or .235.

If any reader is unwilling to take theſe aſſertions for granted, he ſhould conſult the beginning of Mr. *De Moivre*'s, or Mr. *Simpſon*'s Treatiſes on the Doctrine of Chances, where he will find them demonſtrated.

(*a*) See Note (C) Appendix.

For 2 lives at 30—*l.* 32.05—*l.* 18.62—*l.* 7.66.
at 40—*l.* 30.7 —*l.* 15.6 —*l.* 5.45.
at 50—*l.* 29.36—*l.* 12.33—*l.* 3.24.

QUESTION VIII.

" Let the scheme of a society for granting " annuities to widows, be, that, if a member " lives *a year* after admission, his widow shall " be entitled to a life annuity of 20*l.* If " *seven* years, to 10*l.* more, or 30*l.* in the " whole. If *fifteen* years; to another addi- " tional 10*l.* or 40*l.* in the whole. What " ought to be the annual payments of the " members for the ages of 30, 40, and 50; " supposing them of the same ages with their " wives, and allowing compound interest at " 4 *per cent?*"

ANSWER.

According to the *hypothesis*, explained p. 2; and, therefore, very nearly, according to the Tables of observation for *Breslaw, Norwich,* and *Northampton,*

l. 8.44—*l.* 8.69—*l.* 9.05.

According to the *London* observations,

l. 9.41—*l.* 10.17—*l.* 10.92.

These values are easily deduced from the values in the last question. For example. The value of 10*l.* *per annum* for life to 40 after 40, provided the joint lives do not fail in *one* year, is, according to the *hypothesis*, *l.* 30.33. The value of 20*l.* *per annum*, in the same circumstances, is, therefore, *l.* 60.66.—In like manner, the value of 10*l.* after *seven* years, is *l.* 17.44. And of 10*l.* after 15 years *l.* 7.3.—These values together make *l.* 85.4, or the value of the expectation, described in this question, in a *single present payment*; which, divided by 9.82, (the value by Table VII. of two joint lives at 40) gives *l.* 8.69, the value of the same expectation in *annual payments*, during the joint lives.—In the same manner may be found the answer in all cases to any questions of this kind.

These calculations suppose, that the annual payments do not begin till the end of a year. If they are to begin *immediately*, the true *annual payments* will be, as was before observed, the *single* payments, divided by the value of the joint lives increased by unity; and in the present case they will be, by the *hypothesis*,

l. 7.75—*l.* 7.9—*l.* 8.07.

By the *London* observations,

l. 8.52—*l.* 9.06—*l.* 9.51.

By the method of calculation now explained, may be easily found in all cases, supposing the annual payments previously settled, what the reversionary annuities are corresponding to them in value.—Thus, the annuities being the same with those mentioned in this question, the *mean* annual payments for all ages between 30 and 50, are nearly 8 *l.* according to the *highest* probabilities of life; 9 *l.* according to the *lowest*; and 8 guineas the *medium* (*a*); interest being at 4 *per cent.* and the first payment to be made immediately.

If the mean annual payments, beginning immediately, are fixed to five guineas, the corresponding life annuities will be nearly (by the *hypothesis*) 12 *l.* if the contributor lives a year, and 24 *l.* if he lives seven years; or (by the *London* observations) 12 *l*, if he lives a year, and 20 *l.* if he lives seven years (*b*).

(*a*) The value of this expectation, supposing married men 40 years of age, and their wives 30, is, in a *single* payment, 113 *l.* In annual payments beginning immediately *l.* 9.88, by the *hypothesis*. And 107 *l.*—and *l.* 10.93, by the *London* observations.

(*b*) If the annuities in expectation are 14 *l.* provided a member lives a year, and 20 *l.* provided he lives seven years, the proper *mean single* payments for all ages, taken one with another, under 50 or 52, is 50 guineas nearly, according to all the Tables of observation, supposing equality of age between men and their wives. And the addition which ought to be made, on account of excess of age on the man's side is, taking the nearest and the

It is obſervable, that the difference in the values of the annuities, ariſing from difference of ages, and the difference in the probabilities of life, is leſs in this queſtion than in queſtion 4th; and that, conſequently, the plan propoſed in it, is the ſafeſt, as well as the moſt equitable and encouraging, that a ſociety can adopt.

It is neceſſary to remark here further, that *yearly* payments which begin immediately, are more advantageous than *half-yearly* payments which begin immediately. Mr. *Simpſon* (in his Treatiſe on *The Doctrine of Annuities and Reverſions*, pag. 78, and alſo *in his Select Exerciſes*, p. 283) has ſhewn, that, in the caſe of life annuities, *half-yearly* payments, which begin at the end of half a year, are ¼ of a year's purchaſe better than *yearly* payments, which begin at the end of a year. And it is manifeſt, that *half-yearly* payments, which begin immediately, are no

eaſieſt round ſums, about a guinea and ½ for every year as far as 17 years; or, in the annual payments, (ſuppoſed 5 guineas) ½ a guinea *per annum* for five years exceſs, and ½ a guinea more for every four years exceſs beyond five years, till the exceſs comes to be 17 years. And, I believe, that 60 guineas in *ſingle payments*, and ſix guineas in *annual payments* beginning immediately, may very well be ſtated as the *loweſt common* payments proper to be required, ſuppoſing all married men under 52, taken into a ſociety, without enquiring into the difference of age between them and their wives, the annuities being all along ſuppoſed to be *life* annuities, and intereſt reckoned at 4 *per cent.*

more than half a year's purchaſe better than thoſe which begin at the end of half a year. But *yearly* payments, which begin immediately, are a *whole year's* purchaſe better than the ſame payments to begin at the end of a year. The difference of value, therefore, between *yearly* and *half-yearly* payments, ſuppoſing both to begin immediately, is a quarter of a year's purchaſe in favour of the former.

QUESTION IX.

" The value is required of an annuity to
" be enjoyed for what may happen to re-
" main of one life after another, provided
" the life in expectation continues a given
" time?"

ANSWER.

Find by Queſtion VI. the preſent value of the annuity for the remainder of the life in expectation, after the given time, and multiply this value by the probability, that the other life ſhall fail within that time. Find alſo, by Queſtion VII. the value of the reverſion, provided *both* lives continue the given time. Add theſe values to one another, and the *ſum* will be the anſwer in a ſingle preſent payment.

EXAMPLE.

An annuity of 10*l.* for the life of a perſon now 30, is to commence at the end of 11 years (*a*), if another perſon now 40, ſhould be then dead; or, if this ſhould not happen, at the end of any year beyond 11 years in which the former ſhall happen to ſurvive the latter. What is the preſent value of ſuch an annuity, reckoning intereſt at 4 *per cent.* and taking the probabilities of life as they are in Dr. *Halley*'s Table?

The value of 10*l.* *per annum*, for the remainder of the life of a perſon now 30, after 11 years, found by Queſt. VI. is *l.* 69.43.—The probability that a perſon 40 years of age ſhall live 11 years, is, by Dr. *Halley*'s Table, $\frac{335}{445}$. The probability, therefore, that he will die in 11 years, is $\frac{335}{445}$ ſubtracted from unity (*b*), or $\frac{110}{445}$; which multiplied by *l.*69.43, gives *l.* 17.16.—The value of the reverſion, provided *both* live 11 years, found by Queſt. VII. is 17*l.* And this value added to the

(*a*) That is, the title to the annuity is to commence at the end of 11 years, and the firſt payment to be made a year afterwards, in caſe the life in expectation ſhould continue ſo long, and the other fail. But if *both* lives ſhould continue the given term, the firſt payment is always to be made at the end of the year, in which the former life ſhall happen to ſurvive the latter. See Queſt. VI.

(*b*) See the Note, p. 23.

former, makes *l.* 34.16, the value required in a *single present payment*; which payment divided by *l.* 11.43, (the value by Table VII. of two joint lives, aged 30 and 40, with unity added) gives 3*l*; (*a*) or the value required in annual payments during the joint lives, the first payment to be made immediately.——If, every thing else being the same, the assigned term is 15 years, the value required will be 29*l.* in a *single payment*, and *l.* 2.55 in *annual payments*.

QUESTION X.

"What money in hand, and also in annual payments during life, ought a person "of an assigned age to give for a sum of money, payable at his death to his heirs (*b*)?—"In other words, what money in hand, and "in annual payments during life, ought a "person of a given age to pay for an *assurance* of any given sum on his life?"

ANSWER.

Subtract the value of the life from the *perpetuity*. Multiply the remainder by the

(*a*) See the demonstration of this rule in Note (D) Appendix.

(*b*) This question is the same with Problem 16th, in Mr. *De Moivre*'s Treatise on Annuities, and Problem 26th, in Mr. *Simpson*'s Select Exercises; but the answers there given are right only when applied to reversionary *estates*, and therefore must be materially wrong, when applied to reversionary *sums*, as will appear from the *Scholium* to this Question, and from note (E) in the Appendix.

product of the given sum into the interest of 100*l.* for a year: and this last product, divided by 100*l.* increased by its interest for a year, will give the answer in a *single present* payment. And this payment, divided by the value of the life, will give the answer in *annual* payments, during the continuance of the life.

Example. Let the life be 30. The sum 100*l.* The rate of interest 4 *per cent*. And the valuation of lives, that in Table VI. The perpetuity, therefore (*a*), is 25. The interest of 100*l.* for a year, is 4*l.* 100*l.* increased by its interest for a year is 104*l.* And the value of the life 14.68.—The value of the life, subtracted from the perpetuity, gives 10.32, which, multiplied by the product of 100*l.* into 4, or by 400, gives 4128. And this, divided by 104, gives *l.* 39.7, the value of 100*l.* payable at the death of a person aged 30, in a single present payment.—And this payment, divided by 14,68, is *l.* 2.7, the same value in annual payments during the continuance of the life.

These values found in the same way, agreeably to the valuation of lives for *London*, in Table X, are *l.* 45.76, and *l.* 3.49.—If the life is 36, and interest 4 *per cent*. these values are 43*l.* and *l.* 3.1, by Table VI, and *l.* 49.6,

(*a*) That is; the value of the *fee simple* of an estate found by dividing 100*l.* by the rate of interest.

and *l*. 4.1, by Table X.—If interest is reckoned at 3 *per cent.* the same values are, by Table VI, for 30 years of age, *l*. 48.14.—2.86.—For 36 years of age, *l*. 51.43, and *l*. 3.28.

It appears here, that difference of interest makes no considerable difference in the answers to questions of this kind, except when the values are required in a single payment.

If the first of the annual payments is to be made immediately, the single payment is to be divided by the value of the life, with unity added to it, agreeably to what has been already observed; and the annual payments in this case (interest supposed at 4 *per cent.*) will be by Table VI, for a life at 30, *l*. 2.53—At 36, *l*. 2.9.

If the payments are half yearly payments beginning immediately, the single payment must be divided by the value of the life increased by ¾, or .75, (see Quest. VIII.) And the half yearly payments, for the age of 36, will be half 2.9, or 1.45. And half 1.45, or .725, is likewise nearly the proper quarterly payments.

Again; if an annual payment, beginning immediately, of *l*. 2.9, ought (reckoning interest at 4 *per cent.*) to purchase 100 *l*. payable at the failure of a life now 36; 5 *l*. by the rule of proportion, ought to purchase 172 *l*. And in like manner, it may be found, that the same annual contribution, in half-yearly or quarterly payments, beginning immediately, ought to purchase 170*l.*—These sums, according to the *London* observations, are 132*l.* and 130*l.* nearly.

The reason of mentioning these particulars will be seen in the next chapter.

SCHOLIUM.

If the reversion is not a *sum*, but an annuity for ever, or an *estate* in *fee simple*, to be entered upon after a given life, its present value, *in a single payment*, will be "the value "of the life subtracted from the perpetuity, "and the remainder multiplied by the an-"nuity, or the annual rent of the estate."—And the value, in *annual payments*, will be, as before, the single payment divided by the value of the life.—Universally. It ought to be remembered, that a reversionary *estate*, after any given life or lives, is worth as much more than a corresponding reversionary *sum*, as 100*l.* increased by its interest for a year, is greater than 100*l.*—Thus, the present values, in single and annual payments, of 4*l.* *per annum* for ever, and of 100*l.* in money after any assigned life, are to one another, (interest being at 4 *per cent.*) as 104 to 100, or 1.04 to 1.—The reason of this difference is, that the calculations suppose, that the reversionary *sum*, and the first yearly rent of the *estate*, or first payment of the annuity, are to be received at the ſame time, after the extinction of the lives in poſſeſſion. It is eaſy to ſee, that this is a circumſtance which muſt make the latter of moſt value. But to prevent any doubts about it, I ſhall explain it more particularly in a note in the Appendix (*a*).

QUESTION XI.

"A perſon of a given age, having an yearly income which will fail with his life, wants to make proviſion for another perſon of a given age, in caſe the latter ſhould happen to ſurvive. What ought the former to give in a ſingle payment, and alſo in annual payments during their joint lives, for a given ſum, payable at his death to the latter?"

It is manifeſt, that the value of the given ſum in this caſe, muſt be leſs than in the caſe ſtated in the laſt Queſtion; becauſe, here the payment of it is ſuſpended on the contingency, that one life ſhall ſurvive another, whereas in the other caſe, it is *certainly* to be paid at the failure of a given life.

ANSWER.

Find, by the ſolution of problem 32d, p. 297, Mr. *Simpſon*'s Select Exerciſes, the

(*a*) Vid. Appendix note (E).

value of an estate, corresponding to the given sum, and depending on the given survivorship. Divide this value by 1 *l.* increased by its interest for a year, and the quotient will be the value of the given sum in a single present payment. And the single payment, divided by the value of the given joint lives, will be the answer in annual payments during the joint lives.

The solution I have referred to is as follows.

" Find the value of an annuity on two e-
" qual joint lives, whereof the common age
" is equal to the age of the older of the two
" proposed lives; which value, subtract from
" the perpetuity, and take half the remain-
" der. Then say, as the *expectation* of the
" duration of the younger of the two lives is
" to that of the elder, so is the said half re-
" mainder to a 4th proportional, which will
" be the number of years purchase to be gi-
" ven for the estate when the life in expec-
" tation is the oldest of the two. But if this
" life is the youngest, then add the number
" of years purchase just found to the value
" of the joint lives, and let the sum be sub-
" tracted from the perpetuity, and you will
" also have the answer in this case (*a*)".

(*a*) Mr. *Simpson* has given the following examples of this solution, adapted to *London* lives.——Example I. " Suppose the age of the *expectant* to be 40; of the pos- " sessor 30. The rate of interest 4 *per cent.* and the

Let the life in expectation be 30; and the other life 40: The sum, 100*l.* Interest, 4 *per cent.* The valuation of lives, that in Table VI.

The *expectation* of the first life, is 28; of the second life 23, by Mr. *De Moivre's hypothesis*. The value of the joint lives is 10.43,

" given legacy 5000*l.* or 200*l. per annum.* Then the " value of two equal joint lives of 40, being 8.1, by " Table XI, and the perpetuity 25, the remainder or " difference will be here 16.9; whereof the half is 8.45. " Therefore, it will be as 23.6 to 19.6, so 8.45 to 7.02 " years purchase, or *l.* 1404, the required value."

Example II. " Let the age of the *expectant* be 30, of " the *possessor* 40, and the rest as in the preceding example. " Here the value of the joint lives 30 and 40, will " be 8.8; which added to 7.02, (found above) the sum " will be 15.82; whence the answer, in this case, is " 9.18 years purchase, or 1836."

I have shewn, that the values of reversionary *estates*, and reversionary *sums*, are not the same as is here supposed.—The rule gives the true value when applied to the former; but, when applied to the latter, the values given by it must be divided by 1*l.* increased by its interest for a year, as above directed.—The same observation is to be applied to Mr. *Simpson*'s next Problem, or the 33d.

In these Examples, 23.6 and 19.6, are the expectations, in Table IX, of 30 and 40, according to the *London* Tables of Observation; and the method of finding them for any age, and from any Tables of observation, is explained at the beginning of the first Essay.

In Mr. *De Moivre's hypothesis*, the expectation of a life, is always *half* the complement. See note p. 2.—Sometimes the *complement* of a life is mentioned without any view to Mr. *De Moivre*'s hypothesis, and it then means double the *expectation* of the life whatever that may be according to any Table of observations.

by Table VII. The value of two joint lives, both 40, is 9.82, by the same Table. The estate corresponding to 100*l.* is 4*l. per ann.* and the present value of such an estate to be entered upon by a person 30 years of age, provided he survives a person 40 years of age is, by the rule just quoted, *l.* 33.32. And this value, divided by 1*l.* increased by its interest for a year, or by 1.04, is *l.* 32.03. the value in a *single present payment* of the sum of 100*l.* dependent on the given survivorship. And this single payment, divided by 10.43, is *l.* 3.07, the required value in *annual payments*, during the joint lives, if the first payment is not to be made till the end of a year. But if the first payment is to be made immediately, the required value in *annual payments* will be *l.* 32.03, divided by 11.43, or *l.* 2.8.—These values, according to the *London* observations, or Mr. *Simpson*'s Tables founded upon them, are *l.* 35.30, in a *single payment*, and *l.* 3.6, in *annual payments*, beginning immediately.

Mr. *Simpson*, in the Problems following that here quoted, has given solutions of most other Questions, concerning the values of reversions depending on survivorships, where the whole duration of two or three lives is concerned. And I am acquainted with no other solutions of these Questions, which are applicable to all Tables of observations, and which at the same time (proper regard being paid to the correction explained in the last Question) may be considered as sufficiently correct (*a*).

Question XII.

"Suppose an institution for the relief of "widows to extend its assistance likewise "to the families of married men, provided "they leave no widows. Suppose, for in-"stance, that in this case children are to be "entitled to 100*l*. What is such an expec-"tation worth, in present payment, accord-"ing to Dr. *Halley*'s Table, interest being at "4 *per cent*?"

Answer.

If 40 is the mean age at which members are admitted on such an institution, and 32 the mean age of their wives, the answer (supposing no subsequent marriages) is, by the 33d Problem in Mr. *Simpson*'s Select Exercises, p. 298, and the correction already explained, *l*. 13.80 (*b*).

(*a*) See the third Essay.

(*b*) This Problem and its solution are given by Mr. *Simpson* in the following words. "A and his heirs are "entitled to an estate of a given value, upon the decease "of B, provided B survives A; to find the value of "their expectation in *present* money."—Solution. "Find "the value of an annuity on the longest of two equal

But there is a reduction necessary, on account of the chance there is, that a widower may marry again. Suppose, therefore, one half of all widowers to marry a second and third time, and that two fifths of such widowers survive these subsequent marriages. In this case, $\frac{1}{2}$ added to $\frac{2}{5}$ of $\frac{1}{2}$, or $\frac{7}{10}$ of all who become widowers, will die without leaving widows, and therefore $\frac{7}{10}$ of *l.* 13.8, or *l.* 9.66, will be the answer. If only one *fourth* of all who become widowers marry again, and two fifths of these survive, the answer will be *l.* 11.73.

" lives, whereof the common age is that of the older of
" the lives A and B; which value subtract from the
" perpetuity, and take half the remainder; then it will
" be as the expectation of duration of the younger of
" the lives A and B, is to that of the older, so is the
" said half remainder to the number of years purchase
" required, when the life B *is the older of the two*. But
" if B *be the younger*; then to the number thus found,
" add the value of an annuity on the longest of the lives
" A and B, and subtract the sum from the perpetuity, for
" the answer in this case."

If the estate is 4 *l. per annum*, the age of B 40, and of A 32, interest 4 *per cent.* the answer by this rule comes out *l.* 14.35, which divided (as in the preceding question) by 104, gives *l.* 13.80, the value, as above, of 100*l.* in money. If B is 30 and A 40, the same value is 20*l.*

N. B. The value of the longest of two lives is always the *difference* between the value of the *joint* lives, and the *sum* of the values of the two given *single* lives. Thus; the value of a life at 40, is, by Table VI, 13.2. The *sum* of the values of two such lives, is 26.4. The value of two joint lives, whose common age is 40, is, by Table VII, 9.82; and the difference is 16.58, or the value of the *longest* of two lives at 40.

This calculation ſuppoſes all marriages to leave children who ſurvive their parents. If this is conſidered as uncertain, the values now determined muſt be diminiſhed in the proportion of this uncertainty.—Thus; if one marriage in ſeven fails of leaving children (*a*) that ſurvive their parents; theſe values will be reduced a *ſeventh* part, or to *l.* 8.28, if *half*, and *l.* 10.05, if a *quarter* of all widowers marry.

In this way may any other queſtions of the ſame kind be anſwered on any ſuppoſitions that may be thought moſt reaſonable.

QUESTION XIII.

"Let an eſtabliſhment be ſuppoſed which "takes in at once all the marriages in a "country, or all marriages among perſons "of a particular profeſſion within a given "diſtrict, and ſubjects them for perpetuity "to a certain equal and common tax, or an"nual payments, in order to provide life an"nuities for ſuch widows as ſhall reſult from "theſe marriages. What ought the tax to "be, ſuppoſing the annuity 20*l.* and calcu"lating at 4 *per cent.* from Mr. *De Moivre*'s "valuation of lives; or, which is nearly the "ſame, from the probabilities of life in Dr. "*Halley*'s Table of obſervations?"

(*a*) This for many years has been nearly the fact among the miniſters and profeſſors in *Scotland*.

Answer.

Since at the commencement of ſuch an eſtabliſhment, all the oldeſt, as well as the youngeſt marriages, are to be entitled equally to the propoſed benefit, a much greater number of annuitants will come immediately upon it, than would come upon any ſimilar eſtabliſhment, which limited itſelf in the admiſſion of members to perſons not exceeding a given age. This will check that accumulation of money, which ſhould take place at firſt, in order to produce an income equal to the diſburſements at the time when the number of annuitants comes to a *maximum*; and, therefore, will be a particular burden upon the eſtabliſhment in its infancy. For this, ſome compenſation muſt be provided; and the equitable method of providing it, is, by levying *fines* at the beginning of the eſtabliſhment, on every member *exceeding* a given age, proportioned to the number of years which he has lived beyond that age. But in the preſent queſtion, it is ſuppoſed, that ſuch fines cannot be conveniently levied, or that every payment muſt be equal and common, whatever diſparity there may be in the value of the expectations of different members. The fines, therefore, muſt be reduced to one common one, anſwering as nearly as poſſible to the diſadvantage I have mentioned, and payable by every member at the time when the establishment begins. After this, the establishment will be the same with one that takes upon it all at the time they marry; and the tax or annual payment of every member adequate to its support, will be the annual payment during marriage, due from persons who marry at the mean age at which, upon an average, all marriages may be considered as commencing.—There are then two points to be here determined. The *fines* necessary to be paid at first, according to the account I have just given; and the *constant annual payment*, necessary to be made by every member, as an equivalent for the expectation provided by the establishment.—The *fines* to be paid at first are, for every particular member, the same with the difference between the value of the expectation to him at his present age, and what would have been its value to him had the scheme begun at the time he married? Or, they are, for the whole body of members, the difference between the value of the common expectation, to persons at the mean age of all married persons taken together as they exist in the world, and to persons at that age, which is to be deemed their mean age when they marry.

Thus; let 33 for the man, and 25 for the woman, be the mean ages of all that marry annually. Let also 48 be the mean age of all the married men in the world, and 40 of married women (*a*).—Now, he that will calculate for these ages, in the manner directed in Quest. IV. will find, that the value in *annual payments* during marriage, and beginning immediately, of the expectation of an annuity of 20*l*. *per annum*, by a person 25 years of age, after a life whose age is 33, is *l*. 6.64.—And that *l*. 8.04, is the value of the same expectation, the ages being 48 and 40.

The former, therefore, is the payment for perpetuity from every member of the establishment; and the value of the *difference* between it and the latter, or of *l*. 1.4 *per ann.* payable during two joint lives, whose ages are 40 and 48, that is, *l*. 14.2, is the fine necessary to be levied on every married member at the beginning of the establishment (*b*).

It would be easy to extend the benefit of such an establishment, so far as to provide 100*l*. for the children of members, provided

(*a*) I must beg leave to refer to note (F) in the Appendix, for an explanation of what I mean by the mean ages of married men and women, and also for a confirmation of the answer I have given to this question.

(*b*) An annuity for ever, the first payment of which is to be made immediately, is worth 26 years purchase, interest being at 4 *per cent.* *l*. 14.2 therefore, is equivalent in value to 0.55*l*. or 11*s*. *per annum*, for ever. Add this to *l*. 6.64, and it will appear, that *l*. 7.19 *per annum*, beginning immediately, is the answer to this question, supposing the value of the *fine* to be provided for in the perpetual annual payments.

they leave no widows; and the neceſſary addition on this account to the perpetual annual payments, can ſcarcely, in the circumſtances this queſtion ſuppoſes, be much more than about 15*s.* payable during life, and excluding from all benefit ſuch as happen to be widowers at the commencement of the eſtabliſhment, and do not afterwards marry.

If, in ſuch an eſtabliſhment, all perſons of a particular denomination, whether married men, widowers, or batchelors, are ſubjected alike to the taxes and fines; they ought to be as much *leſs*, as the whole number of perſons ſubjected to them, is *greater* than the number of marriages conſtantly exiſting.

In carrying theſe ſchemes into execution, there cannot be a more eaſy, or equitable way of raiſing the neceſſary fines, than by providing, that none ſhall be entitled to any expectation for a few of the firſt years. Thus; an eſtabliſhment, entitling widows to 20*l.* *per annum* for life, and conſiſting of 667 married members, and 344 unmarried, always kept up at an average, ought to begin with a capital of *l.* 14.2 multiplied by 667, or 9471*l.* beſides one payment in hand of the conſtant annual payments. That is, (the proper annual payment of every member being in this caſe $\frac{667}{1011}$, multiplied by *l.* 6.64, or *l.* 4.38) it ought to begin with a capital of 13,899*l.* over and above the payment of *l.*4.38, at the *end* of every year for ever afterwards (*a*).—The exclusion of all the first members from any benefit, unless they survive the first *two* years, or live to make *three* payments, would raise this capital nearly. And such an exclusion for *three* or *four* years, would be an advantage so considerable, that it would probably give security and stability to the scheme for all subsequent time.

In these observations, I have had in view, several schemes of the kind described in it, which are now actually established in this kingdom; but more particularly, one begun among the *London* and *Middlesex* clergy, and another which is established by act of parliament, among the clergy in *Scotland*, of both which, I shall have occasion in the next chapter to take further notice.

I have chosen to calculate here only from Dr. *Halley*'s Table, or Mr. *De Moivre*'s *hypothesis* grounded upon it, because the *London* Table is, by no means, adapted to the cases in view.

The difference of eight years between the ages of men and their wives, as here taken, is probably too little; and for this reason,

(*a*) Or, supposing the value of 9471 *l.* (the fine) provided for in the annual payments, it ought to receive every year, at the *beginning* of the year, a contribution from each member of *l.*4.74.

and alſo on account of the greater mortality of males, the values I have given ſhould be conſidered as the loweſt that any ſcheme ought to provide.

It ſhould be further remembered, that when the mean ages, at which marriages commence, are ſuppoſed to be 33 and 25, all ſecond and third marriages are included; and that it is to be expected, that almoſt all theſe marriages will begin after theſe ages; and likewiſe, that a conſiderable proportion of the firſt marriages will begin a much longer time *after* theſe mean ages, than any of the other firſt marriages will begin before them.—Probably, therefore, theſe mean ages ſhould not be taken younger. One or two years, however, more or leſs, in every ſuppoſition I have made, will make no difference of any conſequence.

QUESTION XIV.

"A perſon of a given age has an eſtate de-
"pending on the continuance of his life for
"a given term. What ought he to give for
"having it *aſſured* to him for that term?"

ANSWER.

From the value of an annuity certain for the given term, found by Table II, ſubtract the value of the life for the given term, found by Queſt. VI. and *reſerve* the remainder.—Multiply the value of 1 *l.* due at the end of the given term, (found by Table I.) by the *perpetuity*, and alſo by the *probability*, that the given life ſhall fail in the given term. The *product* added to the *reſerved* remainder, and the *ſum* multiplied by the given annuity, will be the required value of the aſſurance in one preſent payment (*a*).

EXAMPLE.

An eſtate or annuity of 10 *l.* *for ever*, will be loſt to the heirs of a perſon now 34, ſhould his life fail in 11 years. What ought he to give for the *aſſurance* of it for this term?—That is; what is the preſent value of ſuch an annuity to be entered upon at the failure of ſuch a life, ſhould that happen in 11 years?

The value of the life of a perſon whoſe age is 34 for 11 years, is, by Queſt. VI. (reckoning intereſt at 4 *per cent.* and calculating from Dr. *Halley*'s Table of obſervations) 7.76; which, ſubtracted from 8.760, (the value of an annuity certain for 11 years) leaves 1 *l.* the *remainder* to be reſerved.

The value of 1 *l.* to be received at the end of 11 years, is, 0.6496, by Table I. The probability that the life of a perſon, aged 34,

(*a*) See the demonſtration in note (G) Appendix.

shall fail in 11 years, is, by Dr. *Halley*'s Table, $\frac{101}{756}$; and the perpetuity is 25. These numbers, multiplied by one another, and 1 added to the product, make 4.34, which, multiplied by 10, (the given annuity) gives *l.* 43.4, the required value in a single present payment.

l. 43.4, divided by 1.04, gives *l.* 41.7, the true value, by Scholium to Quest. X. of the assurance of an *equivalent* sum, or of 250*l.* for 11 years on the given life.

Again. 41.7, divided by 8.76, (the value of the given life for the given time with unity added to it) gives 4.76, the same value in annual payments beginning immediately, for 11 years (*a*), subject to failure should the life fail.

Scholium.

In a similar way may the price of assurances on any two joint lives, or the *longest* of two lives for any given terms, be calculated; the rule being as follows:

" From the value of an annuity certain
" for the *given term*, subtract the value of
" the joint lives, or the longest of the two
" lives for the *given term*, found by Scho-
" lium to Quest. VI. and *reserve* the remain-
" der.—Multiply the value of 1*l.* to be re-

(*a*) The last payment to be made at the end of the 11th year; or 12 payments in all.

" ceived at the end of the given term by the " perpetuity, and also by the probability " that the *joint lives*, or the *longest of the two* " *lives*, shall fail within the given term. This " product added to the reserved *remainder*, " and the *sum* multiplied by the annuity to be " assured, will be the value of the assurance " in a single present payment."

EXAMPLE.

" What is the value of 10*l*. *per annum*, to " be entered upon, should *either* of two " persons, one 40 and the other 30 years of " age, die in ten years, reckoning interest " at 4 *per cent*. and calculating from Dr. " *Halley*'s Table."

The value of two joint lives at these ages, for 10 years, (found by *Scholium* to Quest. VI.) is, 6.51; which, subtracted from 8.111, (the value of an annuity certain for 10 years, at 4 *per cent*.) leaves 1.60, the remainder to be *reserved*.

The value of 1*l*. to be received at the end of 10 years, is, .6755, by Table I.

The probability, that the lives of one or other of two persons, aged 30 and 40, shall fail in 10 years, is, $\frac{185}{531}$, by Table III (*a*).

(*a*) The probability taken from the Table, that a person aged 30, shall live 10 years, is, $\frac{445}{531}$. That a person, aged 40, shall live 10 years, is, $\frac{346}{445}$. That they shall *both* live 10 years, is, $\frac{346}{445}$, multiplied by $\frac{445}{531}$, or $\frac{346}{531}$. That they shall *not both* live 10 years, or that *one* or *other* of them shall die in this time, is, $\frac{346}{531}$, subtracted from unity, or, $\frac{185}{531}$. See note p. 23.

And the perpetuity 25. These numbers, multiplied by one another, and 1.60 added to the product, make 7.48, which, multiplied by 10, (the given annuity) gives *l*.74.8, the answer in a single present payment.

l.74.8, divided by 1.04, gives *l*.71.92, the value of the assurance of an *equivalent sum*; or of 250*l*—*l*.71.92, divided by 7.51, (the value of the two joint lives for 10 years with unity added) gives 9.57, the value of the same sum in annual payments beginning immediately, for 10 years, subject to failure should the joint lives fail.

EXAMPLE II.

"What is the value of 10*l*. *per annum*, to be "entered upon, should two persons one 30, "and the other 40, *both* die; that is, should "the *longest* of the two lives fail in 10 years, "reckoning interest at 4 *per cent*. and cal-"culating from Dr. *Halley*'s Table?"

The value of the *longest* of the two lives for 10 years, (that is, the value of the joint lives for 10 years, subtracted from the sum of the (*a*) values of the single lives for 10 years) is, 7.91; which, subtracted from 8.111, the value of an annuity certain for 10 years, leaves .20 the remainder to be reserved.—The value of 1*l*. to be received at the end

(*a*) See Scholium to Quest. VI.

of 10 years, is, .6755. The probability that the lives of two persons, aged 30 and 40, shall fail in 10 years, is, by Table III, $\frac{86}{531}$, multiplied by $\frac{94}{445}$, or $\frac{8084}{236295}$; and the perpetuity 25. These numbers, multiplied by one another, and .20 added to the product, make .740, which, multiplied by 10, (the given annuity) gives 7.4, the answer in a single payment.

7.4, divided by 1.04, gives 11, the value of the assurance of 250*l*.

REMARK I.

The values of single lives for given terms, when these terms are less than 10 years, must, in answering these Questions, and also in answering the following Questions, be found true to at least 2 or 3 places of decimals. But they cannot be found to this exactness by any Tables that are extant; and, therefore, they must be calculated in the following manner:

"Multiply the probability, taken out of "the Table of observations, that the life "shall exist 1, 2, 3, &c. years, by the value "of 1*l*. due at the end of 1, 2, 3, &c. years; "and the sum of the products will be the "value of the life for 1, 2, 3, &c. years."

For Example. The probability, that a person whose age is 34, shall live a year, is, by Dr. *Halley*'s Table, $\frac{490}{499}$. The probability, at the ſame age, of living 2 years, is, $\frac{481}{499}$; 3 years, $\frac{472}{499}$.—$\frac{490}{499}$ multiplied by .9615, (the value, by Table I, of 1 *l.* due at the end of a year, intereſt being at 4 *per cent.*) is, .942; or the value of the life for *one* year.—$\frac{481}{499}$, multiplied by .9245, (the value of 1 *l.* due at the end of 2 years) is, .891. And this added to the former product, gives 1.833; or the value of the life for 2 years.—$\frac{472}{499}$, multiplied by .8890, (the value of 1 *l.* due at the end of 3 years) is, .841; and this product, added to 1.833, makes 2.674, or the value of the given life for 3 years.

When the term exceeds 10 years, the rule in Queſt. VI. will give theſe values with ſufficient exactneſs; and it would do the ſame in all caſes, were the values of lives given true to 3 or 4 places of decimals, and in ſtrict agreement to the Tables of obſervation uſed.

The remark now made is to be extended to the values of *joint* lives for given terms. For theſe values, like thoſe of *ſingle* lives, cannot be found in ſolving theſe Queſtions with ſufficient accuracy, when the terms are ſmall, by any method, except the tedious one, of multiplying the probability that the 2 lives ſhall *both* continue 1, 2, 3, &c. years, by the value of 1 *l.* due at the end of 1, 2, 3, &c. years, and taking the ſum of the products in the manner juſt deſcribed.

Remark II.

If the annuity is to be entered upon, in caſe of the failure within a given time of any life or lives, *at the end of that time*; and not *at the end of the year in which the failure may happen*; its preſent value will be the product ariſing from the continual multiplication by one another of the perpetuity increaſed by unity; the value of 1 *l.* due at the end of the given time; the annuity; and the probability that the life, or lives, ſhall fail within the given time. And care ſhould be taken not to confound theſe two ſorts of Queſtions with one another.—Thus; the value in one payment of 10*l.* *per ann.* to be entered upon eleven years hence, in caſe a perſon aged 34 ſhould not live ſo long, is 26, (the perpetuity increaſed by unity, intereſt being at 4 *per cent.*) multiplied by .6496, and by 10*l.* and alſo by $\frac{101}{495}$; or 34.8.—This value, divided by 1.04, is, 33.5, the value of an equivalent ſum, or of 250*l.* to be obtained on the ſame conditions.

The value of the *aſſurance* of any annuity on the whole continuance of any ſingle life is, by Queſt. X. the *exceſs* of the perpetuity above the value of the life, multiplied by the annuity. And in like manner; the value of the *aſſurance* of any annuity on the whole continuance of any two *joint* lives, or the *longeſt* of two lives, is the exceſs of the *per-*

petuity above the value of the joint lives, or of the longest of two lives, multiplied by the annuity. This is very obvious; but no general method has been yet explained of finding the values of *assurances* on lives and survivorships for terms of years less than the whole continuance of the lives. For this reason, I have been here more explicit than I should otherwise have been; and, as such assurances are now much practised, and may be very useful if their values are rightly determined, I have thought proper to add the two following Questions, which, when joined to Question XI. and Mr. *Simpson*'s 33d *Problem* given in the note p. 39, will, I believe, exhaust this subject as far as two lives can be concerned.

QUESTION XV.

"B, expectant, will lose a given sum, "should he survive A, *within a given time*. "What ought he to pay for the *assurance* of "it?—In other words: "What ought he to "pay for a given sum to be received at the "death of A, should he happen to survive "him within a given time?"

ANSWER.

Divide the *sum* of the decrements of life in the Table of observations from the age of A, for the given time, by the given time; and, by the *quotient*, divide the number of the living in the Table at the age of A; and again, by this *second* quotient (*a*), divide the given sum reserving the *third* quotient.

Find the value of an annuity on the life of B, for the given time. To this value add the *quotient*, that will arise from dividing the value of an annuity certain, for the given time, by twice the *complement* of the life of B; and the *sum*, multiplied by the *reserved quotient*, will be the required value in a single present (*b*) payment.

EXAMPLE.

Let the Table of observations be Mr. *Simpson's* for *London*, or Table VIII. Let the rate of interest be 3 *per cent*. A, seven years of age. B, 30. The given time 14 years. The given sum 100*l*.—The sum of the *decrements*, in Table VIII. for 14 years from the age of seven, is 73, which, divided by 14, gives 5.2. The number of the living at seven is 430, which, divided by 5.2, and 100*l*. divided by the quotient, gives *l*. 1.21, the *quotient* to be *reserved*.

(*a*) When the age of A is under 60, and the term so large as to exceed the difference between it and 70, it will be best, when the *London* Table is used, to divide the given sum, not by the second quotient here mentioned, but by the *complement* of the life of A, taken out of Table IX.

(*b*) See the demonstration of this rule, and also of the rule that will be given for solving the next Question, in the Appendix, note (H).

The value of an annuity for 14 years on the life of B, is, by Quest. VI. 9.5.—The value of an annuity certain for 14 years, is, by Table II. 11.296, which, divided by 94.4, (twice the *complement* of the life of B, by Table IX) (*a*), gives .12, which, added to 9.5, gives 9.62; and this again multiplied by 1.21, the *reserved quotient*, gives 11.64, the *present* value in *one* payment of 100*l.* payable at the death of A aged 37, to B aged 30, should A die and leave B the survivor within 14 years.

The present value for 14 years of two joint lives, one 7 and the other 30 years of age, may be found, by the help of Table XI, and the rule in the *Scholium* to Quest. VI. to be nearly 9 years purchase; and, *l.* 11.64 divided by this value with unity added, or by 10, gives 1.164, the foregoing value in *annual payments* during the joint lives for 14 years, the *first* payment to be made immediately, and the *last* payment at the end of 14 years, should the joint lives not fail.

SCHOLIUM.

It deserves particularly to be remembered, that in this method likewise may be calculated, what sums ought to be paid on any survivorship, within a given time, of one life

(*a*) This Table gives the *expectations* only, but it should be remembered, that twice the *expectation* is always the *complement* of a life. See note, p. 37.

beyond another, in consideration of any given sum now advanced.—The following Example of this is a case which has offered itself in practice.

" A person, aged 30, has in expectation " an estate which is to come to him, pro- " vided he survives a *minor*, aged 7, before " he is out of his minority; that is, pro- " vided he should be himself living at the " time of the minor's death, should that hap- " pen before he is 21.—In these circum- " stances, he wants to borrow 1000*l.* on his " *expectation*. What *reversion* out of the " estate depending on such a survivorship, is " a proper equivalent for this sum now ad- " vanced, interest being reckoned at 3 *per* " *cent.* and the probabilities of life being " supposed the same with those in Mr. *Simp-* " *son*'s Table of *London* observations?"

Answer.

It appears from what has been just determined, that for *l.* 11.64 now advanced, the proper equivalent in such circumstances, is, 100*l.* to be paid, in case the survivorship should take place; or, by the *correction* in page 34, as much of the estate as 100*l.* will buy at 3 *per cent.* supposing the first rent to be received immediately; (that is, supposing the estate worth 34.33 years purchase.) or *l.* 2.912 *per annum.*—By the rule of proportion, therefore, for 1000*l.* the proper equivalent will be 8591*l.* in money, or 250*l.* *per annum* out of the eſtate.

QUESTION XVI.

" 100*l.* will be loſt to B's heirs, ſhould he
" happen to die after A, *within a given time*.
" What is the price of the *aſſurance* of it?—
" That is: What is the preſent value of
" 100*l.* payable at the death of B, provided
" his death ſhould happen *after* A's death,
" *within a given time?*"

ANSWER.

Divide the ſum of the decrements of life in the Table of obſervations from the age of B, for the given time, by the given time; and by the *quotient* divide the number of the living at the age of B; and again, by this *ſecond quotient* (*a*), divide the given ſum, reſerving the *third quotient*.

Find the value of an annuity on the life A for a number of years, leſs by *one* year than the given time, which ſubtract from the value of an annuity certain for the ſame number of years. Multiply the *remainder* by the *reſerved quotient*, and divide the *product* by the amount of 1*l.* for one year, and let this be a *ſecond* reſerved quotient.

(*a*) Or rather, if the *London* Table is uſed, by the *complement* of the life of B, when his age is under 60, and the term exceeds the *difference* between it and 70.

Again. Multiply into one another the *first* reserved quotient, and the value of an annuity certain for the given time; and divide the product by twice the *complement* of A's life. This *last* quotient, added to the *second* reserved quotient, will be the *answer* in a present single payment.

EXAMPLE.

Let the age of B be 40. Of A 30. The sum 100*l.* Rate of interest 4 *per cent.* The given time 20 years. The Table of observations, Mr. *Simpson*'s, or Table VIII.—The sum of the decrements of life, in this Table, from the age of 40 for 20 years, is 127, which, divided by 20, (the given time) gives 6.38.—The number of the living at 40 is 229, which, divided by 6.38, gives 35.8; and 100*l.* (the given sum) divided by 35.8, gives 2.79, the *first* quotient to be reserved.

The value of an annuity for 19 years on a life at 30 years of age, is 10.3; which, subtracted from 13.134, (the value of an annuity *certain* for 19 years, by Table II) and the remainder multiplied by 2.79, gives 7.89. This product divided by 1.04, (the amount of 1*l.* in one year) gives 7.60; the *second* reserved quotient.

2.79 multiplied by 13.59, (the value of an annuity certain for 20 years) gives 37.916; and this *product* divided by 94.4, (twice the complement of A's life by Table IX.) gives .401, which, added to 7.60, gives 8*l.* the *Answer*; or, the value of 100*l.* payable at the death of B, on the contingency of his surviving A aged 30, and *both* dying in 20 years.

It is plain, that this is likewise the sum that ought to be lent to B now, on the expectation of 100*l.* at his death, provided it should happen after A's death in 20 years.

This rule gives the just solution in all cases, except when B, the expectant, is the *youngest* of the two lives, and at the same time the term of years *greater* than the complement of A's life. In this particular case the following rule must be used.

Find, by the preceding rule, the value of the assurance of the given sum for a term of years, equal to the complement of A's life, and let this value be *reserved*. Multiply by one another the given *sum*; the *value* of 1*l.* to be received at the end of a number of years equal to the complement of A's life; and the value of an *annuity certain* for as many years as the given term exceeds this complement. And the *product*, divided by the complement of B's life, and the *quotient* added to the *value reserved*, will be the true value sought.

EXAMPLE.

Let the age of B be 30; of A 40. The term 47 years; and every thing else as in the laſt Example. The complement of A's life, is, by Table IX, 39.2. The value of 100*l.* to be received at the death of B, if he ſurvives A within 39 years, may be found by the preceding rule to be *l.* 16.15; the value to be reſerved.—The value of 1 *l.* to be received at the end of 39 years is, by Table II, .2166. The value of an annuity *certain* for 8 years, (the exceſs of the given term above the complement of the life of B by Table IX.) is, 6.733.

And theſe two values multiplied by one another, and by 100*l.* give 145.83; which, divided by 47.2, (the complement of the life of B) and 16.15, added to the quotient, make *l.* 19.23, the value ſought.

REMARK.

As after finding the preſent value of an eſtate, or annuity, it is neceſſary to *divide* that value by the amount of 1 *l.* in one year, in order to find the preſent value of a *ſum* equivalent to the *annuity*; ſo, after finding the value of a ſum, it is neceſſary to *multiply* that value, by the ſaid amount, in order to find from it the value of an equivalent annuity.

In the firſt Example, therefore, the value of an eſtate of 4*l.* *per annum*, would be *l.* 8.32. In the ſecond Example, 20*l.* And this is, as it ought to be, the value for the whole duration of the lives, agreeably to the Problem in the note page 37.

In ſolving this Queſtion, care alſo muſt be taken not to forget the *firſt* Remark under the foregoing Queſtion.

In the ſame way with that in which the rules in the three laſt Queſtions have been diſcovered, it is poſſible to find rules for calculating the values of *aſſurances, for given terms*, on lives and ſurvivorſhips, where three or more lives are concerned. But this is of leſs importance; and I chuſe to leave to others the further proſecution of this ſubject.

CHAP. II.

Containing an Application of the Questions in the foregoing Chapter to the Schemes of the Societies in Great Britain, *for making Assurances on Lives and Survivorships, and for granting Annuities to Widows, and to Persons in old Age.*

SECT. I.

Of the London Annuity, *and the* Laudable *Societies for the Benefit of Widows.*

THE scheme mentioned in Quest. VIII. is nearly that of the *London Annuity* Society. The *Laudable Society* is also formed on a similar plan. In both, the *annual contribution* of every member is five guineas, payable half-yearly; and for this a title is given to an annuity of 20*l.* to every widow during widowhood, if the husband, after admission, lives *one* year according to the *first* scheme; or *three* years according to the (*a*)

(*a*) In this society a member who lives but *one* year, is entitled to no more than an annuity of 10*l.* for his widow; if he lives two years, 15*l.* If he lives three years, 20*l.* four years, 25*l.* seven years, 30*l.* ten years, 35*l.* thirteen years, 40*l.*

second; of 30*l.* if the husband lives *seven* years, according to both schemes; and 40*l.* according to the *first* scheme, if he lives 15 years, or 13 years, according to the second.— In both schemes also, there is no other premium or fine required, than five guineas extraordinary, at admission, from every member whose age does not exceed 45. The *Laudable Society* admits none above 45, and the *London Annuity* Society obliges every person between 45 and 55 to pay, at admission, five guineas extraordinary, for every year that he is turned of 45.

These are the main particulars in these schemes; and, therefore, both of them, were the annuities to be enjoyed for life, would receive (supposing the members all under 46 at admission, and of the same ages with their wives, and money at 4 *per cent.*) but little more than three fifths of the true value of the annuities; or about one half, supposing wives, one with another, 10 years younger than their husbands; as appears from Question VIII.

It appears further in that Question, that, supposing the annuities to be *life* annuities, and men and their wives of equal ages, the expectation to which an annual payment of five guineas beginning immediately, entitles, is nearly 14*l.* if the contributor lives a year, and 20*l.* if he lives seven years (*a*), taking

(*a*) The same annual payment will, on the same suppositions, entitle to 14*l.* if a member lives a year, and 18*l.* if he lives *three* years.

the medium between the *London* and the other Tables of Obſervation.

It is likely, that many perſons will be very unwilling to believe, that theſe ſchemes are ſo deficient as they have been now repreſented. I will, therefore, endeavour to prove this in a way which, tho' leſs ſtrict, is ſufficiently deciſive, and may be more likely to be intelligible to perſons unſkilled in mathematical calculation.—I ſhall here confine myſelf to the ſcheme of the *London Annuity* Society. The differences between it and the ſcheme of the *Laudable* Society are inconſiderable, and what ſhall be ſaid of the one will be fully applicable to the other.

According to this ſcheme, as it has been juſt deſcribed, all that live 15 years in the ſociety will be entitled to annuities of 40*l.* *per annum* for their widows. Suppoſe the whole ſociety, at admiſſion, to be men of 40 years of age, taken one with another. A perſon of this age has an even chance of *living* 23 years; and he has an even chance of continuing with a wife of the ſame age, (that is, of continuing in the ſociety) 13 years and $\frac{1}{2}$ (*a*). Not much leſs, therefore, than half

(*a*) This is the exact truth according to Mr. *De Moivre*'s Hypotheſis, and the *Norwich* Table. But according to Dr. *Halley*'s and the *Northampton* Table, a man 40 years of age has an even chance of living no more than 22 years, and of joint continuance with a wife of the

half the members will continue in the ſociety 15 years; and, conſequently, not much leſs than half the widows that will come upon the ſociety will be annuitants of 40*l. per annum*. Theſe widows, however, being older than the reſt when they commence annuitants, will continue on the ſociety a ſhorter time; and, thereſore, the number conſtantly in life together, to which they will in a courſe of years increaſe, will be proportionably ſmaller. Putting every thing as favourably as poſſible, let us ſuppoſe, that out of 20 annuitants conſtantly on the ſociety, *five* will be annuitants of 40*l*. *ſix* of 30*l*. and *nine* of 20*l*. To 20 annuitants then the ſociety will pay 560*l*. *per annum*, or the 20th part of this ſum, that is 28*l*. to *every* annuitant at an average. But ſuch an annuity for a life at 40, after another equal life, provided both ſurvive one year, is worth (by Queſt. VII. p. 24.) in a ſingle preſent payment, 85*l*. nearly, according to the *London*, and all the Tables of Obſervations, intereſt being all along ſuppoſed at 4 *per cent*.

It cannot appear improbable to any one, that this ſhould be the true value of ſuch a reverſion.. It is not credible, that there is

ſame age, 13 years.—Forty muſt be more than the mean age of the members of the ſociety at admiſſion, and on this account the number of annuitants of 40*l*. muſt be proportionably greater. The mean age, therefore, has been taken very moderately.

any ſituation in which the decrements of life are ſuch as can make it a tenth part more or leſs.—85*l.* in preſent payment is the ſame with 3*l.* 8*s.* *per annum* for ever.—But is an annual payment of five guineas, which muſt ceaſe as ſoon as either of two lives each 40, fails, equal in value to ſuch a perpetuity? Every one muſt ſee, that there is a great difference.—A ſet of marriages between perſons all 40, will, according to the probabilities of life in Dr. *Halley*'s Table, laſt, one with another, 15 years (*a*); and an annual payment beginning immediately, during the joint continuance of two perſons of this age, is worth 10 years purchaſe (*b*). The compariſon then, in the preſent caſe, is between 3*l.* 8*s.* *per annum for ever*, and five guineas *per annum for* 15 *years*; or between an annuity of 3*l.* 8*s.* worth 25 years purchaſe, and an annuity of five guineas worth only 10 years purchaſe.

But to throw this ſubject into another light.

(*a*) See the beginning of Eſſay I.

(*b*) The value of ſuch an annual payment, by Table XI, or the *London* Obſervations, is 9.1; and 10.8, by Mr. *De Moivre*'s Hypotheſis.—I have not taken into this account the five guineas *fine* paid at admiſſion, becauſe it is obviouſly of too little conſequence to make any conſiderable difference. The allowances I have made in favour of theſe ſchemes are more than equivalent to it. In particular; it ſhould be remembered, that the payments required by theſe ſchemes, are *half-yearly payments* beginning immediately; and that theſe, by Queſt. VIII. are leſs advantageous than the payments I all along ſuppoſe them to require, or, "*yearly payments* beginning imme-"diately."

Let the number to which the society is kept up be supposed to be 200. It has been demonstrated in Quest. II, that at least half this number of widows will in time come to be constantly on the society; and it has also been just now shewn, that the medium of annuities, payable to them, will be at least 28*l*. After a course of years, then, the society will have a constant expence to bear of 2800*l. per annum.*—But what will be its income?—In order to determine this, we must consider, that there are two sources from whence its income will be derived. First, the annual payments of the members. And, secondly, the money accumulated, or the *capital* raised during the time the number of annuitants is coming to a *maximum.*—The first of these sources affords 1000 guineas, or 1050*l. per annum.* This wants 1750*l.* of the annual expence just mentioned; and, therefore, in order to have the income of the society equal to the burden upon it, when the annuitants come to a *maximum,* there must be a fund raised in the mean time equal to 43,750*l.* or to an estate in perpetuity of 1750*l. per annum.*—But 1050*l. per annum* beginning immediately, and forborn 24 years, and improved, without loss or delay, all that time at 4 *per cent.* compound interest, will but just raise such a capital (*a*). There is, therefore,

(*a*) Every Question of this kind may be easily solved in the following manner. In Table I, find the value fore, the fulleſt proof, that the ſcheme I am conſidering is extremely deficient. The truth is, that ſcarcely a *third* of ſuch a capital could be raiſed, as will appear from the following obſervations.

Out of 200 perſons, all 40 years of age, *more* than five, according to the *London* Table of Obſervations, and not ſo many by Dr. *Halley*'s Table, may be expected to die in a year. Suppoſe then five to be the real number of members that will die the firſt year of the ſociety. In ſubſequent years the collective body of members will be continually growing older; and, therefore, the proportion of them that will die every year, will be continually increaſing, till it gets to a *maximum*. I will, however, ſuppoſe, that during the firſt 20 years no more than the

of 1*l.* payable at the end of any number of years; and any given annuity divided by that value, will be the annuity to which the given annuity will in that number of years increaſe. — Thus; the preſent value of 1*l.* payable at the end of 25 years, is .3751, reckoning intereſt at 4 *per cent.* and 1050*l.* *per annum* divided by .3751, gives 2,800*l.* *per annum*, the increaſed annuity ariſing from 1050*l.* *per ann.* In the ſame manner; it may be found, that the ſame annuity, forborn 11 years, will increaſe to 1610*l.* *per annum.* This ſuppoſes the firſt payment of the annuity to be made a year hence. If the firſt payment is to be made immediately, which is the preſent caſe, the annuity will increaſe to the ſame ſums in one year leſs time.—But a more particular account of this will be given in the rules annexed to the Tables at the end of this work.

number just specified will die every year; and that, consequently, no more than *five widows* will come every year on the society. The ages of all these widows, when they commence widowhood, will, it is evident, be between 40 and 60. One with another then, they may be considered as having commenced widowhood at 50 years of age. Now, five widows left every year at this age, will, in 10 years, increase to 43 constantly in life together, according to the expectations of life in Tables III, IV, and V; and, in 20 years, to 70 (*a*). Suppose the true number alive together at the end of 20 years to be only 62. the greater part of these will be annuitants of 30*l*. and 40*l*. *per ann.* and the rest 20*l*. Were the former only equal to the latter, the medium of annuities payable to them would exceed 25*l*. Suppose then this medium to be no more than 26*l*. and it will

(*a*) Every calculation of this kind is easily made by the rule in note (A) in the Appendix.—I have put the number living together at the end of 20 years at 62, not only that the reader may be better satisfied that I have kept low enough, but also to make an allowance for such widows as will be left by those members who die within a year after admission, and who, therefore, according to these schemes, will be entitled to no annuities. This allowance is too large: For, after the first year of the scheme, it will not happen above once in 4 or 5 years, that the death of a member will be so circumstanced, supposing the probability that a man at 40 will live a year, to be, as all but the *London* Tables make it, 50 to 1.

follow, that, at the end of 20 years, the ſociety will have an annual rent to pay of 26*l.* multiplied by 62 or 1612*l.* and, if then able to bear ſuch an expence, it muſt, in the intermediate time, have acquired an increaſe of income equal to the difference between 1050*l.* and 1612*l. per ann.* That is; it muſt, with its ſavings, have accumulated a ſtock equal to 562*l. per ann.* and worth 14,050*l.* But, as during this time, there will be a number of annuitants conſtantly increaſing, to whom yearly payments muſt be made, the ſavings of the ſociety cannot certainly be one half of what they would have been had it been all the time free from all burdens. Suppoſe then the ſtock produced by theſe ſavings, to be equal to the ſtock that would ariſe from an income of 1050*l. per ann.* beginning immediately, and improved perfectly at 4 *per cent.* compound intereſt, for half the time I have mentioned, or for 10 years, without being ſubject to any checks or deductions. Such an income thus improved, would, in 10 years, produce an additional income of 560*l. per annum*, or a capital of 14,000*l.*—According to theſe obſervations, therefore, the annual income of the ſociety at the end of 20 years, and before a third part of the higheſt annuitants could come upon it, would begin to fall ſhort of its expences. About that time then it would neceſſarily run aground; and long before the number of annuitants could riſe to a 100, it would ſpend its whole ſtock, and find itſelf under a neceſſity of either doubling the annual payments of its members, or of reducing the annuities one half.

All I have now ſaid is meant on the ſuppoſition, that the ſociety begins with 200 members at 40 years of age, and is afterwards limited to that number, by admitting no more new members than will juſt ſupply the vacancies occaſioned by the loſs of old members. If it is allowed to increaſe, it may continue a longer time. And, for this reaſon, a ſociety that wants half the income neceſſary to render it permanent, may very well ſubſiſt, and even proſper for 30 or 40 years.—Thus, the *Laudable Society*, was it to keep to its preſent number of members, might poſſibly feel no deficiencies for 20 or 30 years to come; but if it ſhould continue to increaſe at the rate of 70 or 80 every year, it would, at the end of that time, poſſeſs a balance ſo much in its favour, as might enable it to ſupport itſelf for 20 or 30 years more (*a*). But bankruptcy would

(*a*) What has been before demonſtrated in Queſt. III. ſhould be here recollected, that the number of annuitants on ſuch a ſociety as this, muſt go on to increaſe for more than 100 years, after acquiring its greateſt number of members.

The *Laudable* Society, I am informed, took its riſe from a calculation contained in a pamphlet entitled, *The Poſſibility and Probability of a* SCHEME *intended for the Benefit of Widows being able to ſupport itſelf.* The ſcheme here referred to, is the ſame with that which this Society has

come at laſt, and with the more terrible weight the longer it had been deferred.

The rule in the *London Annuity* Society, which obliges every perſon between the ages of 45 and 55, to pay at admiſſion 5 guineas extraordinary, for every year that he exceeds 45, is an advantage to it, but it is a very inadequate, and alſo a very unequitable advantage. For at the ſame time, that it obliges a perſon 55 years of age, to give *more* than the value of his expectation, it takes *above* two fifths *leſs* than the value from a perſon who is 45 years of age.

Should any perſons remain ſtill doubtful about what I have ſaid, I would beg them to attend to one further argument.

It muſt be reckoned upon that every other member of theſe ſocieties, ſuppoſing them to conſiſt of perſons all of the ſame ages with their wives, will leave widows to whom one with another, (as already ſhewn) at leaſt 28*l.*

ſince followed; and I am afraid I ſhall not be credited, when I ſay, that the calculation to prove its capacity of ſupporting itſelf, is founded on the ſuppoſition, that a hundred married men whoſe common age is 36, will leave but *one* widow every year, tho' at the ſame time it is ſuppoſed that two of them will die every year.

This miſtake has made the whole calculation one half wrong.—Nothing can be plainer than that, if the death of a married man does not leave a widow at the end of the year, the reaſon muſt be, that both himſelf and his wife have happened to die in the year. But it is always very improbable this ſhould happen.

per ann. must be allowed, for as many years as there have been payments from each member. For every 10 guineas then received they must some time or other hereafter pay 28*l.* But let it be well considered what can enable them to do this. Did money bear no interest, for any given sum now received, they could not afford at any time hereafter to pay more than an *equal* sum. That is; (since the duration of *survivorship* is in the present case, by Quest. II, equal to the duration of *marriage*) the proper consideration for any given reversionary annuity, to be allowed to *all* the survivors of a set of marriages, would be, supposing no interest of money, an equal annuity payable by each marriage during its existence; and just *half* the reversionary annuity, if it is to be allowed only to half the survivors, or to widows exclusive of widowers. The annual payment then of *five* guineas, during marriage, can entitle widows to no more than an annuity of *ten* guineas, supposing money to bear no interest. But if it does bear interest, the same payment will entitle them to more, in proportion to the degree in which it is capable of being improved, during the time between that in which the annual payments begin, and the commencement of widowhood. Now, it is easy to see, that unless money bears very high interest, this improvement cannot be likely in any circumstances to produce a capital, the interest of which shall be equal to the annual payment itself. Any given annual payment perfectly improved at 4 *per cent.* compound interest, requires 17 years to double itself, supposing the first payment made immediately; or, near 18 years (*a*), if the first payment is not made till the end of a year. But no marriages are *likely* to last so long as this, except those among persons who are very young. A marriage between two persons, both 40, will not *probably* last longer than 13 years, according to the probabilities of life in Dr. *Halley*'s Table. A marriage between two persons, both 50, will not probably, by the same Table, last longer than *eleven* years; nor a marriage between two persons, both 30, longer than 16 years. Such marriages, it is true, may possibly last 30 or 40 years. But this circumstance is more than balanced by the fact, that no less possibly they may not last *one* year. The annual payments, then, being incapable of such an improvement as shall produce an additional income equal to themselves; it is obvious, that no society ought to go so far as to allow to widows annuities twice as great as those which might be allowed, supposing no

(*a*) At 3 *per cent.* the period of doubling money by compound interest, is nearly 23 years. At 5 *per cent.* 14 years.

interest of money (*a*); so far, for instance, as to allow, instead of 10 guineas, 20 guineas for an annual payment of five guineas. In the circumstances of most of these societies three fifths addition may be the full allowance. That is; supposing the annual payment of each member to be five guineas, time may be expected for gaining from hence a capital of 75 guineas, or that shall produce three guineas *per annum* interest; and the proper reversionary annuity will be 16 guineas; or six guineas more than the proper reversionary annuity, did money admit of no improvement.

The preceding observations have gone on the supposition, that the reversionary annuities are to be *for life*. What difference in favour of these societies arises from the circumstance, that the annuities are to be paid only *for widowhood*, cannot be exactly determined. Some judgment, however, may be formed of it from what has been said at the conclusion of Quest. II. Were even one half

(*a*) The money accumulated will not be exactly the same with that to which the annual payment would increase, if improved at compound interest for a number of years, equal to that which the joint lives have an *equal chance* of existing. Much less will the increase be the same with that which would arise from the annual payment forborn, and improved for a number of years equal to the *expectations* of the joint lives. It will be less than either of these, for a reason explained in note (L) Appendix.

of the widows to marry, ſtill the ſchemes I have been conſidering would probably be inſufficient. But in the circumſtances of theſe ſocieties it cannot be expected, that above one in 10, or perhaps one in 20, will marry. The perſons moſt likely to enter into them, are ſuch as have not the proſpect or ability of making competent proviſions for their widows in other ways. The widows left, therefore, will in general be unprovided for, and being alſo left with families of children, it is quite unreaſonable to expect, that any conſiderable proportion ſhould marry. This is true of ſuch as may happen to be left young; but when a ſociety has ſubſiſted ſome time, the *greater* part will not be young when left, and theſe, at the ſame time that no advantage can be expected from their marrying, will be in general the *higheſt* annuitants, and, therefore, the *heavieſt burdens.*—Moreover, the proſpect of the loſs of their annuities will have a particular tendency to check marriage among them.—For all theſe reaſons it ſeems to me likely, that the benefit, which theſe ſocieties will derive from marriage among their annuitants, will not be very conſiderable; or at leaſt not *ſo* conſiderable as to be equal to the advantages I have allowed them, by calculating on the ſuppoſitions, that the money they receive will be *always improved perfectly, without loſs or delay, at the rate of* 4 *per cent. compound intereſt*; that the probabilities of life among males and females are the ſame, and all huſbands likewiſe of the ſame ages with their wives, and that conſequently the *maximum* of widows on ſuch ſocieties can amount to no more than half the number of marriages (*a*).—With reſpect to the laſt of theſe ſuppoſitions, it deſerves to be particularly obſerved, that by an enquiry made ſome years ago in *Scotland*, it was found, that the widows of *miniſters* and *profeſſors* there, (*b*) notwithſtanding the diminution occaſioned by their marrying, did exceed half the number of marriages. And certainly it would be unreaſonable in theſe ſocieties not to reckon that the ſame will happen among them.—Indeed it ſeems certain that, notwithſtanding

(*a*) Care ſhould be taken in theſe ſocieties, not to judge of the proportion of widows that will marry, from the proportion that may happen to marry during their firſt years. For moſt of the widows that will be left at firſt will be young; whereas the greater part will not be young when they commence widowhood, after a ſociety has ſubſiſted 30 or 40 years; and, therefore, tho' one in 3 or 4 ſhould marry at firſt, it will not be reaſonable to expect, that half ſo many ſhould marry after the affairs of the ſociety become ſtationary.

(*b*) 364 widows, all living at one time, were counted; and the number of married miniſters and profeſſors for many years paſt has been, at an average, 667.—Twenty widows likewiſe are left one year with another; and, for 10 years, ending in the year 1767, but nine of theſe had married.—Of the annuitants likewiſe (about 160 in number) on the fund eſtabliſhed among the Diſſenters in *London*, for relieving the widows of indigent miniſters, it is found that few ever marry. See the latter end of the 4th Eſſay; and note (A) in the Appendix.

the hazards that attend child-bearing, the probability, that the woman ſhall ſurvive in marriage, and not the man, is much greater (*a*) than is commonly imagined. It will be ſhewn in the laſt Eſſay, that it is not leſs than the odds of 3 to 2; and had I calculated agreeably to this fact, the values of annuities for widows, would have been given near a quarter greater than they have been given on the ſuppoſition, that the chance of ſurvivorſhip is equal between men and their wives.—It muſt be added, that I have made no account of any expences attending the execution and management of the ſchemes of theſe ſocieties. Some ſuch expences there muſt be, and ſome advantages ſhould be always provided in order to compenſate them.

There are in this kingdom ſeveral inſtitutions for the benefit of widows, beſides the two on which I have now remarked; and in general, as far as I have had any information concerning them, they are founded on plans

(*a*) Partly, as obſerved in page 8, on account of the greater mortality of males, but chiefly on account of the exceſs of age on the man's ſide.—According to the printed articles of agreement, the *Laudable Society* pays no regard to this exceſs of age; and the allowance required on this account by the *London Annuity* Society is ſo trifling that it deſerves no notice.

In March 1770, thirty-two huſbands had died in the *Laudable Society*, and 27 wives. They ſeem, therefore, to be already beginning to experience, that the chances of ſurvivorſhip in marriage are in favour of the wife.

equally inadequate. The motives which influence the contrivers of these institutions are, without doubt, *laudable*; but they ought, I think, to have informed themselves better. This appears sufficiently from what has been said, but I will just mention one further proof of it.

The *London Annuity Society* promises that, if in 21 years; and the *Laudable Society* that, if in 25 years, it shall appear that there has been all along an annual surplus in favour of the societies, it shall be employed in either raising the *annuities*, or in sinking the *annual payments*. Now, they may be assured, that, if at the end of these periods, they should not be possessed of a considerable surplus, the true reason will be, their having granted much higher annuities than the annual contributions are able permanently to support: For it has been demonstrated, that the number of annuitants, and consequently the amount of the annual expences, will go increasing for a long course of years beyond these periods. The effect, therefore, of carrying into execution this regulation will be, precipitating that bankruptcy which would have come too soon had there been no such regulation.

It has been said in defence of these Societies, that the deficiencies in their plans cannot be of much consequence, because their rules oblige them to preserve a constant equality between their income and expences, by reducing the annuities as there shall be occasion.

And from hence it is inferred, that they can never be in any danger of a bankruptcy.—In anſwer to this, it has appeared, that the time when they will begin to feel deficiencies is ſo diſtant, that it will be too late to remedy paſt errors, without ſinking the annuities ſo much, as to render them inconſiderable and trifling. All that is given too much to *preſent* annuitants is ſo much taken away from *future* annuitants. And if a ſcheme is *very* deficient,. the firſt annuitants may, for 30 or 40 years, receive ſo much more than they ought to receive, as to leave little or nothing for any who come after them. Deficient ſchemes, therefore, are attended with particular injuſtice; and this injuſtice will be the ſame, if, inſtead of *reducing* the annuities, the annual payments ſhould be increaſed; for all the difference this can make will be, to cauſe the injuſtice to fall on *future contributors*, inſtead of *future annuitants*.

But what requires moſt to be conſidered here is, that, after either the annuities have been for ſome time in a ſtate of reduction, or the contributions in a ſtate of increaſe, it will be ſeen that theſe Societies have gone upon wrong plans, and, therefore, they will be deſerted and avoided; the conſequence of which will prove ſtill greater deficiencies in their annual income, and a more rapid deſertion and decline, 'till a total diſſolution and bankruptcy take place.—This will be the death of most of the present societies for providing for widows, if they continue to be encouraged, and do not soon alter their plans: And at that period the number of *annuitants* will be greater than ever; whose annuities, having no other support than the poor remains of a stock always insufficient, will be soon left, without the possibility of relief, to lament that ignorance and credulity which gave rise to these societies, and which had so long supported them.

In the *London* Annuity Society, there is an encouragement to *batchelors* and *widowers* to join them, arising from the additional annuities to which they will be *immediately* entitled, when they marry, in consequence of having made their payments a greater number of years; and it is imagined, that particular advantages will be derived from such members. But even these will in general pay much less than the value of their expectations.—A person who begins an annual contribution of five guineas at the age of 24 will, should he live 11 years, and marry a woman of the same age at the end of that time, entitle her immediately to 35*l.* *per ann.* during survivorship, and to 41*l.* *per annum* should he live four years after marrying. (interest being at 4 *per cent.*) (*a*). In this par-

(*a*) The value of five guineas *per annum* (first payment made immediately) for 11 years, subject to failure should a life now 24 fail; and, after 11 years, for the joint lives

particular caſe, therefore, a perſon will pay nearly the true value of his expectation. But *all* at all ages who *marry*; and *moſt* of thoſe who *die*, in leſs time than 11 years after admiſſion, will pay leſs than the value of their expectations.

SECT. II.

Of the Aſſociation among the London *Clergy, and the Miniſters in* Scotland, *for providing Annuities for their Widows.*

IN April, 1765, the clergy within the bills of mortality, and the county of *Middleſex*, at a general meeting in *Sion-College*, agreed to form themſelves into a ſociety for the ſupport of their widows and orphans. Many in this reſpectable body may be capable of doing, in a better manner, what I have attempted in this Treatiſe; and they are, perhaps, already ſenſible of the deficiencies in the plan which they have eſtabliſhed. I ſhall not, however, I hope, do wrong, in taking the liberty to recite briefly this plan, in order to introduce a few obſervations upon it.

of two perſons both 35, is, by the Table of *London Obſervations*, *l.* 69.3.—By Dr. *Halley*'s Table *l.* 76.44.—The preſent value of 35 *l. per annum* for life to the widow of a perſon now 24, ſhould he live 11 years, and marry a woman of the ſame age with himſelf at the end of that time; and alſo of 6 *l.* more, or 41 *l. per annum* in all, ſhould he live after marriage four years; is, by the Table of *London* Obſervations, *l.* 69.36,—By Dr. *Halley*'s Table, *l.* 76.03.

According to the printed articles, every clergyman poſſeſſed of any benefice, lectureſhip, or licenſed curacy, within the bills of mortality, and the county of *Middleſex*, who ſubſcribes annually one guinea, or two guineas, or more, ſhall entitle his widow to an annuity; or, if he leaves no widow, he ſhall entitle any ſuch children as he ſhall leave, to the ſame annuity for ſeven years as his widow would have had. And, in caſe a widow poſſeſſed of an annuity, ſhould either *die* or *marry* before the lapſe of 10 years, from the commencement of her annuity, ſuch children of her former huſband, as ſhall be then alive, are to be entitled to as many of the ten years payments of the annuities as ſhe ſhall not have received.—The annuity is fixed to no particular ſum, but inſtead of this, it is ordered, that a fourth part of the annual ſubſcriptions and intereſt ſhall be divided the firſt three years after the eſtabliſhment of the ſociety; half only the next four years; and 3-4ths the next 5 years; provided, however, that in no one of theſe 12 years the dividend ſhall exceed 20*l*. to the widows and orphans of the clergy ſubſcribing two guineas or more; and 10*l*. to the widows and orphans of the ſubſcribers of one guinea. And, after the expiration of 12 years, the whole amount of the ſubſcriptions, and of the intereſt of the capital ſtock, is to be divided proportionably for ever.—It is further provided, that every clergyman, who ſhall be married, or have children, at the time of his ſubſcription, ſhall pay a fine of two guineas towards a capital ſtock, if a ſubſcriber of two guineas or more, and 40 years of age or upwards. If 50 years of age or upwards, he ſhall pay a fine of three guineas; if 60 or upwards, five guineas. But, if not married at the time of his ſubſcribing, and ſhall afterwards marry, he ſhall pay a fine according to the age he ſhall be of at the time of his marrying. The obligation laid upon all, whether married or unmarried, to become ſubſcribers, is, an incapacity of being admitted members without the conſent of a general court, unleſs, within two years after becoming poſſeſſed of any eccleſiaſtical employment, they ſubſcribe.

Every one who has attended to the obſervations in this and the preceding chapter, muſt know what judgment to form of theſe regulations.

Let us ſuppoſe, that all the clergy in *London* and *Middleſex* came into this aſſociation from the firſt; and that one with another they are ſubſcribers of two guineas annually; and that there are among them as many unmarried perſons as married.

In this caſe, it may be learnt from Queſt. XIII, that the annuity to which widows ſhould be entitled, (ſuppoſing no allowance to the children of any that die) ought not to exceed 10 or 11 guineas at moſt, and that, beſides the annual ſubſcriptions, there ought to have been a fine paid at the commencement of the ſcheme, by every married perſon, of ſix guineas at leaſt, or, by the whole number of ſubſcribers, three guineas. If the number of married members is double the unmarried, the annuity ought not to exceed eight guineas; and the fine from every member ſhould be about four guineas.—The order, that only a fourth part of the annual ſubſcriptions and intereſt ſhall be divided the firſt three years, half the next four years, and three quarters the next five, is without reaſon; becauſe the number of claimants, for the firſt 12 years of the ſcheme, will be ſo few, that it will not be poſſible, during that time, that there ſhould be occaſion for dividing any proportions ſo large of the annual ſubſcriptions and intereſt, unleſs they are indeed beyond all bounds too little. —After 12 years, the number of annuitants will go on increaſing for near 50 years, as appears from Queſt. III. The conſequence, therefore, of dividing, after this time, the whole amount of the annual ſubſcriptions and intereſt, will be a conſtant yearly diminution in the dividends for near 50 years; and making the payments to the firſt claimants much more conſiderable than they ought to be, at the expence of all ſubſequent claimants.—For theſe reaſons; it appears to me out of all doubt, that this ſcheme is by no means likely to anſwer the good ends propoſed by it; and that, therefore, it will be beſt to lay it aſide.

At the time it was ſettled it was, I find, further agreed, that the annual ſubſcriptions of the *laity*, together with the intereſt of their benefactions, unleſs otherwiſe directed by the donors; and the annual ſubſcriptions of ſuch of the clergy as ſhall ſo direct, ſhall make a *charitable fund* to be applied to the relief of the diſtreſſed widows or children of all the clergy within the limits I have mentioned, whether ſubſcribers or not, provided that in no one year of the firſt twelve more than 20*l.* be given out of the fund to any one family.— This is an excellent deſign; and if the money ariſing from all the ſubſcriptions is thrown into this fund, an important means of relief may be provided, for ſuch of the more indigent widows and families as will accept the help of charity.

There is one more aſſociation of particular conſequence, which it is neceſſary I ſhould take notice of. I mean, the *aſſociation* among the miniſters and profeſſors in *Scotland*, for making proviſions for their widows and orphans. The laſt-mentioned aſſociation, and alſo ſeveral others of the ſame kind (*a*) in this kingdom, have been formed on the

(*a*) There is one among the Diſſenting Miniſters in the counties of *Cheſter* and *Lancaſhire*, and another among the Diſſenting Miniſters in *Cumberland*, *Northumberland*, *Weſtmoreland*, and *Durham*.—Even the *London Annuity Society*, tho' its plan is totally different, profeſſes to form itſelf on the principles of the *Scotch* eſtabliſhment, and to derive encouragement from it.

model of this establishment; and the success with which it has been hitherto attended, has been the principal cause to which they owe their rise. — I am afraid of being too tedious, and therefore I will not attempt to recite all the particulars contained in the plan of this establishment. It may be sufficient to observe, that for " an annual " payment, which begun immediately, of " five guineas from 1011 contributors, 667 " of whom are married persons; besides a " tax on weddings producing about 142*l.* " *per annum*; it entitles every widow to an " annuity of 20*l.* during widowhood; and also, every family of children that shall be " left by such members as die without leaving widows, to 200*l.*" Now, by particular enquiry at the commencement of the scheme, it had been found, that there was reason to believe that, for many years back, 20 widows had been left annually by the whole body of ministers and professors; and that, also, six had died annually and left children without widows; and these facts have been since confirmed by the experience of 25 years.—Substract, therefore, from 5,450*l.* (the whole annual income) 1,200*l.* payable every year to six families of children; and 4,250*l.* *per ann.* (the first payment of which was made (*a*) immediately) or *l.* 4.2 *per annum*

(*a*) The truth is, that a double payment was made at the beginning of the second year. This is of less value than

annum from each member, will remain as the ſtanding proviſion for bearing the burden of the annuitants.—This proviſion, according to the calculation in Queſt. XIII, and note (F) Appendix, ought to be at leaſt 4,745*l. per annum*, from each member; from whence it ſeems to follow, that this eſtabliſhment has not a ſufficient income to afford it a *permanent* ſupport.—But I do not by any means deſign to aſſert this. The difference between the real and calculated incomes, as it has been now ſtated, is not conſiderable enough to give ſufficient reaſon for ſuch an aſſertion. This eſtabliſhment may have ſome advantages that I know nothing of, and that are not mentioned in the printed accounts; or, in conſequence of the increaſe of luxury, and the higher price of all the means of ſubſiſtence, marriage may decline among the miniſters; or, poſſibly, the probabilities of life among them, tho' much higher 'till towards 50, than is common among mankind in towns, may yet afterwards decreaſe much faſter. The income, therefore, of this eſtabliſhment, properly improved, may continue to be adequate to all its expences and burdens.—One obſervation, however, ought to be carefully attended to. The ſucceſs it has hitherto met with, is no good reaſon for en-

two payments, one of which is made immediately, and the other a year hence; but, the difference not being conſiderable, I have reckoned them the ſame.

tertaining this expectation, with any degree of confidence. It appears from Quest. III, that the number of annuitants, on such an establishment, must go on increasing for 60 years, from the time of its commencement; and it is obvious, that the *continuance* of a success which has not lasted *half* this period, cannot be absolutely depended on. I know, indeed, that, according to the calculations which were made when this establishment begun (*a*), the number of widows upon it will not increase sensibly after the year 1780, or for more than 10 years to come; and, were this true, all diffidence about it would, perhaps, be unreasonable. But these calculations cannot, in this instance, be right; for they imply, that none are left widows under 52 years of age. 'Tis certain, on the contrary, that many are left widows under 32; and that, consequently, the whole body in life together must go on to increase for 25 years, beyond the period assigned in these calculations; or till the year 1805 (*b*). It is ne-

(*a*) See Table III, in a book printed at Edinburgh in 1748, entitled, Calculations, with the Principles and Data on which they are instituted, relative to a late act of parliament, entitled, *An act for raising and establishing a fund for a provision for the widows and children of the ministers of the church, and of the heads, principals and masters of the universities of* Scotland; shewing the rise and progress of the fund.

(*b*) This is said on the supposition, that all the ministers and professors acceded to the scheme from the first.

ceſſary I ſhould add, that the whole number alive, when the increaſe ſtops, will, moſt probably, be greater than the number provided for in theſe calculations. They are made on the ſuppoſition, that 52 is the mean age at which women commence widows. If this ſuppoſition is right, it is impoſſible that, according to the probabilities of life in Dr. *Halley*'s Table, the number of widows living together at one time, derived from 20 left annually, ſhould increaſe to more than 323, if none marry; or about 300, if one marries every year (*a*): Nor does it appear likely, that

135 did not accede; but all their ſucceſſors have been obliged to accede. This circumſtance muſt add 30 or 35 years to the period of increaſe which I have mentioned; that is, as many years as are neceſſary to cauſe all the non-contributors to die off. See Queſt. III.

(*a*) The *expectation* of a perſon at the age of 52 is, when taken exactly from Dr. *Halley*'s Table, 16.16; and this number multiplied by 20, gives the *maximum*, to which 20 widows left annually, at 52, will increaſe in 34 years, ſuppoſing 86 the utmoſt limit of life. Vid. Eſſay I.—In the calculation to which I have referred, there is no account taken of thoſe that die in the year in which they are left widows; and, for this reaſon, they are made to increaſe to a greater number than is conſiſtent with the ſuppoſition, that 52 is their mean age when they commence widowhood.—It ſhould be remembered here, that ſuppoſing this mean age, as explained in note (F) Appendix, rightly taken, the *maximum* of widows will be rightly found in the manner juſt ſpecified. But the period, in which they would attain to that *maximum*, would be as many years greater than the difference between the mean age and the utmoſt limit of life, as the mean age is greater

this establishment will be able to bear the expence of above 30 or 40 more than the

than the *least* age at which widowhood ever commences. The calculation, therefore, which I have in view must be very wrong. It supposes not only, that all the widows left at all ages, will increase to a *maximum* in the same time with those left at the mean age; but that all left in the course of every year will certainly live to the beginning of the next year. It supposes, likewise, that no widows will marry; and those concerned will understand me when I add, that it supposes further, that *acceders*, tho' mostly young ministers unmarried, will leave widows as fast as the *noncontributors* whom they succeed. In consequence of these omissions it has all along given the numbers in life much higher than they ought to have been given; but yet the event has been, that these numbers have in fact corresponded nearly to the calculation. From whence it follows, that the widows in life have hitherto increased at a much greater rate than they could have done, according to Dr. *Halley*'s Table, had their mean age, when left, been 52. Either, then, their mean age has been considerably less than 52; or, their probabilities of life must be considerably greater than those in Dr. *Halley*'s Table; and, it ought, therefore, to be expected, that they will at last increase to higher numbers than those assigned in this calculation.

I cannot help here mentioning one more reason for entertaining this expectation.—Were the decrements of life *uniform*, and the chances of survivorship between men and their wives *equal*, the number of widows and widowers in the world, if none married, would also be equal; and both together equal to the whole number of marriages. See Quest. II, and note (F) Appendix.

If the chances for the survivorship of the wife are greatest, the number of widows in the world will be also greatest, and the whole number of widows and widowers greater than the whole number of marriages. In the present case experience proves, that the chances of survivorship in marriage are as 5 to 3 at least, in favour of

last-mentioned number. But it was found, by enquiry, that the number of widows liv-

the wife; or that there are 20 widows left to 12 widowers. (See note (F) Appendix, and the end of the last Essay). The number of widows and widowers then would certainly, if none married, exceed 667, the whole number of marriages. Suppose, however, that they would be only equal; which is the same with supposing, that *widows* would not increase to more in life together, in proportion to the number left, than *widowers*; or that one with another they are of equal ages. 667 then being the number of marriages, this will likewise be the number of widows and widowers, 416 of whom must be widows and 250 widowers; that is, 5 to 3. Now as *widows* are certainly, one with another, younger than *widowers*; and likewise, very probably, more long-lived at equal ages; and as also, in the present case, but *one* marries of the *twenty* left annually; it follows, with demonstrative evidence, that if the annuitants on this establishment should not increase to 400, the reason must be, that the decrease in the probabilities of life, instead of continuing always uniform, is slow in the first stages of mature life, and accelerated afterwards, to a degree of which there is no example in any Tables. And this, possibly, may be indeed the case; for it is uncertain whether, in this particular situation, life may not waste according to a law not yet observed. This uncertainty it is in the power of the conductors of this scheme to remove, by keeping an account of the ages at which all the ministers and professors enter upon their offices and die; and also of the ages of their wives when they marry and die. From such an account kept for a course of years, Tables of Observation, adapted to the best sort of lives of both sexes, might be formed, which would contribute much to the improvement of this part of knowledge.

I have said nothing above of the advantage which this establishment derives from the marriages among widows. This advantage, it has appeared, were it enjoyed without abatement, would not be considerable; but it is in some measure given up by the order which makes a part of this

ing in 1748, was *at least* 364; (*a*) and it may be learnt from notes (A and F) in the *Appendix*, that, according to Dr. *Halley*'s Table, 20 widows left annually, must in time increase to near 400, tho' one of the youngest married every year. And it may be further learnt from note (A) Appendix, that the widows on this establishment have not hitherto increased more slowly, than is consistent with their actually increasing to 400: Nor, indeed, (as the probabilities of life in this case are higher than those given by Dr. *Halley*'s Table) should I much doubt of their increasing to *more* than this number, were it not that 364 has been given as the number found upon enquiry. With respect to this, however, it ought to be mentioned, that another account had been taken which made the number of widows only 321. As, therefore, a more careful enquiry discovered 43 new widows; perhaps, an enquiry yet more careful would have made yet further discoveries. In taking such accounts, none can well be added;

establishment, that such children of an annuitant as are under 16, shall be entitled, if she marries, to as much as shall happen to be then unpaid of ten years purchase of her annuity. The same provision is made for the children of annuitants that die. There are other *burdens* on this establishment, and it has also *advantages* of which I have taken no notice; but, as far as I am acquainted with them, they are of no particular consequence, and they also nearly balance one another.

(*a*) See Calculations, with their Principles and Data, &c. Introduction.

but in the strictest search it can hardly be possible to avoid omitting some.

The result of the last enquiry, in particular, is said to have been; not that it was found that there were *no more* than 364 widows, but that they did *exceed* this number. (*a*) However, let 364 be the true number living in 1748. Before that time, there had probably been more marriages among them, than there have been since; and this may have rendered their number less than it would otherwise have been, and less than it will be hereafter: For it seems to me, that this establishment, at the same time that it encourages marriage among the ministers, has a tendency to check it among their widows, by making the consequence of marrying to be the loss of their annuities.

I hope the venerable ministers and professors concerned in these remarks, and at present so eminent in all the departments of science, will excuse what has been now said. It may, perhaps, be of service, if not to them, yet at least to some in this part of the united kingdoms, by shewing them, that this establishment has been copied in it much too rashly; and that, however successful it may in the end prove, it is yet too soon to make it a model and an authority for similar establishments.

(*a*) See Calculations with their Principles, &c. p. 44.

SECT. III.

Of the best Schemes for providing Annuities for Widows.

INstitutions for providing widows with annuities would, without doubt, be extremely useful, could such be contrived as would be *durable*, and at the same time *easy* and *encouraging*. The natures of things do not admit of this in the degree that is commonly imagined. The calculations and rules, in the preceding chapter, will enable any one to determine in all cases to what reversionary annuities any given payments entitle, according to any given valuation of lives or rate of interest. From Quest. VII and VIII, in particular, it may be inferred that (interest being at 4 *per cent.* and the probabilities of life as in Mr. *De Moivre's* Hypothesis, or the *Breslaw*, *Norwich*, and *Northampton* Tables) for an annual payment beginning immediately of *four* guineas during marriage; and also for a guinea and half in hand, on account of each year that the age of the husband exceeds the age of the wife, every married man, under 40, might be entitled to an annuity, during life, for his widow of 5*l.* if he lives a year, 10*l.* if he lives *three* years, and 20*l.* if he lives *seven* years. Money can scarcely now in this kingdom be improved at ſo high a rate as 4 *per cent.* But, perhaps, it might be reaſonably expected, that an advantage, ſufficient to compenſate this diſadvantage, would be derived, from changing the annuities I have mentioned into annuities during widowhood. One may, at leaſt, venture to pronounce, that nothing much worſe could befall a ſociety that went on this plan, than the neceſſity of ſome time or other adding half a guinea to the annual payments.

If ſuch a ſociety chuſes, that thoſe who ſhall happen to continue members the longeſt time, ſhall be intitled to ſtill greater annuities, ſix guineas, additional to all the other payments at admiſſion, would be the full payment for an annuity of 25*l.* and 12 guineas for an annuity of 30*l.* if a member ſhould live 15 years.

All batchelors and widowers might be encouraged to join ſuch a ſociety, by admitting them on the following terms.—*Four guineas* to be paid on admiſſion, and *three guineas* every year afterwards, during celibacy; and, on marriage, the ſame payments with thoſe made by perſons admitted after marriage; in conſideration of which, 1*l. per annum*, for every ſingle payment before marriage, might be added to the annuities, to which ſuch members would have been otherwiſe entitled.

For example. If they have been members four years, or made five payments before marriage, instead of being entitled to life-annuities for their widows of only 5*l.* 10*l.* 20*l.* 25*l.* and 30*l.* on the conditions I have specified, they might be entitled to annuities of 10*l.* 15*l.* 25*l.* 30*l.* and 35*l.* Or, if they have been members nine years, and made 10 payments, they might, instead of the same annuities, be entitled to annuities of 15*l.* 20*l.* 30*l.* 35*l.* and 40*l.*—In this case, the contributions of such members as should happen to desert, or die in celibacy, would be so much profit to the society, tending to give it more strength and security.

This is one of the best schemes that I am able to think of, or would chuse to recommend. There are, however, others no less safe and encouraging which some may prefer, and which therefore, I will just propose.

Let the probabilities of life be the same with those in the Tables just mentioned. Let money be supposed to be improved at no higher interest than 3 *per cent.* Let the reversionary annuities promised to widows be 10*l.* *for life*, if a member lives five years after admission, and 15*l.* more, or 25*l.* in all, if he lives 11 years. The proper payments for such an expectation, from married men not exceeding 50 years of age, will, in the nearest and most convenient round sums, be four guineas *in annual payments* beginning immediately, and two guineas in hand for every year that his age exceeds his wife's, not admitting any greater excess than 15 years: Or, if the whole value is given in *one present payment*, 40*l.* added to a guinea, for every year that his age falls short of 50, besides the payment just mentioned on account of disparity of age.—For example. Four guineas in annual payments, besides 10 or 20 guineas in hand, according as the age of the husband exceeds the wife's 5 or 10 years. Or, if the whole value of the expectation is given in one payment, 10 guineas added to 40*l.* (that is 50*l.* 10*s.*) from a man whose age is 40; and, in like manner, 20 guineas added to 40*l.* (that is 61*l.*) from a man whose age is 30; besides the payment just mentioned on account of disparity of age.

If money is improved at 4 *per cent.* or, on account of any advantages attending a scheme, may be justly considered as so improved, the full payments for the expectation I have mentioned will be about one eighth, or half a guinea, less in the *annual payments* during marriage; and a quarter less in all the other payments. That is: A married man, *at* or *under* 50, would, besides three guineas and half in annual payments during marriage, be bound to add a guinea and half for every year he is older than his wife: Or, if he chuses to give the value of his expectation in one payment; besides the common contribution of 30*l.* and a guinea and half for every year his age exceeds his wife's; he would be bound to pay three quarters of a guinea, for every year he is less than 50 years of age; that is, 53*l.* 12*s.* 6*d.* in all, supposing him 40 years of age, and 10 years older than his wife.—All these payments doubled would entitle to double annuities.

There is one particular advantage which societies formed on a plan of this kind would enjoy (*a*)—Persons who know themselves subject to disorders, which are likely to render them short-lived, will have no great temptations to endeavour to gain admission into such societies; and, if admitted, the danger from them will be less than on any other plan. Were it not for this danger, one might recommend the following plan, as one of the most inviting.

In the plans hitherto mentioned it is implied, that, if either a member or his wife dies within any of the periods specified, the additional annuities, that would otherwise have become due, will be lost. But it would be much more agreeable to a purchaser, that they should be made certain to his wife, provided she lives to the end of these periods,

(*a*) See another advantage mentioned under Quest. VIII, p. 28.

tho' in the mean time his own life ſhould fail. The value of ſuch annuities may be computed by the rule in Queſt. IX.

Suppoſe for inſtance, the *ſcheme* to be "that a wife ſhall be entitled certainly to a "life-annuity of 20*l.* the firſt payment of "which ſhall be made at the end of 12 years, "provided ſhe ſhould be then alive, and her "huſband dead; or at the end of any year "beyond this term in which ſhe may hap-"pen to be left a widow." Suppoſe it alſo ſtipulated, "that ſhe ſhall be entitled to "10*l.* more, or 30*l.* in all, on the ſame "terms, provided ſhe ſhould live 16 years." —The value of ſuch an expectation (intereſt being at 3 *per cent.* and the probabilities of life as in Mr. *De Moivre*'s Hypotheſis) will be, in the moſt convenient round ſums, ſuppoſing none admitted above 50 years of age, ſeven guineas in annual payments to be continued during marriage, and to begin immediately; beſides four guineas in preſent money for every year, as far as 15 years, that the huſband's age exceeds the wife's, if he is between 40 and 50, and three guineas on the ſame account if he is under 40: Or, if the whole value of the expectation is given in one preſent payment, 70*l.* added to a guinea and half, for every year that the huſband's age falls ſhort of 50, beſides the payment juſt mentioned on account of diſparity of age.

If the annuities are made to be annuities during *widowhood*, and not during *life*, and the advantage arising from hence, is supposed equivalent to the difference between the improvement of money at 4 *per cent.* and its real improvement; the value of the expectation just mentioned, (that is, its value at 4 *per cent.*) will be six guineas in annual payments; besides three guineas in present money, for every year that the husband's age exceeds the wife's, if he is between 40 and 50; and 2 guineas, if he is under 40: Or, if the whole value of the expectation is given in one present payment, 56*l.* added to 1*l.* 5*s.* for every year that his age falls short of 50, besides the payment last mentioned on account of inequality of age. (*a*)

(*a*) Supposing 16 years the only term, the annuity 20*l.* and interest at 4 *per cent.* the proper payments will be nearly, in the case of equal ages and *single* payments, 46*l.*—40*l.*—29*l.* as the age of the man is 30, 40, or 50. Or, in *annual* payments, *l.*3.80.—*l.*3.66.—*l.*3.13.—Supposing the woman's age 10 years less than the man's, the same values will be, in *single* payments, *l.*58.92.—*l.*56.56.—*l.*53.66.—In *annual* payments *l.*4.63.—*l.*5.—*l.*5.41.—It appears, therefore, that a society, supposing money improved at the rate of 4 *per cent.* might entitle all married men *indiscriminately*, who are under 50 years of age, to such an expectation as this for their wives, for either 60*l.* in *one* payment, or five guineas in *annual* payments. — But equity requires, that different payments should be made, according to the different comparative ages of men and their wives; and Tables might be formed for shewing, at one view, what these different payments ought to be in all cases. If such Tables are wanting, recourse must be had to some such easy rules as those I have stated above.

He that will give himself the trouble to calculate, agreeably to the directions in the Questions to which I have referred, will find that, taking all particular cases together, the rules now given come as near the truth as there is reason to desire in an affair of this nature, the *defects* in some cases being nearly compensated by the *excesses* in others.

I have calculated here, as well as in most other places, from Mr. *De Moivre*'s *Hypothesis*, because its conformity to the three Tables which I have so often mentioned, convinces me, that it gives a proper *medium* between the different values of *town* and *country* lives, In the country the probabilities of life are much higher; but in *London*, and probably in all *great* towns and some *smaller* ones, they are much lower.

It is proper to add, that, according to the values of lives and survivorships deduced both from the *London* and Dr. *Halley*'s Table, and taking interest as low as 3 *per cent.* all women whose husbands are under 50 years of age, might be entitled to an annuity of 24*l.* during *life* (the first payment to be made at the end of the year in which they shall be left widows) for the sum of 100*l.* supposing 3*l.* additional given on account of every year that they are younger than their husbands.— At 4 *per cent.* an annuity of 30*l.* might be granted on the same terms.

In the year 1690, the company of *Mercers* in *London*, adopted ſuch a ſcheme as that laſt mentioned. For 100*l.* in *one preſent payment*, they entitled every ſubſcriber to a *life annuity* for his widow of 30*l.*; and this, at that time, (when money bore 6 *per cent.* intereſt) was conſiderably leſs than the value of the money advanced, ſuppoſing men and their wives of equal ages. As the intereſt of money ſunk, they ſunk alſo the annuity, firſt to 25*l.* and then to 20*l.* and 15*l.* But at laſt, after carrying on the ſcheme for above 50 years, finding the burden of the annuitants too heavy, and likely to go on increaſing, they were obliged to drop the ſcheme and to ſtop payment. In a little time, however, by a parliamentary aid of 3000*l. per ann.* which they are now enjoying, they were reſtored to a capacity of making good all their engagements, and of paying their arrears.—Their failure, is, indeed, much to be lamented; for, in conſequence of it, the public has loſt the benefit of an inſtitution, that for many years promiſed the happieſt effects, by encouraging marriage, and affording relief to indigence. The rapid fall of the intereſt of money; their admitting purchaſers at too advanced ages; and, particularly, their paying no regard to the difference of age between huſbands and their wives, muſt have contributed much to hurt them. Some of the principal cauſes, therefore, which have rendered them unsuccessful, may be now avoided; and for this reason I should be glad to see some similar scheme, providing, as this did, annuities for *life*, and not for *widowhood*, undertaken. If well planned it would, I think, be a proper object of *parliamentary* encouragement.

It must, however, be remembered, that the issue of the best schemes of this kind must be in some degree uncertain. For want of proper observations, it is not possible to determine what allowances ought to be made, on account of the higher probabilities of life among females than males. No prudence can prevent all losses in the improvement of money; nor can any care guard against the inconveniencies to such schemes, which must arise from those persons being most ready to fly to them who, by reason of concealed disorders, feel themselves most likely to want the benefit of them.

The societies, therefore, on which I have remarked in the first Section of this chapter, would have reason to take warning from what has happened to the *Mercer's Company*, were the schemes on which they are formed perfectly unexceptionable. But I have demonstrated that these schemes are very defective; and that the longer they are carried on, the more mischief they must produce. 'Tis vain (as appears from Quest. III.) to form such establishments with the expectation of seeing their fate determined soon by experience. If not more extravagant than any ignorance can well make them, they *will* go on prosperously for 20 or 30 years; and, if at all tolerable, they *may* support themselves for 50 or 60 years; and at last end in distress and ruin. No experiments, therefore, of this sort should be tried hastily. An unsuccessful experiment must be productive of very pernicious effects. All inadequate schemes lay the foundation of *present* relief on *future* calamity, and afford assistance to a *few* by disappointing and oppressing *multitudes*.

As the persons who conduct these schemes can mean nothing but the advantage of the public, they ought to listen to these observations. At present their plans are capable of being reformed; but they cannot continue so always; for the greater number of exorbitant payments they now make to annuitants, the more they consume the property of future annuitants, and the less practicable a retreat is rendered to a rational and equitable and permanent plan (*a*). They should, therefore, *immediately* (*b*) either *reduce*

(*a*) See p. 82, 83. Sect. I.

(*b*) Thus; was the *London* Annuity Society to make their lowest annuity 10*l.* the next 20*l.* and the highest 30*l.* they would probably be safe. But, after proceeding on their present plan some years longer, such a reduction would by no means be sufficient.

their ſchemes, or change them into one of thoſe which I have propoſed. But, I am afraid, this is not to be expected. The neglect with which they have received ſome remonſtrances that have been already made to them, gives reaſon to fear, that what has been now ſaid will be in vain; and that thoſe who are to come after them, muſt be left to *rue* the conſequences of their miſtakes.

SECT. IV.

Of Schemes for providing Annuities for Old Age.

A General diſpoſition has lately ſhewn itſelf, to encourage ſchemes for granting *annuities* to perſons in the latter ſtages of life; and this has occaſioned the 6th Queſtion in the former Chapter; and, as a further and more particular direction in caſes of this kind, I have thought it neceſſary here to give the following Table.

Values of 1*l. per ann.* for life, after 50, to persons whose ages are	Values in one *present payment*, interest 4 *per cent.*	Interest 3 *per cent.*	Values in annu*al payments*, till 50, to begin at the end of a year, interest 4 *pr ct.*	Interest 3 *per cent.*
10	1.235	2.015	.0789	.113
15	1.583	2.444	.106	.146
20	2.028	2.989	.146	.193
25	2.594	3.644	.203	.259
30	3.369	4.508	.297	.366
35	4.446	5.667	.466	.559
40	5.953	7.232	.822	.950
Values of the same annuity, after 55, to ages				
30	2.114	2.937	.167	.211
35	2.722	3.632	.241	.297
40	3.732	4.708	.394	.464
45	5.088	6.115	.703	.803
Values of the same annuity after 60, to ages				
35	1.667	2.290	.135	.168
40	2.234	2.923	.203	.245
45	3.043	3.811	.327	.384
50	4.255	5.061	.600	.679

The numbers in the 2d and 3d columns of this Table, multiplied by any annuity, will give the value of that annuity in a *single* payment, to be enjoyed for life, by the ages corresponding to those numbers in the first column, *after* the age mentioned at the head of that column.—And in the same manner; the numbers in the 4th and 5th columns will give the values in *annual* payments.—Thus. The value of 44*l.* *per annum*, to be enjoyed for life, after 50, by a person now 40, (interest at 4 *per cent.*) is 5.95, multiplied by 44, or *l.* 261.9, in a *single* payment; and .822, multiplied by 44, or *l.* 36.16, in *annual* payments till 50, the first payment to be made at the end of a year.

In order to find the same values, partly in *annual payments*, and partly in any given *entrance* or *admission-money*; say; "As the value of the *given annuity* in a *single* payment, "(found in the way just mentioned) is to the "given *entrance-money*; so is its value in *annual* payments, to a fourth proportional; "which, subtracted from the value in *annual* "*payments*, the *remainder* will be the annual "payment due, over and above the given entrance-money."

EXAMPLE.

Suppose a person now 40, to be willing to pay 200*l.* entrance-money, *besides* such an annual payment for 10 years as shall, together with his entrance-money, be sufficient to entitle him to a life annuity of 44*l.* after 50. What ought the annual payment to be?

ANSWER.

*L.*8.55.—For, *l.*261.9, is to 200*l.* as *l.*36.16, to *l.*27.61; which, ſubtracted from *l.*36.16, the remainder is *l.*8.55.

This Table has been calculated from the *probabilities* and *values* of lives in Tables III. and VI. The probabilities of life among the inhabitants of *London*, are (as I have often had occaſion to obſerve) much lower than among the generality of mankind; and the values in the preceding Table, had they been given agreeably to the *London* Obſervations, would have been leſs. But, certainly, an office or ſociety, that means to be a permanent advantage to the public, ought always to take higher rather than lower values, for the ſake of rendering itſelf more ſecure, and gaining ſome *profits* to balance *loſſes* and *expences*.

There have lately been eſtabliſhed, in *London*, ſeveral ſocieties for granting ſuch annuities as thoſe now mentioned; and he that will compare their true values, as they may be learnt from the preceding Table, with the *terms* of admiſſion into theſe ſocieties, as given in their printed *Abſtracts* and

Tables, muſt be ſurpriſed and ſhocked. They are all impoſitions on the public, proceeding from ignorance, and encouraged by credulity and folly.

It has been ſhewn; that the proper payment, (allowing compound intereſt at 4 *per cent.*) for an annuity of 44*l.* to be enjoyed by a perſon now 40, for what may happen to remain of his life after 50, is 200*l.* in *admiſſion-money*; beſides *l.*8.55, or 8*l.* 11*s.*, in annual payments till he attains to 50, the firſt of theſe payments to be made at the end of a year.—The conditions of obtaining this annuity, according to the Tables of the *Laudable Society of Annuitants for the benefit of age*, are 76*l.* 17*s.* in *admiſſion-money*; and 6*l.* 14*s.* in *annual payments.*—According to the Tables of the ſociety of *London Annuitants for the benefit of age*, the conditions of obtaining the ſame annuity are 30*l.* in *admiſſion-money*, and 10*l.* in *annual payments.*—The *Equitable* Society of Annuitants requires for the ſame annuity 38*l.* 10*s.* in *admiſſion-money*, and 13*l.* in *annual* payments. The true value is, over and above the *admiſſion-money* juſt mentioned, an *annual payment* of 30*l.* 17*s.* (intereſt reckoned at 4 *per cent.*) or an *annual payment* of 36*l.* 15*s.* intereſt reckoned at 3 *per cent.*—The *London Union Society for the comfortable ſupport of aged members* promiſes an annuity of no leſs than 50 guineas for life, after 50, to a perſon now 40 for 40*l.* 10*s.* in admiſſion-money, and 7*l.* in annual payments.

The *Amicable Society of Annuitants for the benefit of age*, promiſes an annuity of 26*l. per annum*, for life, to a perſon now 40, after attaining to 50, for 28*l.* 16*s.* in *admiſſion-money*, and 6*l.* in *annual payments.*—The true value of this annuity is 28*l.* 16*s.* in *admiſſion-money*, and 17*l.* 8*s.* in *annual payments*, (intereſt ſuppoſed at 4 *per cent.*); or the ſame ſum in *admiſſion-money*, and 20*l.* 18*s.* in *annual payments*, intereſt ſuppoſed at 3 *per cent.*

The *Provident Society for the benefit of age* promiſes an annuity of 25*l.* to a perſon now 40, after attaining to 50, for 34 guineas in admiſſion-money, and eight guineas in annual payments. The true value is, 34 guineas in *admiſſion-money*, and 15*l.* 12*s.* in *annual* payments, intereſt at 4 *per cent.*; or, the ſame ſum in *admiſſion-money*, and 19*l.* in *annual* payments, intereſt being at 3 *per cent* (*a*).

But I will not tire the reader, by going, in this manner, thro' the ſchemes of all theſe ſocieties. The contrivers of them, it is certain, can know nothing of the principles on which the rule in Queſt. VI, and the demonſtration of it in the *Appendix* is founded; and, therefore, if unwilling to be guided by the autho-

(*a*) The account here given of the terms on which a perſon whoſe age is 40, is admitted into theſe ſocieties, I have taken from their printed Tables as they ſtood at the end of the year 1770.—In the younger ages the deficiencies are greater.

rity of mathematicians, it may not be possible to convince them of their mistakes. I will, however, offer to them the following demonstration, which will be understood, without difficulty, by every one who knows how to compute (*a*) the increase of money at compound interest.

The value of a life at 50, (interest being at 4 *per cent.*) is 11⅓ years purchase by Table VI. For an annuity, therefore, of 44*l. per annum* for life, to be enjoyed by a person at this age, 498*l.* ought to be given. *Two* in *three* of a number of persons at the age of 32 will, (by Tables III, IV, and V,) live to 50; and therefore, in order to be able to pay an annuity to them of 44*l.* for life, after 50, the money now advanced by every *three*, ought to be such as will, in consequence of being laid up to be improved, increase in 18 years to double 498*l.* or to 996*l.*—From the preceding Table it may be learnt, that the money which ought to be advanced by every single person is 165*l.* or by *three* persons 495*l.* and this, in 18 years, will double itself, or increase to just the sum that will then be the value of the annuities to be paid. —But the money required in this case by the *Laudable Society*, is 14*l.* 11*s.* 9*d.* from each member at admission, besides an *annual* payment of 4*l.* The admission-money, therefore, of two members, being 29*l.* 3*s.* 6*d.*

(*a*) The easiest method of doing this, is taught in the rules annexed to the Tables in the APPENDIX.

may be increafed to twice this fum, or to 58*l.* 7*s.* An annual payment of 4*l.* for 18 years will, if perfectly improved at 4 *per cent.* compound intereft, increafe to 102*l*; and two fuch annual payments will increafe to 204*l.*

The whole pay, therefore, of *two* members will produce at the end of 18 years 262*l.* 7*s.*—A third part, I have faid, will die without attaining to 50, and thefe will live one with another 10 years. An annuity of 4*l.*, for this time, will produce a capital of 48*l.* and this capital improved for eight years more will increafe to 66*l.* The whole profit, therefore, from the member who will die is, his admiffion-money doubled and added to 66*l.* or 95*l.* 3*s.* 6*d.* And this fum added to 262*l.* 7*s.* makes 357*l.* 10*s.* 6*d.* the *whole* money with which the fociety can be provided, at the end of 18 years, to bear the expence of *two* life-annities, worth together 996*l.*

By a fimilar computation it may be found, that the improvement of money at only 3 *per cent.* will *fink* the *former* fum to 329*l.* at the fame time that the value of the *annuities* will be *raifed* to 1100*l.*

The deficiencies in the fchemes of all the other focieties, except the *Provident Society*, are no lefs confiderable (*a*).—What confu-

(*a*) Some of thefe focieties tell us, that the payments on admiffion fhall increafe, as the number of members increafes; and they have practifed on this rule juft as if

ſion then muſt they produce ſome time or other? How barbarous is it thus to draw mo-

the value of an annuity was nothing determinate in itſelf, but depended on the number of perſons who have been purchaſers. But the true deſign may perhaps be, to quicken the public in their applications.

Should any of theſe ſocieties, ſenſible of their miſtakes, reſolve to reform themſelves, they ought to conſidor, that this cannot be done by only obliging *future* members to pay the juſt values of the annuities promiſed them. All the *preſent* members muſt likewiſe, beſides raiſing their payments, make compenſation for what they have hitherto paid too little; and this compenſation is to be calculated in the following manner.—"Find the whole "amount to the preſent time of the payments which have "been made. Subtract this from the whole amount of "the payments which *ſhould* have been made; and the "*remainder* will be the compenſation required."

EXAMPLE. In the *Laudable Society of Annuitants*, the condition of a title to 44*l. per annum* for life, after 50, to a perſon at the age of 40, was, 4 years ago, 34*l.* 17*s.* in admiſſion-money, beſides an annual payment of 6*l.* 14*s.* 'till he attained to 50.—The admiſſion-money will, (reckoning compound intereſt at 3 *per cent.*) amount in four years to 39*l.* 4*s.* and the annual payment to 28*l.* The whole amount, therefore, of the payments of a member admitted 4 years ago, is 67*l.* 4*s.*—But the value of the annuity was 37*l.* 4*s.* in annual payments, beſides 34*l.* 17*s.* in admiſſion-money; and theſe payments, during the 4 years, would have amounted to 195*l.* The difference, therefore, between theſe two amounts, or 127*l.* 16*s.* is the *compenſation* which ſuch member ought to pay; and if he continues a member without paying it, (beſides raiſing his annual contribution to 37*l.* 4*s.*) he muſt either loſe his annuity, or owe it to injuſtice.

I have taken intereſt here at 3 *per cent.* becauſe I think theſe ſocieties cannot reaſonably depend on always improving the money they receive at a higher rate.

Since I writ the above, I have found, that the admiſſion-money required by this ſociety has lately received

ney from the public by promiſes of advantages that *cannot* be obtained? Have we not already ſuffered too much by *bubbles*; and, if nothing elſe can check the frenzy that encourages them, ought not the legiſlature to interpoſe its authority?

I do not, however, mean to condemn all inſtitutions of this kind. They may be very uſeful, if the full values are taken, and proper care is uſed in the *improvement* of money. Intereſt, in theſe caſes, ought not to be reckoned higher than 3 *per cent.* and, ſuppoſing money improved at this rate, a perſon, for a ſingle payment of 50*l.* before he is 40, might be entitled to a life-annuity of 10 guineas *after* 55; or, if he chuſes it, to a life-annuity of 17*l.* *after* 60. But if he pays the ſame ſum before he is 34, he might be entitled to a life annuity of 14*l.* *after* 55, or 22*l.* *after* 60. 25*l.* might purchaſe for him *half* theſe annuities; and 100*l.* *double.*

A ſociety or office that would go on this plan, might do great ſervice. Perſons in

another advance. At the age of 40, in particular, it is advanced to 108*l.* 7*s.*—when they have further either advanced the admiſſion-money to *double* this ſum, or *tripled* the annual payments, they will be *almoſt* right with reſpect to this particular age, provided the *compenſation-money*, juſt mentioned, has been paid.

These ſocieties, tho' their plans are ſo inſufficient, may, after beginning their payments to annuitants, continue them 15, or, perhaps, 20 years; but it will be by robbing all the younger members.

the lower ſtations of life might be brought to a habit of induſtry, in the beginning of life, by ſtriving to get 25*l.* or 50*l.* beforehand in order to purchaſe ſuch annuities, and thus to make proviſions for themſelves in the more advanced parts of life, when they will be incapable of labour.

There are now eſtabliſhed in *Holland* ſome inſtitutions of this kind.—Any poor perſons there, I am informed, who can, before they attain to a particular age, lay up 50*l.* may make uſe of it in buying for themſelves a right to be admitted, when 50, or at any time afterwards, to houſes prepared on purpoſe, for providing them with all the conveniencies of lodging and board. This is an excellent inſtitution; and I wiſh there was ſome imitation of it in this kingdom.

Conſiderable profits would, in this, caſe be received, from the payments of *ſome* who would chuſe to *delay* going into ſuch houſes; and of others who would grow rich enough to be above them.

It is proper to obſerve here, that inſtitutions of this kind would furniſh one of the *ſafeſt* ways of providing for widows.—A married man might, by paying 100*l.* before his wife attained to 40, entitle her, after 55, or 60, to a life annuity of 21*l.* or 34*l.* Or, by paying the ſame ſum before ſhe attained to 34, he might entitle her, after the ſame ages, to a life annuity of 28*l.* or 44*l.* (*a*); and in this caſe he would have a chance of ſharing himſelf in the benefit of the annuity.

I have called this the *ſafeſt* way of providing for widows, becauſe attended with none of the dangers ariſing from diſproportion of age between men and their wives, and from the admiſſion of perſons labouring under concealed diſtempers.

I cannot conclude this Section, without mentioning the following plan of a proviſion for Old Age.

Let 13 guineas be given as *entrance-money*; and let beſides 1*l.* 2*l.* 3*l.* 4*l.* &c. be given at the beginning of the 1ſt, 2d, 3d, 4th, &c. years, as the payments for theſe years reſpectively; and let the laſt payment be 16*l.* at the beginning of the 16th year. All theſe payments put together will, according to the probabilities of life in the 3d, 4th and 5th Tables, (intereſt being at 4 *per cent.*) entitle a perſon, whoſe age was 40 when he begun them, to an annuity, after 15 years, beginning with 15*l.* and increaſing at the rate of 1*l.* every year, 'till, at the end of 15 years more, or (*b*) when he has attained to 70, it

(*a*) The ſame payment before 30, would entitle to an annuity of 22*l.* after 50.

(*b*) According to the probabilities of life in the *London* Table, this annuity ſhould be greater.—A *Theorem* for finding what the annuity ought to be in theſe caſes, is given in the Appendix, Note (I).

becomes a ſtanding annuity of 30*l.* for the remainder of his life.

If the addition of three guineas is made to the *entrance-money*, for every year that any life between 30 and 40 falls ſhort of 40, the value will be obtained nearly, of the ſame annuity to be enjoyed by that life, after the ſame number of years, and increaſing in the ſame manner, 'till, in 30 years, it becomes *ſtationary* and *double*.—This plan is particularly inviting, as it makes the *largeſt* payments become due, when the *near* approach of the annuity renders the encouragement to them *greateſt*; and as, likewiſe, the annuity is to increaſe continually with age, till it comes to be higheſt (*a*), when life is moſt in the de-

(*a*) The lower part of mankind are objects of particular compaſſion, when rendered incapable, by accident, ſickneſs, or age, of earning their ſubſiſtence. This has given riſe to many very uſeful ſocieties among them, for granting relief to one another, out of little funds ſupplied by *weekly* contributions. A ſociety of this kind, formed on the following plan, would probably thrive, and might, on ſome accounts, be even more uſeful than the inſtitutions in *Holland*, mentioned in p. 118.

Let the ſociety, at its firſt eſtabliſhment, conſiſt of 100 perſons, all between 30 and 40; and whoſe mean age may therefore be reckoned 36; and let it be ſuppoſed to be always kept up to this number, by the admiſſion of new members, between the ages of 30 and 40, as old members die off. Let the contribution of each member be four-pence *per* week, making, from the whole body, an annual contribution of 85*l.* 17*s.*—Let it be further ſuppoſed, that ſeven of them will fall every year into diſorders, that ſhall incapacitate them for ſeven weeks.—

cline, and when therefore it will be moſt uſeful. — It is further a recommendation of this plan, that leſs depends in it on the *improvement* of money than in moſt other plans. — But I muſt leave theſe hints to be purſued by others.

SECT. V.

Of the Amicable Society for a perpetual Aſſurance Office: And the Society for equitable Aſſurances on Lives and Survivorſhips.

THE 10th Problem has been given, with a particular view to the corporation of the *Amicable Society*, for a perpetual Aſſu-

30*l.* 12*s.* of the annual contribution will be juſt ſufficient, to enable the ſociety to grant to each of theſe 12*s.* *per* week, during their illneſſes. And the remaining 55*l.* *per annum*, laid up and *carefully* improved, at $3\frac{1}{2}$ *per cent.* will increaſe to a capital that ſhall be ſufficient, according to the chances of life in Tables III, IV, and V, to enable the ſociety to pay to every member, *after* attaining to 67 years of age, or *upon* entering his 68th year, an annuity, beginning with 5*l.* and increaſing at the rate of 1*l.* every year for ſeven years, 'till, at the age of 75, it came to be a ſtanding annuity of 12*l.* for the remainder of life.

Were ſuch a ſociety to make its contribution *ſevenpence per* week, an allowance of 15*s.* might be made, on the ſame ſuppoſitions, to every member during ſickneſs; beſides the payment of an annuity beginning with 5*l.* when a member entered his 64th year, and increaſing for 15 years, 'till, at 79, it became fixed for the remainder of life at 20*l.*

If the probabilities of life are lower among the labouring poor, than among the generality of mankind, this plan will be ſo much the more ſure of ſucceeding.

rance-office on ſingle lives, kept in *Serjeant's-Inn*. This ſociety was eſtabliſhed in 1706, and is the only one I am acquainted with, which has ſtood any conſiderable trial from time and experience. The annual payment of each member uſed to be 6 *l.* 4 *s.* payable quarterly; but it has been lately reduced to 5 *l.* The whole annual income, hence ariſing, is equally divided among the *nominees*, or heirs of ſuch members as die every year; and this renders the dividends among the *nominees* in *different* years, more or leſs, according to the number of members who have happened to die in thoſe years. But the ſociety now engages, that the dividends ſhall not be *leſs* than 150 *l.* to each claimant, tho' they may be *more*. — None are admitted whoſe ages are *greater* than 45, or *leſs* than 12; nor is there any difference of contribution allowed on account of difference of age.

This ſociety has, I doubt not, been very uſeful to the public; and its plan is ſuch, that it cannot well fail to *continue* to be ſo. It might, however, certainly have been much more uſeful, had it gone from the firſt on a different plan. It is obvious, that regulating the dividends among the *nominees* by the number of members who die every year, is not *equitable*; becauſe it makes the benefit which a member is to receive to depend, not on the value of his contribution, but on a *contingency*; that is, the number of members that ſhall happen to die the ſame year with him. This regulation must also have been disadvantageous to the society; as will appear from the following account of the natural progress of the affairs of such a society, when established on a right plan.

Suppose a *thousand* persons, whose common age is 36, to form themselves into a society for the purpose of *assuring* a particular sum at their deaths, to such persons as they shall name, in consideration of a particular annual-contribution to be continued during their lives. Suppose the annual contribution to be 5*l.* and the first payment (*a*) to be made immediately. Suppose, likewise, the original number of the society to be constantly kept up by the admission of new members, at 36 years of age, in the room of such as die.—In Quest. X. p. 33, it appears, that an annual payment, beginning immediately, of 5*l.* during a life at the age of 36, should entitle, at the failure of such a life, to 172*l.* reckoning interest at 4 *per cent.* and taking Mr. *De Moivre*'s valuation of lives.—A *thousand* persons, all 36 years of age, will die off at the rate of 20 every year. The disbursements, therefore, of such a society will be, the first year, 20 times 172*l.* or 3,440*l.* and its income will be 5000*l.* It will, therefore, at the end of the year, have a surplus

(*a*) Such payments, it has been shewn, Quest. VIII. p. 28, are better than any *half* yearly or *quarterly* payments, and at the same time they save some trouble.

of 1560*l.* to put to intereſt.—In conſequence of the yearly acceſſions to ſupply vacancies, the number dying annually will be always increaſing after the firſt year. In 50 years it will attain to a *maximum*; and then, the affairs of the ſociety will become *ſtationary*, and the number dying annually will be 40, and its annual expence will be 6,880*l.* exceeding the annual contribution 1,880*l.* But, in the mean time, by improving its ſurplus moneys, it will have raiſed a capital equal to this exceſs, and, conſequently, its affairs will be fixed on a firm baſis for all ſubſequent times.

Suppoſe now, that ſuch a ſociety, at its eſtabliſhment, ſhould reſolve to divide its whole yearly income among the *nominees* of deceaſed members. The effect of this would be, that no capital could be raiſed; that the dividends payable to *nominees* would diminiſh continually, till, at the time that the greateſt number of members came to die *annually*, or at the end of 50 years, they would be reduced to half; and all claimants, after this period, receive too little, becauſe the firſt claimants had received too much (*a*).

(*a*) The reverſe of this will take place, if ſuch a ſociety *begins* with admitting all at all ages, and afterwards changes its plan, and *limits* the age of admiſſion. In this caſe, the number of *yearly deaths* will be *greateſt* at firſt, and the *dividends ſmalleſt*. In conſequence of altering its plan, the *yearly deaths* will leſſen gradually, and the *dividends* riſe; but in time *both* would return again to their original ſtate.

At the time of the institution of the *Amicable Corporation*, the interest of money was at 6 *per cent.* and, as they admit all between 12 and 45, the mean age of admission cannot probably be so great as 36. It appears, therefore, that had they avoided the error now mentioned, and gone from the first on the plan I have described; they might have all along paid to each *nominee* 172*l.* besides raising a capital much greater, in proportion to the number of members, than that I have specified; by the help of the excess of their annual payments above 5*l.* and some other advantages which they have enjoyed (*a*). Indeed, I cannot doubt but that, with these advantages, they might, before this time, have found themselves able to pay at least 200*l.* to each *nominee*; and at the same time

The following facts incline me to suspect, that this remark may be applicable to the *Amicable Corporation*.

First. In their *original charter*, as it is given in their printed abstracts, there is no limitation of age mentioned; but 31 years afterwards, I find a bye-law made against admitting any person who should be above the age of 45, or under 12.—Secondly. In their printed advertisements in 1770, it is said, that in 59 years they had paid, among 3643 claimants, 378,184*l.* from whence it follows, that tho' the average of their dividends, for the last 17 years, has been 154*l.* the same average, for 59 years, is only 104*l.*

(*a*) A surplus from a *thousand* members of only *five shillings per annum*, duly improved, at 4 *per cent.* would, in 41 years, produce a capital of 25,000*l.*

reſtricted themſelves, as they now do, to an annual payment of 5 *l.* (*a*).

I have already mentioned one inſtance in which the plan of this ſociety is not equitable. Another inſtance of this is, their requiring the ſame payments from all perſons under 45, without regarding the differences of their ages; whereas, the annual payments of a perſon admitted at 45, ought to be double the annual payment of a perſon admitted at 12.

Further. The plan of this ſociety is ſo narrow, as to confine its uſefulneſs too much. It can be of no ſervice to any perſon whoſe age exceeds 45. It is, likewiſe, far from being properly adapted to the circumſtances of perſons, who want to make aſſurances on their lives, for only ſhort terms of years.—Thus; the true value of the aſſurance of 150 *l.* for 10 years, on the life of a perſon whoſe age is 30, is, by Queſt. XIV, (intereſt being at 3 *per cent.*) 2 *l.* 13 *s.* in annual payments for 10 years, to begin at the end of the firſt year; and ſubject to failure when the life fails. But ſuch an aſſurance could not be made, in this ſociety, without an annual payment of 5 *l.*—Neither is the plan of this ſociety at all

(*a*) It ſhould be remembered, that all this is ſaid on the ſuppoſition, that proper care has been taken to keep out unhealthy perſons; and that the probabilities of life among the members of this ſociety, are the ſame with thoſe in the 3d, 4th, and 5th Tables, in the *Appendix*.

adapted to the circumstances of persons, who want to make assurances on particular survivorships. — For example. A person possessed of an estate, or salary, which must be lost with his life, has a person dependent upon him, for whom he desires to secure a sum of money, payable at his death. But, he desires this only as a provision against the danger of his dying *first*, and leaving a wife, or a parent, without support. In these circumstances, he enters himself into this society; and by an annual payment of 5*l.* entitles his *nominee* to 150*l.* In a few years, perhaps, his *nominee* happens to die; and, having then lost the benefit he had in view, he determines to forfeit his former payments, and to withdraw from the society. In this way, probably, this society must have gained some advantages. But the right method would have been, to have taken from such a person the true value of the sum assured, "on the supposition of non-payment, provided he should survive." In this way he would have chosen to contract with the society; and had he done this, he would have paid for the *assurance*, (supposing interest at 3 *per cent.* his age 30, the age of his *nominee* 30, and the probabilities of life as in the 3d, 4th, and 5th Tables) 3*l.* 8*s.* (*a*) in annual payments, to begin immediately, and

(*a*) The value of 150*l.* payable at the death of a person, aged 30, *provided* he survives another person of the

to be continued during the *joint* continuance of his own life, and the life of his *nominee*.

All these objections are removed by the plan of the society kept in *Nicholas-Lane, Lombard-Street*, which has justly stiled itself the Society for *Equitable Assurances on Lives and Survivorships*. This Society, if due care is taken, may prove a very great public benefit. It was founded, in consequence of proposals which had been made, and lectures, recommending such a design, which had been read by Mr. *Dodson*, the author of the *Mathematical Repository*. It assures any sums, or reversionary annuities, on any lives, for any number of years, as well as for the whole continuance of the lives, at rates settled by particular calculation, and in any manner that may be best adapted to the views of the persons assured. That is; either by making the assured sums payable *certainly* at the failure of any given lives; or on *condition* of survivorship; and also, either by taking the price of the assurance in *one present payment*; or in *annual payments*, during any single or

same age, is, by Quest. XI. Chap. I. *l.* 45.65; and this value divided by 13.43, (the value increased by unity, of two joint lives both 30) gives *l.* 3.4, or 3*l.* 8*s.* — The value of the same reversion, according to the probabilities of life in *London*, is, *l.* 49.19, in *one* payment; and 4.16, in *annual* payments, during the joint lives, the first payment to be made immediately.

joint lives, or any terms less than the whole continuance of the lives.—In short; the plan of this society is so extensive, and so important, that I cannot satisfy my own mind, without offering to the gentlemen concerned in the direction of it, the following observations, hoping they will not think them impertinent or improper.

First. They should consider what distress would arise from the failure of such a scheme in any future time; and what dangers there are, which ought to be carefully guarded against in order to secure success. I have already more than once observed, that those persons will be most for flying to these establishments, who have feeble constitutions, or are subject to distempers, which they know render their lives particularly precarious; and it is to be feared, that no caution will be sufficient to prevent all danger from hence.

Again. In matters of chance, it is impossible to say, that an unfavourable run of events will not come, which may hurt the best contrived scheme. The calculations only determine probabilities; and, agreeably to these, it may be depended on, that events will happen on the whole. But at particular periods, and in particular instances, great deviations will often happen; and these deviations, at the commencement of a scheme, must prove either very favourable, or very unfavourable.

But further. The calculations ſuppoſe, that all the monies received are put out immediately to accumulate at compound intereſt. They make no allowance for loſſes, or for any of the expences attending management. On theſe accounts, the payments to a ſociety of this kind, ought to be ſomewhat more than the calculations will warrant. The intereſt of money ought to be reckoned low; and ſuch Tables of Obſervations uſed as give the higheſt values. Mr. *Dodſon*, I find, has paid due attention to all this, by reckoning intereſt, in his calculations for this ſociety, at 3 *per cent*. and taking the loweſt of all the known probabilities of life, or thoſe deduced from the *London* bills of mortality (*a*). There is, beſides, a liberty provided of making a call on all the members, in caſe of any particular emergency. It is, therefore, highly probable, that this ſociety is ſecure. The laſt expedient, however, would be a very diſagreeable one, ſhould there be ever any oc-

(*a*) It ought, however, to be remembered here, that in ſelling life-annuities to commence either immediately, or after given terms; and alſo in ſome other caſes, the values come out *leſs* in conſequence of *lower* probabilities of life. Would it, in *ſuch* inſtances, be taking an unfair advantage, to eſtimate the values by the 3d, 4th, or 5th Table in the Appendix, rather than the *London* Table?— Thus; was the ſociety to ſell 20*l*. *per annum*, for life, to a perſon now 30, after attaining to 50, the value, according to Dr. *Halley*'s Table, would, reckoning intereſt at 3 *per cent*. be 90*l*. in a ſingle payment; but, according to the *London* Table, the value would be only 70*l*.

casion for having recourse to it; and, in order to guard still more effectually against danger, it would not, I think, be amiss to charge a profit of 3 or 4 *per cent.* on all the payments. —Should the consequence of this prove, that in some future period the society shall find itself possessed of too large a capital, the harm will be trifling, and future members will reap the advantage. But this leads me to repeat an observation of particular consequence.

As this society is guided in every instance, by strict calculation, it is not to be expected that it can meet with any difficulties for many years; because, not till the end of many years after it has acquired its *maximum* of members, will the *maximum* of yearly claimants and annuitants come upon it? Should it, therefore, thro' inattention to this remark, and the encouragement arising from the possession of a large surplus, be led to check or stop the increase of its stock by enlarging its dividends too soon, the consequences might prove pernicious.

Again; I would observe, that it is of great importance to the safety of such a society, that its affairs should be under the inspection of able mathematicians. Melancholy experience shews, that none but mathematicians are qualified for forming and conducting schemes of this kind.—In short; dangerous mistakes may sometimes be committed if the affairs of ſuch a ſociety are not managed carefully and prudently. One inſtance of this I cannot avoid mentioning.

A perſon, who deſires to aſſure a particular ſum, to be paid at the failure of his life, on condition of the ſurvivorſhip of another life, may chuſe to pay the value in annual contributions during the continuance of his own ſingle life, rather than during the continuance of the joint lives, becauſe the annual contributions, in this caſe, ought to be much leſs. But a ſociety that would practiſe ſuch a method of *aſſurance* would hurt itſelf; for, as ſoon as the life, on whoſe ſurvivorſhip the aſſurance depends, is extinct, the perſon aſſured, if then living, would have no longer any benefit in view; and, therefore, would make his payments with reluctance, and, in time, perhaps, entirely withdraw them; the conſequence of which would be, that the ſociety would ſuffer a loſs by being deprived of the juſt value of the expectation it had granted. The plan of a ſociety ought always to be ſuch, as that the loſſes ariſing from diſcontinuance of payment, ſhould fall on the purchaſer, and never on the ſociety.

I muſt not forget to add, that it is neceſſary, that ſuch a ſociety ſhould be furniſhed with as complete a ſet of Tables as poſſible. This will render the buſineſs of the ſociety much more eaſy, and alſo much more capable of being conducted by perſons unſkilled in mathematics. It will alſo contribute much to its *ſafety*. For in all caſes to which Tables can be extended, there would be no occaſion for employing any calculators; and, conſequently, a danger would be prevented to which, tho' it is not *now*, it may *hereafter* be expoſed; I mean, the danger of happening to truſt unſkilful, or careleſs calculators.—-Mr. *Dodſon*, I find, has furniſhed this ſociety with ſome important Tables; and his ſkill was ſuch, that there is no reaſon to doubt, but they may be depended on. They have alſo others which, I believe, are ſafe and accurate. But there are ſome ſtill wanting which ſhould be ſupplied; and all ſhould be ſubjected to the examination of the beſt judges, and afterwards publiſhed; together with a minute account of the principles aſſumed, and the method taken in compoſing them. Such a publication would be a valuable addition to this part of ſcience; and it would alſo be the means of increaſing and eſtabliſhing the credit of the ſociety.

In Queſtions 4th, 6th, 10th, 11th, 14th, 15th, and 16th, I have, with a particular view to this ſociety, given rules, by which may be formed every Table it can want, for ſhewing the values of aſſurances on the *whole duration*, or any *terms*, of any *one* or *two* lives, in all poſſible caſes; and nothing but care and attention can be neceſſary to enable any good arithmetician to calculate from them.

Perhaps, this may be as much buſineſs as any one ſociety ſhould undertake. Rules, however, for finding the values of *aſſurances*, in moſt caſes, where the whole duration of any *three* lives is concerned, may be found in Mr. *Simpſon*'s Select Exerciſes, from pag. 299 to p. 307; and it is not poſſible they ſhould follow a better guide.

ESSAY II.

On Mr. De Moivre's *Rules for calculating the Values of* Joint *Lives.*

THE calculation of the values of *ſingle* and *joint* lives, from given Tables of Obſervation, being tedious and troubleſome; Mr. *De Moivre* has had recourſe to two *Hypotheſes*, which give eaſy rules for this purpoſe; and which, he thought, correſponded with ſufficient exactneſs to Obſervations.— The firſt of theſe *Hypotheſes* is, that the probabilities of life decreaſe, as we advance from childhood to old age, in an *arithmetical progreſſion*; or in ſuch a manner, that the *difference* is always the ſame, between the number of perſons living at the beginning of any one year, and the number living at the beginning of the next following year.—The other *Hypotheſis* is, that the probabilities of life decreaſe in a *geometrical* progreſſion; or in ſuch a manner, that the *proportion* is always the ſame, between the number of perſons living at the beginning of any one year, and the number living at the beginning of the next following year.—All the Tables of Obſervation ſhew, that the real law, according to which human life waſtes, comes much nearer to the former *Hypothesis*, than the latter.—In Tables III, IV, and V, in the *Appendix*, it is so near the former *Hypothesis*, that the difference is scarcely worth regarding. According to this *Hypothesis*, therefore, (accommodated to the *Breslaw* Table, in the manner mentioned in the note, page 2.) Mr. *De Moivre* calculated the values of *single* lives; and the rules founded upon it for this purpose are so easy, that an operation which would otherwise take up much time, may be performed almost immediately.

By proceeding on the same principles, the values of *joint* lives might have been calculated; but the rules for this purpose derived from these principles, are far from being equally easy in practise. Here, therefore, Mr. *De Moivre* quitted his *first* Hypothesis; and finding, that the *second* Hypothesis afforded, in the case of *joint* lives, rules that were as easy, as the rules given by the other Hypothesis were in the case of *single* lives, he chose to adopt this *Hypothesis*; believing at the same time, that the values of *joint* lives, obtained by rules derived from it, would not deviate much from the truth. But in this he was greatly mistaken. The values of *two joint* lives obtained by these rules are so wrong, that in finding the present value, in a *single payment*, of one life after another, they generally give results which are near $\frac{1}{4}$ of the true value too great; and about *two-*

fifths too great, when the value is ſought in *annual payments* during the joint lives.— Theſe are errors ſo conſiderable, that I think it is of particular importance that the public ſhould be informed of them, in order to prevent the inconveniencies and perplexities they may occaſion.

Mr. *Simpſon* (in the Appendix to his Treatiſe on the *Doctrine of Annuities and Reverſions*) has obſerved, that Mr. *De Moivre*'s rules for finding the values of joint lives are wrong. But I don't know, that it has been ever attended to, that they are *ſo* wrong as I have found them. Mr. *Simpſon*'s remarks point out chiefly the errors in theſe rules, when the values of *three* or more joint lives are calculated by them; but, 'till I was forced to a particular examination of this ſubject by ſome difficulties into which I found myſelf brought by following Mr. *De Moivre* too implicitly, I did not at all ſuſpect, that any ſuch errors as I have mentioned, could ariſe from theſe rules, when the values of only *two* joint lives are calculated by them. Mr. *De Moivre*, in conſequence of other remarks contained in Mr. *Simpſon*'s *Appendix*, altered in the 4th edition of his Treatiſe ſome of his rules. It is ſurprizing he did not ſee reaſon at the ſame time to alter theſe.

That there may be no doubt about the truth of theſe obſervations, I will juſt mention a few examples of the difference between the values of a given reversionary annuity, according to the rules to which I have objected, and the *true* values, according to the exact method of deducing them from Mr. *De Moivre's first Hypothesis.*

Let the proposed annuity be 30*l.*, to be enjoyed for what shall happen to remain of the life of a person now 40 years of age, after the life of another person of the same age. The value of the joint lives (interest being at 4 *per cent.*) is, by problem 2d of Mr. *De Moivre's* Treatise on Life-annuities, 8.964; which subtracted from 13.196, (the value by Table VI, of a single life at 40) gives 4.23; which remainder, multiplied by 30, gives *l.*126.9, or the value of the reversion in a single present payment. And 126.9, divided by the foregoing value of the joint lives, is *l.* 14. 16; or, the value of the reversion in annual payments during the joint lives.—But the *true* values are *l.* 101.1 in a *single* payment, by Quest. I. chap. I.; and *l.* 10.3, in *annual* payments, by Quest. IV.—The former values, therefore, are near a *quarter* of the true value too great in the *single* payment; and near *two-fifths* too great in the *annual* payments.

The *true* value of the same annuity for a life at 66, after another life of the same age, is, (reckoning interest as before, at 4 *per cent.*) 68*l.* in a *single* payment; and 13.5, in *annual* payments.—But these values, according to the Problem just quoted, are 91*l.*, and 21*l.* one of which is near a *third*, and the other above *half* the true value too great.

In *unequal* lives these errors may be no less considerable.—Thus; if the value of the proposed annuity be required for a life at 70, after a life at 30 years of age; it will, by the same Problem, be *l.* 26.5, in a *single* payment; and *l.* 5.1, in *annual* payments during the joint lives. But the *true* values are 17*l.* and *l.* 3.05.

Where 3 or more lives are concerned the errors will be still greater.

The true values of the joint lives, mentioned in these Examples, have been calculated by a rule in pag. 16, of Mr. *Simpson's* Treatise on the Doctrine of *Annuities* and *Reversions*, and explained in note (M) *Appendix.*—To save, however, a great deal of trouble hereafter, I have thought proper to calculate Table VII, which gives the exact values, according to Mr. *De Moivre's first* Hypothesis, of two joint lives, for every five years of human life from, 10 to 70.

This *Hypothesis*, I have observed, does not differ much from the Tables of Observation in the *Appendix*, for *Breslaw*, *Northampton* and *Norwich*. Between the ages of 30 and 40, it gives the values of *single* lives almost the same with the *Breslaw* Table. Under 30, it gives them somewhat *less*; and above 40, somewhat *greater*. But it ought to be remembered, that wherever it does this, it gives, at the ſame ages, the values of the *joint* lives alſo too little or too great; and that, conſequently, the reſults from it, in calculating the values of *Reverſions*, and of the *longeſt* of given lives, come ſo much nearer to exactneſs.

The rules to which I have objected are the only ones given by Mr. *De Moivre*, in all the editions of his Treatiſe on Life-Annuities. But it ſeems, this great mathematician became at laſt ſenſible, that they were too incorrect; and, therefore, at the end of the laſt edition of his Treatiſe on the *Doctrine of Chances*, pag. 320, (a work which gets into comparatively few hands) he has given other rules which come nearer the truth. But even theſe rules produce errors ſo great in many caſes, (particularly when combined with the errors of the Hypotheſis) that it will be beſt never to uſe them.

ESSAY III.

Of the Method of calculating the Values of Reverſions depending on Survivorſhips.

ALL Queſtions relating to the values of lives and reverſions, are at preſent of particular importance in this kingdom. Much buſineſs is continually tranſacted in this way; and any conſiderable errors in the methods of ſolving ſuch queſtions, muſt in time produce very bad conſequences.—The deſign of the following obſervations is to point out a particular error, into which there is danger of falling, in finding the values of ſuch reverſions as depend on ſurvivorſhips. In doing this, I ſhall, in order to be as plain as poſſible, take the following caſe. "A, aged "40, expects to come to the poſſeſſion of "an eſtate, ſhould he ſurvive B, aged like-"wiſe 40. In theſe circumſtances he offers, "in order to raiſe a preſent ſum, to give ſe-"curity for 40*l. per annum*, out of the eſtate "at his death, provided he ſhould get into

" possession; that is, provided he should survive B. What is the sum that ought now " to be advanced to him, in consideration of " such security, reckoning compound interest " at 4 *per cent?*"

Mr. *De Moivre*'s directions in his Treatise on Annuities, Problems 17th and 20th, lead us to seek the required sum in this case, by the following process.

Find first, the present sum A should receive, for the reversion of 40*l. per annum* for ever after his death; supposing it *not* dependent on his surviving B. The present value of such a reversion is " the (*a*) value of the life " subtracted from the *perpetuity*, and the *re-* " *mainder* multiplied by the annual rent."— The value of the life is, by Table VI, 13.196. This subtracted from 25, the *perpetuity*, leaves 11.80; which, multiplied by 40, gives *l.*472; the value of the supposed estate, after the life of A. But, as Mr. *De Moivre* observes, the lender having a chance to lose his money, a compensation ought to be made to him for the risk he runs, which is founded on the possibility, that a man of 40 years of age may not survive another person of the same age. This chance is an *equal* chance; and, therefore, half the preceding sum, or 236*l.* is the money which should be advanced now on the expectation mentioned.

(*a*) By *Scholium*, p. 34, and Problem 26th, p. 293, of Mr. *Simpson*'s Select Exercises.

This ſolution carries a plauſible appearance; and moſt perſons will, probably, be ready to pronounce it right; nor will this be at all wonderful, as ſo great a maſter of theſe ſubjects as Mr. *De Moivre* appears to have been miſled by it.—Nothing more is neceſſary to prove it to be fallacious, than proceeding in the ſame way to ſolve the following ſimilar Queſtion.

" A, aged 40, offers to give ſecurity for " 40*l. per annum*, to be entered upon at his " death, provided it ſhould happen *before* the " death of B, aged likewiſe 40. What ſum " ſhould now be advanced to him for ſuch a " reverſion, intereſt being reckoned at 4 *per* " *cent?*"

In ſolving this Problem, agreeably to the method juſt deſcribed, we are to find the value of 40*l. per annum*, to be entered upon *certainly* at the death of A; and then to multiply this value by the chance that A ſhall *not* ſurvive B, or by $\frac{1}{2}$; and in this way the anſwer comes out the ſame with that already given.

Now it may be eaſily ſeen, that this muſt be wrong. The value of a reverſion, to be received when a perſon of a given age dies, cannot be the ſame, whether the condition of obtaining it is, that he ſhall die *before*, or that he ſhall die *after* another perſon. That is, whether it is provided, that a purchaſer, if he ſucceeds, ſhall get into poſſeſſion *ſooner* or *later*. The reverſion in the latter caſe muſt, without doubt, be of leſs value than in the former.

The firſt Queſtion here propoſed, reſolves itſelf into the following general Queſtion.

"What is the preſent value of a given re-" "verſionary eſtate, to be entered upon after" "the failure of two lives, provided one *in*" "*particular* of them ſhould be the *longeſt*" "*life?*"

Now, the preſent value of an eſtate to be enjoyed for ever, after the failure of the *longeſt* of two lives, is "the value of the *longeſt*" "of the two lives, ſubtracted from the *per-*" "*petuity*; and the remainder multiplied by" "the annual rent of the eſtate."—The value of the *longeſt* of two lives is, (as is well-known) the value of the two *joint* lives, ſubtracted from the *ſum* of the (*a*) values of the two *ſingle* lives. In the preſent caſe, therefore, it is 9.82, (the value of two joint lives at the age of 40 by Table VII,) ſubtracted from twice 13.196; (the value of a *ſingle* life at the ſame age by Table VI,) that is, 16.57 year's purchaſe. And this ſubtracted from 25, (the perpetuity) gives 8.43; which, multiplied by 40, gives *l*.337.2, the value of the given eſtate were it *certainly* to be enjoyed, after the ex-

(*a*) See Mr. *De Moivre* on Annuities, Problem IV; or Mr. *Simpſon's Doctrine of Annuities and Reverſions*, Prob. II.

tinction of the longest of two lives both 40; that is, whether *one* or *other* of them failed last. But that A's life in particular should fail last, rather than B's, is an even chance. The true value of the reversion, therefore, is half the last value, or *l.* 168.6.

In like manner. The second Question is the same with the Question, " What is the pre-" sent value of 40*l. per ann.* for ever, to be en-" tered upon after the extinction of two *joint* " lives both 40; that is, whenever *either* of " them shall fail; provided the first that fails " should happen to be A's life in particular?" —And the answer is found by subtracting the present value of the *two joint* lives from the *perpetuity*, and multiplying the remainder by $\frac{1}{20}$, or by the chance that A in particular shall die first: And this will give the required value, *l.* 303.4 (*a*).

In short. It appears in *both* these cases, that, according to the first method of solution, we are to subtract from the *perpetuity* the value of *one* of the single lives; when, in the *former* case, the value of the *longest* of the two lives; and, in the *latter* case, the value of their *joint continuance*, ought, in reality, to be subtracted. I need not say what prodigious errors may often arise from hence; and how unfit such a method of solution is for practice.

(*a*) I have, tho' scarcely necessary, given a demonstration of these Solutions in the Appendix, note (N).

Mr. *Simpson*, in p. 322, of his Select Exercises, speaks on this subject in the following manner.—" I have been very particular " on these kinds of Problems; and the more " so, as there has been no method before published, that I know of, by which they can " be rightly determined. 'Tis true, the manner of proceeding, by first finding the probability of survivorship, (which method is " used in my former work, and which a celebrated author has largely insisted on in three " successive editions) may be applied to good " advantage, when the given ages are nearly " equal; but then it is certain, that this is " not a genuine way of going to work, and " that the conclusions hence derived are at " best but near approximations."

This excellent mathematician has here expressed himself much too favourably of the method of solution on which I have remarked.—In both the cases I have specified the ages are equal; and yet, in one of them the error is a good deal above a *third* of the true value, and in the other, a *fifth*: And, it is obvious, that in cases where three equal lives are taken, the errors will be much greater. —Mr. *Simpson*'s Observations in this passage are true only, when applied to a *different* method used by himself, in the 28th and following Problems of his Treatise on the *Doctrine* of *Annuities* and *Reversions*. This method is exact when the lives are equal; but, it gives results which are too far from the truth, when there is any considerable inequality between the lives.

It is with reluctance I have made some of these remarks. Mr. *De Moivre* has made very important improvements in this branch of science; and the highest respect is due to his name and authority. This, however, only renders these remarks more necessary.

In the first Chapter (Questions 10th, 11th, 12th, 14th, &c.) I have given a minute account of the method of finding, in all cases, the values of the reversions which have been the subject of this Essay.

Obſervations on the proper Method of conſtructing Tables for determining the Rate of human Mortality, the Number of Inhabitants, and the Values of Lives in any Town or Diſtrict, from Bills of Mortality in which are given, the Numbers dying annually at all Ages.

IN every place that juſt ſupports itſelf in the number of its inhabitants, without any recruits from other places; or where, for a courſe of years, there has been no increaſe or decreaſe, the number of perſons dying every year at any particular age, and above it, muſt be equal to the number of the living at that age.—The number, for example, dying every year, at all ages, from the *beginning* to the utmoſt *extremity* of life, muſt, in ſuch a ſituation, be juſt equal to the whole number *born* every year. And for the ſame reaſon, the number dying every year at *one* year of age and upwards; at *two* years of age and upwards; at *three* and upwards, and ſo on; muſt be equal to the numbers that attain to thoſe ages every year; or, which is the ſame, to the numbers of the living at thoſe ages. It is obvious, that unleſs this happens, the number of inhabitants cannot remain the ſame. If the former number is greater than the latter, the inhabitants muſt *decreaſe*; if leſs, they muſt *increaſe*.—From this obſervation it follows, that in a town or country, where there is no increaſe or decreaſe, bills of mortality which give the ages at which all die, will ſhew the exact number of inhabitants; and alſo the exact law, according to which human life waſtes in that town or country.

In order to find the number of inhabitants; the mean numbers dying annually, at every particular age and upwards, muſt be taken as given by the bills, and placed under one another in the order of the ſecond column of the 12th Table in the Appendix. Theſe numbers will, it has appeared, be the numbers of the living at 1, 2, 3, &c. years of age; and, conſequently, the ſum, diminiſhed by half the number born annually (*a*), will be the

(*a*) This ſubtraction is neceſſary for the following reaſon.—In a Table formed in the manner here directed, it is ſuppoſed, that the numbers in the ſecond column are all living together at the beginning of every year. Thus; the number in the *ſecond* column oppoſite to 0 in the *firſt* column, the Table ſuppoſes to be all juſt born together on the firſt day of the year. The number, likewiſe, oppoſite to 1, it ſuppoſes to attain to one year of

whole number of inhabitants.—In ſuch a ſeries of numbers, the exceſs of each number above that which immediately follows it, will be the number dying every year, out of the particular number alive at the beginning of the year; and theſe exceſſes ſet down regularly as in the third column of the Table to which I have referred, will ſhew the different rates at which human life waſtes thro' all its different periods, and the different probabilities of life at all particular ages.

It muſt be remembered, that what has been now ſaid goes on the ſuppoſition, that the place whoſe bills of mortality are given, ſupports itſelf, by procreation only, in the number of its inhabitants. In towns this very ſeldom happens, on account of the luxury and debauchery which generally prevail in them. They are, therefore, commonly kept up by a conſtant acceſſion of ſtrangers or *ſettlers*,

age juſt at the ſame time that the former number is born. And the like is true of every number in the ſecond column.—During the courſe of the year, as many will die at all ages as were born at the beginning of the year; and, conſequently, there will be an exceſs of the number alive at the beginning of the year, above the number alive at the end of the year, equal to the whole number of the annual births; and the true number conſtantly alive together, is the arithmetical mean between theſe two numbers; or, agreeably to the rule I have given, the *ſum* of the numbers in the ſecond column of the Table, leſſened by *half* the number of annual births. See Eſſay I, page 174.

who remove to them from country parishes and villages. In these circumstances, in order to find the true number of inhabitants, and probabilities of life, from bills of mortality containing an account of the ages at which all die; it is necessary, that the proportion of the annual births to the annual settlers should be known; and also the period of life at which the latter remove.—Both these particulars may be discovered in the following method.

If for a course of years there has been no sensible increase or decrease in a place, the number of annual settlers will be equal to the excess of the annual burials above the annual births. If there is an *increase*, it will be *greater* than this excess. If there is a *decrease*, it will be *less*.

The period of life at which these settlers remove, will appear in the bills by an increase in the number of deaths at that period and beyond it. Thus; in the *London* bills, the number of deaths, between 20 and 30, is generally above double; and between 30 and 40, near triple the number of deaths between 10 and 20: And the true account of this is, that from the age of 18 or 20, to 35 or 40, there is an afflux of people every year to *London* from the country, which occasions a great increase in the number of inhabitants at these ages; and, consequently, raises the deaths for all ages *above* 20, considerably above their due proportion, when compared with the number of deaths *before* 20.—This is observable in all the bills of mortality for towns with which I am acquainted, not excepting even the *Breslaw* bills. Dr. *Halley* takes notice, that these bills gave the number of deaths, between 10 and 20, too small. This he considered as an irregularity in them, owing to chance; and, therefore, in forming his Table of Observations, he took the liberty so far to correct it, as to render the proportion of those who die to the living in this division of life, nearly the same with the proportion which, he says, he had been *informed* (*a*) die annually of the young lads in *Christ-Church Hospital*. But the truth is, that this irregularity in the bills was derived from the cause I have just assigned.—During the five years for which the *Breslaw* bills are given by Dr. *Halley*, the births did, indeed, a little exceed the burials; but, it appears, that this was the effect of some peculiar causes that happened to operate just at that time; for, during a complete century from 1633 to 1734, the annual medium of *births* was 1089 (*b*), and of bu-

(*a*) See *Lowthorp*'s Abridgment of the Philosophical Transactions, vol. III. p. 670.—Dr. *Halley*'s information in this instance was not right, as will appear presently; and, therefore, he has by no means sufficiently corrected the irregularity I have mentioned.

(*b*) See Dr. *Short*'s Comparative History, p. 63.

rials 1256 (*a*). This town, therefore, must have been all along kept up by a number of yearly recruits from other places, equal to about a *seventh* part of the yearly births.

What has been now observed, concerning the period of life at which people remove from the country to settle in towns, would appear sufficiently probable, were there no such evidence for it as I have mentioned; for it might be well reckoned, that these people in general, must be single persons in the beginning of mature life, who, not having yet obtained settlements in the places where they were born, migrate to towns in quest of employments.

Having premised these Observations, I shall next endeavour to explain distinctly, the effect which these accessions to towns must have, on Tables of Observation formed from their bills of mortality. This is a subject proper to be insisted on, because mistakes have been committed about it; and because also, the discussion of it is necessary to shew, how near to truth the values of lives come as deduced from such Tables.

The following general rule may be given on this subject.

(*a*) It appears from the account in the *Philosophical Transactions*, (Abridgment, vol. VII, No. 380, p. 46, &c.) that from 1717 to 1725, the annual medium of births at *Breslaw* was 1252, of burials 1507; and also, that much the greatest part of the births died under 10 years of age.

If a place has, for a courſe of years, been maintained in a ſtate nearly ſtationary, as to number of inhabitants, by recruits coming in every year, to prevent the decreaſe that would ariſe from the exceſs of the burials above the births; a Table formed on the principle, "that the number dying annually, after every "particular age, is equal to the number liv- "ing at that age," will give the number of inhabitants, and the probabilities of life, too *great*, for all ages preceding that at which the recruits ceaſe; and after this, it will give them *right*.—If the acceſſions are ſo great as to cauſe an *increaſe* in the place, ſuch a Table will give the number of inhabitants, and the probabilities of life, too *little*, after the age at which the acceſſions ceaſe (*a*); and too great, if there is a decreaſe. *Before* that age it will in *both* caſes give them too great; but moſt conſiderably ſo in the former caſe, or when there is an increaſe.

(*a*) Agreeably to theſe Obſervations; if a place increaſes, not in conſequence of acceſſions from other places, but of a conſtant exceſs of the births above the deaths; a Table, conſtructed on the principle I have mentioned, will give the probabilities of life too low through the *whole extent* of life; becauſe, in ſuch circumſtances, the number of *deaths* in the *firſt* ſtages of life muſt be too great, in compariſon of the number of deaths in the *latter* ſtages; and more or leſs ſo, as the *increaſe* is more or leſs rapid. — The contrary, in all reſpects, takes place where there is a decreaſe, ariſing from the exceſs of the *deaths* above the *births*.

For example. Let us ſuppoſe, that 244 of thoſe born in a town, attain annually to 20 years of age; and that 250 more, all likewiſe 20 years of age, come into it annually from other places; in conſequence of which, it has, for a courſe of years, been juſt maintained in the number of its inhabitants, without any ſenſible increaſe or decreaſe. In theſe circumſtances, the number of the living in the town of the age of 20, will be always 244 *natives* and 250 *ſettlers*, or 494 in all; and, ſince theſe are ſuppoſed all to die in the town, and no more recruits are ſuppoſed to come in; 494 will be likewiſe the number dying annually at 20 and upwards.—In the ſame manner; it will appear on theſe ſuppoſitions, that the number of the living, at every age, ſubſequent to 20, will be equal to the number dying annually at that age and above it; and, conſequently, that the number of inhabitants and the decrements of life, for every ſuch age, will be given exactly by the Table I have ſuppoſed. But for all ages *before* 20, they will be given much too great. For let 280 of all born in the town, reach 10. In this caſe, 280 will be the true number of the living in the town at the age of 10; and the recruits not coming in 'till 20, the number given by the bills, as dying between 10 and 20, will be the true number dying annually of the living in this diviſion of life. Let this number be 36; and it will follow, that the Table ought to make the numbers of the living at the ages between 10 and 20, a ſeries of decreaſing means between 280 and (280 diminiſhed by 36, or) 244. But in forming the Table on the principle I have mentioned, 250 (the number above 20 dying annually in the town who were not born in it) will be added to each number in this ſeries; and, therefore, the Table will give the numbers of the living, and the probabilities of life in this diviſion of life, almoſt twice as great as they really are.—This obſervation, it is manifeſt, may be applied to *all* the ages under 20.

It is neceſſary to add, that ſuch a Table will give the number of inhabitants, and the probabilities of life, equally wrong before 20, whether the recruits all come in at 20, agreeably to the ſuppoſition juſt made, or only *begin* then to come in. In this laſt caſe, the Table will give the number of inhabitants, and probabilities of life, too great throughout the whole extent of life, if the recruits come in at all ages above 20. But if they ceaſe at any particular age, it will give them right only from that age; and before, it will err all along on the ſide of exceſs; but leſs conſiderably between 20 and that age, than before 20. ——For example. If, of the 250 I have ſuppoſed to come in at 20, only 150 then come in, and the reſt at 30; the numbers of the living will be given 100 too high, at every age between 20 and 30; but, as juſt ſhewn, they will be given 250 too high at every age before 20.—In general, therefore, the number of the living *at* any particular age, muſt be given by the ſuppoſed Table, as many too great as there are annual ſettlers *after* that age; and, if theſe ſettlers come in at all ages indiſcriminately, during any certain interval of life; the number of inhabitants and the probabilities of life will be continually growing leſs and leſs wrong, the nearer any age is to the end of that interval. —Theſe obſervations prove, that Tables of Obſervation formed in the common way, from bills of mortality for places, where there is an exceſs of the burials above the births, muſt be erroneous, for a great part of the duration of life, in proportion to the degree of that exceſs. They ſhew likewiſe, at what parts of life the errors in ſuch Tables are moſt conſiderable, and how they may be in a great meaſure corrected.

All this I ſhall beg leave to exemplify and illuſtrate a little further, in the particular caſe of *London*.

The number of deaths, between the ages of 10 and 20, is always ſo ſmall in the *London* bills, that it ſeems certain few recruits come to *London* under 20; or at leaſt, not ſo many as before this age are ſent out for education to ſchools and univerſities. After 20, great numbers come in 'till 30, and ſome, perhaps, 'till 40 or 50. — But, at every age after 50, it is probable, that more retire from *London* than come to it.—The *London* Tables of Obſervation, therefore, being formed on the principle I have mentioned, cannot give the probabilities of life right 'till 40. Between 30 and 40 they muſt be a little too high; but more ſo between 20 and 30; and moſt of all ſo before 20.—It follows alſo, that theſe Tables muſt give the number of inhabitants in *London* much too great.

Table XII, in the Appendix, is a Table formed in the manner I have explained, from the *London* bills for 10 years, from 1759 to 1768; and adapted to a 1000 born as a *radix*. The ſum of the numbers in the ſecond column, diminiſhed by half the number born, is 25,757. According to this Table then, for every 1000 deaths in *London*, there are $25\frac{3}{4}$ as many inhibitants; or, in other words, the expectation of a child juſt born is $25\frac{3}{4}$; and the inhabitants are to the annual burials, as $25\frac{3}{4}$ to 1. —But it has appeared, that the numbers in the ſecond column being given on the ſuppoſition, that all who die in *London* were born there, muſt be too great; and we have from hence a DEMONSTRATION, that the probabilities of life are given in the common Tables of *London* Obſervations, too high, for, at leaſt, the firſt 30 years of life; and alſo, that the number of inhabitants in *London* muſt be *leſs*, than $25\frac{3}{4}$, multiplied by the annual burials. —The common Tables, therefore, of *London*

Obſervations, undoubtedly want to be corrected (*a*); and the way of doing this, and in general, the right method of forming genuine Tables of Obſervation for towns, may be learnt from the following rule.

"From the ſum of all that die annually, "*after* any given age, ſubtract the number "of annual ſettlers *after* that age; and the "remainder will be the number of the liv-"ing *at* the given age."

This rule can want no explication or proof, after what has been already ſaid.

If, therefore, the number of annual ſettlers in a town at every age could be aſcertained; a perfect Table of Obſervations might be formed for that town, from bills of mortality, containing an account of the ages at which all die in it. But no more can be learnt in this inſtance, from any bills, than the whole number of annual *ſettlers*, and the general diviſion of life in which they enter. This, however, may be ſufficient to enable us to form Tables that ſhall be tolerably exact.— For inſtance. Suppoſe the *annual deaths* in a town which has not increaſed or decreaſed,

(*a*) The ingenious and accurate Mr. *Simpſon* ſaw that it was neceſſary to correct the *London* Tables, and he has done it with great judgment; but, I think, too imperfectly, and without going upon any fixt principles, or ſhewing particularly, how Tables of Obſervation ought to be formed, and how far in different circumſtances, and at different ages, they are to be depended on.

to have been for many years, in the proportion of 4 to 3, to the *annual births.* It will hence follow, that $\frac{1}{4}$ of the persons who die in such a town are *settlers*, or *emigrants* from other places; and not *natives:* And the sudden increase in the deaths after 20, will also shew, agreeably to what was before observed, that they enter after this age. In forming, therefore, a Table for such a town, a *quarter* of all that die at all ages throughout the whole extent of life, must be deducted from the sum of all that die after every given age before 20; and the remainder will be the true number living at that given age. And if, at 20, and every age above it, this deduction is omitted, or the number of the living at every such age is taken the same with the sum of all that die after it, the result will be (supposing *most* of the settlers to come in before 30, and *all* before 40) a Table exact 'till 20; too high between 20 and 30; but nearly right for some years before 40; and after 40 exact again.—Such a Table, it is evident, will be the same with the Table last described at all ages above 20; and different from it only under 20.—It is evident also that, on account of its giving the probabilities of life too great for some years after 20, the number of inhabitants deduced from it may be depended on as somewhat greater than the truth; and more or less so, as the annual recruits enter in general later or sooner after 20.

Let us now consider, what the result of these remarks will be, when applied particularly to the *London* bills.

It must be here first observed, that, at least, one *quarter* of all that die in *London* are *settlers* from the country, and not *natives*.—The medium of annual burials for 10 years, from 1759 to 1768, was 22,956; of births 15,710. The excess is 7246; or near a *third* of the burials.—The same excess, during 10 years, before 1750, was 10,500; or, near *half* the burials. *London* was then *decreasing*. For the last 12 or 15 years it has been *increasing*. This excess, therefore, agreeably to the foregoing observations, was then *greater* than the number of annual settlers; and it is now *less*. I have chosen, however, to suppose the number of annual settlers to be now, no more than a *quarter* of the annual burials, in order to allow for more omissions in the births than the burials; and also, in order to be more sure of obtaining results that shall not exceed the truth.

Of every thousand then who die in *London*, only 750 are *natives*, and 250 are *settlers*, who come to it after 18 or 20 years of age: And, consequently, in order to obtain from the bills a more correct Table than the 12th in the *Appendix*, 250 must be subtracted from every one of the numbers in the second column 'till 20; and the numbers in the third column must be kept the same, the bills always giving these right.—After 20, the Table is to be continued unaltered; and the reſult will be, a Table which will give the numbers of the living at all ages in *London* much nearer the truth, but ſtill ſomewhat too high.—Such is the 13th Table in the Appendix.—The ſum of all the numbers in the ſecond column of this Table, diminiſhed by 500, is 20,750. For every 1000 deaths, therefore, in *London*, there are, according to this Table, 20,750 living perſons in it; or for every ſingle death, 20¾ inhabitants. It was before ſhewn, that the number of inhabitants in *London* could not be ſo great as 25 times ¾ the deaths. It now appears, (ſince the numbers in the ſecond column of this Table are too high) that the number of inhabitants in *London* cannot be ſo great as even 20 times ¾ the deaths. And this is a concluſion which, I believe, every one who will beſtow due attention on what has been ſaid, will find himſelf forced to receive. It will not be amiſs, however, to confirm it by the following fact, the knowledge of which I owe to the particular enquiry, and kind information of Mr. *Harris*, the ingenious maſter of the Royal Mathematical School in Chriſt-Church Hoſpital.—The average of lads in this ſchool has, for 30 years paſt, been 831. They are admitted at all ages between ſeven and eleven; and few ſtay beyond 16. They are, therefore, in general lads between the ages of eight and 16. They have better accommodations than it can be ſuppoſed children commonly have; and about 300 of them have the particular advantage of being educated in the country. In ſuch circumſtances it may be well reckoned, that the proportion of children dying annually, muſt be leſs than the general proportion of children dying annually at the ſame ages in *London*. — The fact is, that, for the laſt 30 years, $11\frac{4}{5}$ have died annually; or *one* in $70\frac{2}{5}$.

According to Table XIII, *one* in 73 dies between 10 and 20, and *one* in 70 between eight and 16. That Table, therefore, probably gives the decrements of life in *London*, at theſe ages, too little, and the numbers of the living too great: And, if this is true of theſe ages, it muſt be true of all other ages *under* 20; and it follows demonſtrably, in conformity to what was before ſhewn, that more people ſettle in *London* after 20, than the $\frac{3}{4}$ I have ſuppoſed; and that from 20 to at leaſt 30 or 35, the numbers of the living are given too great, in proportion to the decrements of life.

In this Table the numbers in the ſecond column are doubled at 20, agreeably to what really happens in *London*; and the ſum of the numbers in this column diminiſhed by half the whole number of deaths, gives the *expectation* of life, not of a child juſt born, as in other Tables, but of all the inhabitants of *London* at the time they enter it, whether that be at birth, or at 20 years of age. The *expectations*, therefore, and the *values* of *London* lives under 20, cannot be calculated from this Table. But it may be very easily fitted for this purpose, by finding the number of births which, according to the given decrements of life, will leave 494 alive at 20; and then adapting the intermediate numbers in such a manner to this radix, as to preserve all along the number of the living, in the same proportion to the numbers of the dead. This is done in the 14th Table in the Appendix; and this Table may, I fancy, be recommended as better adapted to the present state of *London* than any other Table. The values of lives, however, deduced from it, are in general nearly the same with those deduced by Mr. *Simpson*, from the *London* bills as they stood 40 years ago. The main difference is, that after 52, and in old age, this Table gives them somewhat lower than Mr. *Simpson*'s Table.

It has sufficiently appeared, what judgment we are to form of the values of lives thus deduced. During the greatest part of the interval of life, in which the annual recruits that keep up *London* come to it, these values err on the side of *excess*; and after that interval, they err, perhaps, a little on the side of *defect* (*a*), on account of retirements from *London* in the last stages of life.

(*a*) I have not taken into account the effect of migrations *from* towns, on Tables formed in the manner I have

The number of inhabitants in *London* may alſo be learnt from what has been offered,

explained; becauſe, towns in general being kept up by recruits from the country, the migrations *from* them are of little conſequence, compared with the migrations *to* them.—Thus; in LONDON, it appears, from the much greater number of deaths between 40 and 50, than in any other equal interval of life after 10, that more people come to it than leave it, at every age between 20 and 50. After 50, it is probable, that the contrary happens. But, it ſhould be conſidered, that *emigrants* from LONDON after 50, are chiefly perſons who, having got fortunes in buſineſs, chuſe to leave off, and to ſpend the latter part of their lives in country retirements. But how few are theſe compared with the multitudes who, tho' poſſeſſed of good fortunes, never retire; and with the bulk of the inhabitants in lower ſtations, who never can be able, without the greateſt inconveniencies, to quit the ſettlements by which they are ſupported? It is, however, likely, that retirements from LONDON are now more numerous than they ever were; and that they have *ſome* effect on the bills of mortality, and on *Tables* formed from them; by cauſing theſe Tables to give the number of the living too little, in compariſon with the *decrements* of life, at every age, from that at which the migrations *to* and *from London* become equal, to the age at which the latter ceaſe.—To explain this; let us ſuppoſe, that none ſettle in LONDON after 50; but that, between 35 and 50, as many come to it as retire from it at all ages after 35; and that theſe retirements ceaſe at 70. In this caſe, the Tables will give the proportion of the living to the decrements of life too high *'till* 35. *At* 35, this proportion will be given right. *After* 35, it will begin to be given too low; and this error will increaſe 'till 50; from which age it will decreaſe gradually 'till it vaniſhes at 70: And after 70, the Tables will be exactly right again.—This is the exact ſtate of the effect of retirements from *London*, on the *London* Table of Obſervations. But this effect appears, indeed, to be inconſiderable; for,

more nearly than by any method which has been hitherto taken. It cannot, it has been shewn, exceed 20 times $\frac{1}{4}$ the number of annual deaths. Could, therefore, the annual deaths be ascertained, we should know the number of inhabitants within pretty narrow limits. But the omissions in the bills are such, that it is not possible to ascertain, with exactness, the annual deaths. Dr. *Brakenridge* supposed these omissions to amount to 2000 annually. The result of a very minute enquiry by Mr. *Maitland* is, that in the year 1729, they amounted to 3038. But they are probably now much more considerable, than either of these writers have reckoned them (*a*). Let them be 6000; and the number of inhabitants will be 601,750 at most.

All the preceding Observations are, it is plain, applicable to bills of mortality for towns in general; and point out the way of deducing from them genuine Tables of Ob-

after 50, the values of lives by the *London* Table, are continually approaching nearer and nearer to the same values by other Tables; which could not happen were retirements attended with any *great* effect.—It is proper to add, that in summing up, as above-explained, the numbers of the living, in order to find the number of inhabitants in *London*, the circumstance that these numbers may be too small for some years after 40 or 50, in consequence of retirements, is, undoubtedly, much more than balanced by their being given too high between 20 and 40.

(*a*) Vid. Preface to a Collection of the Bills of Mortality from 1657 to 1758, p. 4, &c.

ſervations, which ſhall give the true probabilities and values of lives, and the true number of inhabitants, in the town whoſe bills are given.—I ſhall beg leave to confirm and illuſtrate this, in the particular caſe of the town of NORTHAMPTON.

In this town, containing four pariſhes, namely, *All-Saints*, *St. Sepulchre's*, *St. Giles*, and *St. Peter's*, an account has been kept ever ſince the year 1741, of the number of males and females that have been chriſtened and buried (Diſſenters included) in the whole town. And in the pariſh of *All-Saints*, containing the greateſt part of the town, an account has been kept ever ſince 1735, of the *ages* at which all have died there.

In 1746, an account was taken of the number of *houſes*, and of *inhabitants* in the town. The number of *houſes* was found to be 1083; and the number of *inhabitants* 5136.—In the pariſhes of *All-Saints* and *St. Giles*, the number of *male* and *female heads* of families, *ſervants*, *lodgers*, and *children*, were particularly diſtinguiſhed.—The *heads of families* were, 707 males; and 846 females.—*Children*, males 624; females 759.—*Servants*, males 203; females 280.—*Lodgers*, males 137; females 287.—In *St. Peter's*, males 99; females 129.—In *St. Sepulchre's*, *adults* 638; *children* 427. In this pariſh the ſexes were not diſtinguiſhed.

The *Christenings* and *Burials* in the *whole town* for 28 years, from 1741 to 1770, have been as follows.

Christened	Males 2361 / Fem. 2288	4649	— Annual medium 155
Buried	Males 2869 / Fem. 2878	5747	— Annual medium 191

In the parish of *All-Saints*, from 1735 to 1770, or 36 years,

Christened	Males 1632 / Fem. 1610	3242	—Annual medium 90
Buried	Males 1856 / Fem. 1834	3690	—Annual medium 102½

Of these died,

Under 2 years of age —	1206
Between 2 and 5 —	276
Between 5 and 10 —	155
Between 10 and 20 —	155
Between 20 and 30 —	297
Between 30 and 40 —	257
Between 40 and 50 —	297
Between 50 and 60 —	300
Between 60 and 70 —	293
Between 70 and 80 —	285
Between 80 and 90 —	155
Between 90 and 100 —	14
Total	3690

A Table formed from these *data* in the manner of Table XII; or, on the supposition, that all who *die* in *Northampton* were *born* there, would give the expectation of a child just born 28.83 years; or, the proportion of the inhabitants to the annual deaths, as 28.83 to 1. It has been shewn, that this proportion, in a place where the burials exceed the births, must be *greater* than the *true* proportion of the number of inhabitants to the annual deaths: And this appears to be the real case. For the bills shew, that, from 1741 to 1750, or for 10 years, about the time when the number of inhabitants was 5136, the annual medium of burials was 197.5; which, multiplied by 28.83, gives 5693; or a 9th part more than the *true* number.

A Table formed in the manner of Table XIII, would give the proportion of inhabitants to the annual deaths, as 26.41 to 1; and this makes the inhabitants 5216; or very near the true number.

The IVth Table, in the *Appendix*, is formed in the same manner with Table XIV, for *London:* And this is the genuine Table of Observations for *Northampton*, from which may be calculated the true probabilities and values of lives, at all ages, in that town.

At NORWICH, bills of mortality, of the same kind with those in *London* and *Northampton*, have been kept for many years. I have been favoured with a copy of these bills for 30 years, from 1740 to 1769. The annual medium of *christenings*, during this period, has been 1057 (*a*), of *burials* 1206. And from hence, together with the account of the numbers dying in the several decads of life, after 10, I have formed Table V, which shews the true probabilities of life in this town.

The following particulars seem to deserve notice here.

First. Had these Tables been formed from the NORTHAMPTON and NORWICH bills, for no longer time than any 10 years taken together, of the periods I have mentioned; they would have given the probabilities and values of lives nearly the same. These Tables, therefore, are founded on a sufficient number of Observations; and it appears, that there is an invariable law which

(*a*) In this register all that die before baptism, and also all that are born and die among *Quakers*, *Jews*, &c. are omitted. There are also some other omissions; and the true annual medium of births and burials must be greater than they are given in the bills. But this will have no effect on a Table of Observations, supposing the *proportions* of the births to the burials, and of the numbers dying in the different stages of life, given right. —It is proper I should mention further here, that these bills give only the whole number of children dying under 10, without specifying the numbers dying under two years of age, between 2 and 5, and between 5 and 10, as in other bills. I have, therefore, in forming the Table for NORWICH, supposed the proportions of these numbers the same that they are at NORTHAMPTON.

governs the waſte of human life in theſe towns.—The ſame remark might be made concerning LONDON (*a*). See p. 251.

Secondly. An account was taken at SHREWSBURY, in 1750, of the *whole* number of inhabitants; diſtinguiſhing, particularly, the number at the age of 21 and upwards.—The former number was 8141; and the latter, 5187.—According to a Table formed for NORTHAMPTON, in the ſame manner with Table XIII, for LONDON, the whole number of the living is to the number of the living at 21 and upwards, as 26,411 to 16,586; that is, as 8141 to 5113.—According to a like Table for NORWICH, theſe numbers are to one another, as 24,500 to

(*a*) Some have entertained a very wrong notion of the imperfections in the LONDON bills. They do, indeed, give the *whole* number of births and deaths much too little; but the concluſions with reſpect to the probabilities of life in LONDON, and the proportion of inhabitants dying annually, depend only (agreeably to the obſervation in the laſt note) on the *proportions* of the numbers dying in the ſeveral diviſions of life; and theſe are given *right* in the LONDON bills.—For firſt. There ſeems nothing in this caſe, that can be likely to cauſe the deficiencies in the bills to fall in one diviſion of life more than in another: But what decides this point is, that theſe proportions, as given by the bills for *any* ten, or even *any* five years, come out nearly the ſame with one another; and always very different from the proportions given by other bills.—There are no other variations, than ſuch as muſt ariſe from the fluctuations of LONDON, as to increaſe and decreaſe; and alſo from ſome improvements in its ſtate, which have lately taken place. See Eſſay I. p. 190, 191, 201.

15,680; that is, as 8141 to 5210.—These Tables, therefore, give the proportion of the *whole* number of inhabitants, to the number of the living at 21 and upwards, almost exactly the same with the true proportion, as it is at SHREWSBURY (*a*): And this affords a kind of demonstration of the rectitude of the principles on which these Tables have been formed.

In the parish of HOLY-CROSS near SHREWSBURY, an account was taken, in 1760 and 1770, of the *whole* number of inhabitants; distinguishing, *both* times, the number at the age of 70 and upwards; and the *last* time, the number at 10 and upwards: And, I find, that a Table formed from the *Register* of this parish, mentioned p. 192, gives, likewise, *these* numbers as nearly the same as could possibly be expected.

But further.—The number of inhabitants, not reckoning children, in the parishes of *St.*

(*a*) The annual medium of births at SHREWSBURY, for 7 years, from 1762 to 1768, was 301; of burials, 329. It appears, therefore, that one in 24$\frac{1}{4}$ of the inhabitants die annually. But it should be remembered, that in 1766, the small-pox and measles increased very much the mortality in this town; and I find also, that, since 1750, a nursery for *foundlings* from LONDON, was established here; and that in 1768 this nursery contained 660 children and servants. It seems, therefore, probable, that the true *medium* of burials about the year 1750, must have been less than 329; and that the proportion of inhabitants dying annually, may not be much greater than it is at NORTHAMPTON; or 1 in 26.41.

Giles and *All-Saints*, NORTHAMPTON, was, in 1746, 2460; and the *whole* number of inhabitants in these two *pariſhes* was 3843. See p. 254.—In the account I have received, the particular age at which the limit of childhood was fixed in taking this ſurvey, is not mentioned; but there is ſufficient reaſon to believe, that it was 21: And, taking this for granted, the number of inhabitants, not children, will come out, (by ſuch a Table for NORTHAMPTON, as Table XIII for LONDON) 2414; or, nearly the ſame with the number *really* found in theſe pariſhes.—Had this number been computed, from a Table formed for NORTHAMPTON, in the manner of Table XII, *Appendix*, it would have come out only 2176. This remark is applicable to the Table for *Breſlaw*, formed by Dr. *Halley*, compared with the ſame Table, corrected for all the ages under 20 (*a*), by the rule, p. 246.

(*a*) I have given Dr. *Halley*'s Table in the Appendix juſt as he framed it. A correction of it might be made from the proportion of births to burials, mentioned p. 239. And it would then appear, that a 25th part of the inhabitants at *Breſlaw* die annually; and that half the number born die there under ſix, as well as at *Norwich*. This Table, as we now have it, makes half live to 16; but the account mentioned in the note, page 240, ſhews this not to be the truth. It likewiſe makes the number of inhabitants at SHREWSBURY, above the age of 21, to be 4730; and in the pariſhes of *All-Saints* and *St. Giles* in NORTHAMPTON, 2230. It gives, therefore, theſe numbers wrong; whereas, as obſerved above, a corrected Table would give them true.

The neceſſity, therefore, of this correction is verified by facts; and it appears, abundantly, that the Tables I have given for NORTHAMPTON and NORWICH may be depended on.

But, thirdly. In comparing theſe two Tables, it may be obſerved, that there is a difference between them in favour of NORTHAMPTON, *fewer* dying there in childhood, and *more* in old age. The ſame would be found to be true, were the NORTHAMPTON Table to be compared with a corrected BRESLAW Table. It appears, therefore, agreeably to what might have been expected, that NORTHAMPTON, being a ſmall town compared with BRESLAW and NORWICH, is leſs unfavourable to health and longevity. The difference, however, is not conſiderable. After the age of 20, there is a ſtriking conformity between all the three Tables, which gives them great weight and authority.

Further. It ought to be particularly noted, that theſe Tables prove, the *decrements* of life in moderate towns, to be nearly *equal* thro' moſt of its ſtages. At NORTHAMPTON it appears that, of a given number of perſons alive at 20, the ſame number die every year 'till 78, without any interruption worth notice, except between the ages of 30 and 40.—A like uniform decreaſe in the probabilities of life appear in the BRESLAW and NORWICH Tables; but not ſo remarkably. It was this circumſtance in the BRESLAW Table, that led Mr. *De Moivre* to the *Hypotheſis*, deſcribed in p. 2, and ſo often mentioned in this work.—The values of lives, I have ſaid, deduced from this *Hypotheſis*, agree ſo nearly with the ſame values deduced immediately from the Tables, that it is ſcarcely worth while to diſtinguiſh them. But that every one may be able to judge of this for himſelf, I have calculated (*a*) the following Table.

	Value of a life at the age	By *Breſlaw* Table.	By *Norwich* Table.	By *Northampton* Table.	By Mr. *De Moivre's Hypotheſis*.
Reckoning intereſt at 4 *per cent.*	12	17.617	17.48	17.20	16.69
	20	16.49	16.41	15.93	15.89
	30	14.77	15.15	14.85	14.68
	40	12.90	13.36	13.10	13.19
	50	10.87	11.13	11.25	11.34
	60	8.58	8.54	9.02	9.01
	70	5.59	5.99	6.26	6.06
	75	4.21	4.86	4.79	4.29

It may be obſerved in this Table, that the values, by the *Hypotheſis*, come nearer to the true values by the NORTHAMPTON and NORWICH Tables, than by the BRESLAW Table; and alſo, that, before the age of 60, they are *all* much higher than the values for

(*a*) Every calculation of this kind may be made without much labour, by a rule explained in note (O) *Appendix*.

the ſame ages in LONDON by Table X; the inhabitants of *London*, (as Mr. *De Moivre* obſerves) being "for cauſes (*a*) too well known, "more ſhort-lived than the reſt of mankind." —The *Hypotheſis*, therefore, is by no means applicable to LONDON lives. It is proper to add, that neither can it be applied to the valuation of COUNTRY lives.—It appears, from the regiſter of the pariſh of *Holy-Croſs* (*b*), that the *expectations* of lives there are much greater than the *expectations* by the *Hypotheſis*. —The *expectation* there of a life (*c*)

At 20	is 38	By *Hypoth.* 33	In *Lond.* 28.9
27	33.9	29.5	25.1
30	32	28	23.6
40	25.7	23	19.6
50	20	18	16
60	14.5	13	12.4
70	10	8	8.8

(*a*) Doctrine of Chances, p. 347.

(*b*) See Eſſay I. p. 191.—I have not given the Table of Obſervations from whence theſe concluſions are deduced, becauſe it is poſſible, ſome may think 20 years not a period long enough, to afford *data* in this caſe of ſufficient authority. I have in p. 257, mentioned a fact which ſeems to prove the contrary. It is, however, certain, that the ſame regiſter continued 10 or 20 years longer, will afford *data* more to be depended on.

(*c*) The expectation of a child juſt born in this pariſh, is 33. At NORTHAMPTON, 25½. At NORWICH, 23. In LONDON, 18.—In this pariſh, 1 in 11 dies at 80, and upwards. In NORTHAMPTON; 1 in 22. In NORWICH; 1 in 27. In LONDON; 1 in 40. See Eſſay I. p. 200.

From this comparison it appears, that the *Hypothesis*, from 20 to 60, gives nearly the

I will add, that the probabilities of life here, appear to be much the same, with the probabilities of life among the ministers and professors in SCOTLAND.—This is a fact of some consequence; and, therefore, I shall beg leave to give a brief account of it.

The mean age at which the ministers and professors enter into benefices and professorships in *Scotland*, is reckoned to be 27. Their number is 974. The establishment among them for providing for their widows, begun on the 25th of *March* 1744; from which time to *November* 22, 1768, 721 have died: That is, 29.23 annually; or 1 in 33$\frac{1}{7}$. The *expectation*, therefore, of a life among them, at the age of 27, is 33$\frac{1}{7}$; which is nearly the same with the *expectation*, as given above, of a life of the same age in the parish of *Holy-Cross*; and 3$\frac{1}{2}$ years more, than the *expectation* of the same age by Tables III, IV and V. —Now, the *expectation* at a given age, being composed of all the probabilities of life from that age to the extremity of life; there arises from hence reason for concluding, that the probabilities of life among the ministers in *Scotland*, cannot differ much in any part of life, from those in this parish.—But there is another fact that confirms this observation.

The annual average of weddings among the ministers and professors in SCOTLAND, for the last 24 years, has been at most 32. The average of married persons among them, for 17 years ending in 1767, had been 667. This number, divided by 32, gives 20.84, the *expectation* of marriage among them; which is 2$\frac{1}{4}$ years more than the *expectation* of marriage would be, by Dr. *Halley*'s Table, on the supposition, that all 1st, 2d and 3d marriages may be justly considered as commencing, one with another, so early as the age of 30.—The *expectation* of two equal *joint* lives is to the *expectation* of a *single* life of the same age, as 2 to 3, by note (L) *Appendix*. It follows, therefore, that among the ministers in *Scotland*, the *expectation* of a *single* medium between the *expectations* of LONDON and COUNTRY lives; and for this reason it is excellently adapted to general use.—After 60, the *expectations* and *values* of lives in LONDON approach nearer and nearer to the *expectations* and *values* of lives in *Northampton, Norwich* and *Breslaw*; 'till, at 70, they come to be almost the same. This is a circumstance which, I believe, has not been attended to: And it is the more surprizing, as there is no cause known, which can produce any error in the values of lives after 60, deduced from the LONDON Table, except migrations from *London*; and the effect of these must be to *diminish* these values.

The following observations will, perhaps, account for this.

It has been proved, that at least *half* the inhabitants of LONDON, turned of 20 years of age, are *emigrants* to LONDON from the country. So great a change as that, from the *country* air and modes of life, to the air and modes of life in *London*, must be parti-

life at 30 cannot be less than 31.26. Most probably it is more; on account of the later commencement of marriage in the situation of the *Scotch* ministers. — I reckon also, that 27 must be less than the mean age at which they enter their benefices and professorships; meaning by it, not the age on each side of which equal numbers enter; but the age at which, the excess of the interval of time taken to enter on one side, is just such as to compensate the greater numbers who enter on the other side. See the conclusion of note (F) *Appendix*.

cularly hurtful to these persons; and, therefore, (except *infants*) it is in them, probably, that the pernicious influence of *London* on its inhabitants chiefly appears. They come in at every age 'till near 50; and this is the reason why the deaths continually increase in *London* 'till that age; but, after that age, the inhabitants consisting chiefly of persons, who (like men *used* to drink) have been *seasoned* to *London*, or with whom it does not happen particularly to disagree; the number of deaths becomes less, and the values of lives begin to approach nearer to the common standard in other towns.

There is one more fact which I shall here take notice of; and which deserves more attention than has been hitherto bestowed upon it. I mean; "the difference between the "probabilities of life among *males* and *fe*-"*males*, in favour of the latter."

From the account in p. 254, it appears, that at NORTHAMPTON, tho' more *males* are born than *females*, and nearly the same number die; yet the number of living *females* is greater than the number of *males*, in the proportion of 2301 to 1770, or 39 to 30. This cannot be accounted for, without supposing, that *males* are more short-lived than *females*.—One obvious reason of this fact is, that *males* are more subject to untimely deaths by accidents of various kinds; and also, in general, more addicted to the excesses and irregularities which ſhorten life. But this is by no means the *only* reaſon. For it ſhould be obſerved, that at NORTHAMPTON the number of *female* children was, in 1746, greater than the number of male children, in the proportion of 759 to 624.—The greater mortality of males, therefore, takes place among *children.*—But this, together with the greater mortality in general of males at all ages, will more particularly appear from the following recital of facts.

In the pariſh of *Holy-Croſs, Salop*, the ingenious Vicar, Mr. *Gorſuch*, in 1760, and again in 1770, took the number of male and female inhabitants turned of 70. In 1760, the number of females turned of this age, was 35; of males, 8. In 1770, theſe numbers were, females, 35; males, 26. And for the laſt 10 years 11, out of 365 have died between the ages of 85 and 102; and they were all females.

At BERLIN, it appeared, from the accurate account which was taken of the inhabitants in 1747, and which has been mentioned in p. 219, that the number of *female* citizens exceeded the number of *male* citizens, in the proportion of 459 to 391: And yet, out of this ſmaller number of males, more had died, for 20 years preceding 1751, in the proportion of 19 to 17 (*a*).

(*a*) Vid. *Suſmilch*, p. 8, and p. 32, &c. where a minute account is given of the number of males and females at BERLIN in 1747; and alſo, of the numbers of each ſex that had died from 1722 to 1750.

At EDINBURGH, in 1743, the number of *females* was to the number of *males*, as 4 to 3; (See Essay I. p. 211) but the females that died annually, from 1749 to 1758, were to the males, in no higher proportion than $3\frac{1}{7}$ to 3. Before 1749, the bills give the totals of burials, without distinguishing them into the totals of males and females dying every year.

Mr. *Kerseboom*, in his Essay on the numbers of people in HOLLAND, informs us, that from the Tables of assignable Annuities for lives in HOLLAND, which had been kept there for 125 years, wherein the ages of the persons dying are truly entered; it appears, that females have, in all accidents of age, lived about 3 or 4 years longer than the same number of males. See *Philosophical Transactions* abridged, Vol. IX, p. 326.

In Volume the 7th of the *Philosophical Transactions* abridged, Part IV, p. 46, &c. there is an account of the numbers of *male* and *female* still-born children and chrysoms, and of boys and girls under 10, of married men and married women, and of widows and widowers, who died for a course of years at *Vienna*, *Breslaw*, *Dresden*, *Leipsic*, *Ratisbon*, and some other towns in GERMANY.

He that will take the pains to examine these accounts will find that, though in these towns the proportion of males and females born is no higher than 19 to 18, yet the proportion of boys and girls (*a*) that die is 8 to 7; and that, in particular, the *ſtill-born* and *chryſom males*, are to the ſtill-born and chryſom *females*, as 3 to 2.

In theſe accounts it appears alſo, that of 7270 *married* perſons who had died in theſe towns (*b*), 4336 were married *men*, and but 2934 married *women*; that is, *three* married *men* died to *two* married *women*.—The ſcheme for making proviſion for the widows and orphans of the miniſters in SCOTLAND, has obliged them to keep an account of the number of *weddings* among them, and the number of *widows* left annually; and it appears, from the *reports* of the *truſtees* for carrying this ſcheme into execution, that the annual medium of *weddings* (*c*), is (as obſerved in the note, p. 264) at moſt 32. And the annual

(*a*) In the accounts from *Breſlaw* it is particularly mentioned, that by *boys* and *girls* are meant children to 10 years of age, of whom, for 8 years from 1717 to 1725, *ſeven* males died to *ſix* females, excluſively of the *ſtill-born* and *chryſoms*.

(*b*) In *Breſlaw* alone, for the eight years mentioned in the laſt note, 1891 married men died, to 1196 married women; that is 5 to 3.—In *Dreſden* alone, for five years, theſe numbers were 1080 and 849.

(*c*) The annual medium of weddings, among the miniſters admitted to benefices, has been, for 24 years from the commencement of the ſcheme, 27. Beſides theſe I find there have been 4 weddings annually among them, *before* admiſſion to benefices. The whole annual medium, therefore, is no more than 31. But I have ſuppoſed it 32, in order to go upon more ſure grounds.

medium of widows, who have come upon the ſcheme for 24 years, is 20. Of 32 marriages then contracted annually, 20 become extinct by the deaths of *huſbands*; and but 12 by the deaths of *wives*. That is; among the miniſters and profeſſors in SCOTLAND, 20 married men die to 12 married women; or 5 to 3. It appears, therefore, that there is the chance of 3 to 2, and in ſome circumſtances even a *greater* chance, that the *woman* ſhall be the ſurvivor of a marriage, and not the *man*. In order to account for this by the difference of age between men and their wives, this difference ought to be at leaſt 12 years (*a*). That is; ſuppoſing the mean age at which women marry to be 23, the mean age at which men marry ought to be 35. But this ſeems to exceed the bounds of credibility; and, therefore, very probably, the greater mortality of males muſt operate in this caſe.

It is further obſervable in the accounts from *Germany*, to which I have referred, that the number of *widows* dying annually, is four times the number of *widowers* (*b*); and, as

(*a*) The chance of ſurvivorſhip between two perſons aged 21 and 34, is nearly 3 to 2 in favour of the former. There is the ſame chance of ſurvivorſhip between 25 and 37; and 28 and 39. This may be learnt from Problem XVI, in Mr. *De Moivre*'s Treatiſe on *Life-Annuities*.

(*b*) In *Dreſden* alone, the number of *widows* who died, in four years, was 584. The number of *widowers*, 149. That is; 4 to 1.—It appears from note (*b*) in the laſt

widows are certainly, one with another, ſeveral years younger than *widowers*; it may be concluded from hence, that the number of the former in life together could not be leſs than five times the latter.—This fact is likewiſe confirmed, by the obſervations which have been made among the miniſters in *Scotland*. At the commencement of the ſcheme which I have ſo often had occaſion to mention, an account was taken of the number of the *widows* of miniſters in the whole country. 364 were counted; and, probably, the true number was greater. See p. 95 and 96. On the contrary; the number of *widowers* among the miniſters has, one year with another, been ſcarcely 90; that is, not ſo much as a *quarter* of the number of *widows*.—It may be eaſily ſeen, and it would not be difficult to demonſtrate, that neither the greater number of perſons left widows, nor any probable ſuppoſition concerning the greater frequency of marriages among widowers, can completely account for this, without admitting the *greater mortality of males*.—This, therefore, appears, on the whole to be a fact

page, that the chance of ſurvivorſhip in this city in favour of the *wife*, is leſs than among the miniſters in *Scotland*.—Does not this fact afford a reaſon, additional to that mentioned above, and in p. 92, 93, 94, &c. and notes (A) and (F), for *believing*, or at leaſt *ſuſpecting* that the number of *widows* on the *Scotch* eſtabliſhment, if marriage does not decline among the miniſters, will not at laſt be found to be ſo little as 400?

well eſtabliſhed: And it follows from it, that in order to calculate the values of *Life-Annuities* and *Reverſions* with exactneſs, there ought to be diſtinct Tables of the probabilities of life for *males* and *females*. But there are no ſuch Tables extant; nor, indeed, has it been ſuſpected, that there is ſo much occaſion for them as the facts I have mentioned ſeem to ſhew. All that is neceſſary to obtain the proper *data* for forming ſuch Tables is, that the *ſexes* as well as the *ages* of the dead ſhould be ſpecified in the bills; and this is an improvement of bills (*a*) of mortality which would give little trouble, and which, therefore, I hope, will be ſome time or other made.

It has been obſerved, that the author of nature has provided, that more *males* ſhould be born than *females*, on account of the particular waſte of *males*, occaſioned by wars and other cauſes. Perhaps it might have been added, that this proviſion had alſo in view, that particular weakneſs or delicacy in the conſtitution of males, which makes them more ſubject to mortality; and which, con-

(*a*) This improvement would be rendered more complete, by diſtinguiſhing the *males* that die, under the denominations of *married men*, *widowers*, and *batchelors*; and the *females*, under the denominations of *married women*, *widows*, and *virgins*.—The uſe I have made of ſome accounts of this kind which have been kept in *Germany*, ſhews that this would be of conſiderable ſervice.

fequently, renders it neceffary, that more of them fhould be produced, in order to preferve in the world a due proportion between the two fexes.

In the courfe of this Effay, it has often appeared, that I have been particularly indebted to an information which I have received from NORTHAMPTON.—I fhould be inexcufable, did I not mention, that I owe this information to Mr. *Lawton*, an ingenious gentleman in that town, who has preferved the bills of mortality there with much care, and been very obliging in communicating them to me.—It is much to be defired, that like accounts were kept in every town and parifh. It would be extremely agreeable to learn from them the different rates of human mortality in different places, and the number of people and progrefs of population in the kingdom. The trouble of keeping them would be trifling; but the inftruction derived from them (*a*), would be very important.—I have already propofed one improvement of fuch accounts. I will add, that they would be ftill more ufeful, did they give the ages of the dead after 10, within periods of *five*, inftead of *ten* years. — During every period, fo fhort as *five* years, the decrements of life may, in conftructing Tables, be fafely

(*a*) See Effay I. p. 207, 208.

taken to be *uniform*. But this cannot be equally depended on, in periods ſo long as ten years.

There is yet another improvement of theſe accounts, which I will take this opportunity to mention. They ſhould contain not only a liſt of the diſtempers of which all die, like that in the *London* bills; but they ſhould ſpecify particularly the numbers dying of theſe diſtempers, in the ſeveral diviſions of life. Accurate regiſters of mortality kept in this manner, in all parts of the kingdom; and compared with records of the ſeaſons, and of the weather, and with the particular circumſtances which diſcriminate different ſituations, might contribute, more than can be eaſily imagined, to the increaſe of *phyſical* knowledge. — But to proceed no farther in theſe Obſervations; I ſhall now beg leave to ſhut up this whole work with the following general reflexion.

I have repreſented particularly, the great difference between the probabilities of human life in towns and in country pariſhes; and from the facts I have recited, and the obſervations I have made, it appears, that the further we go from the artificial and irregular modes of living in great towns, the fewer of mankind die in the *firſt* ſtages of life, and the more in its *laſt* ſtages. The lower animals (except ſuch (*a*) as have been taken under human management) ſeem in general to enjoy the full period of exiſtence allotted them, and to die chiefly of old age: And were any obſervations to be made among *ſavages*, perhaps the ſame would be found to be true of them.—DEATH is an evil to which the order of providence has ſubjected every inhabitant of this earth; but to man it has been rendered unſpeakably more an evil than it was deſigned to be. The greateſt part of that black catalogue of diſeaſes which ravage human life, is the off-ſpring of the tenderneſs, the luxury, and the corruptions introduced by the vices and falſe refinements of civil ſociety (*b*). That delicacy which is in-

(*a*) Calves are the only animals taken under our peculiar care immediately after birth; and, in conſequence of then adminiſtring to them the ſame ſort of phyſic that is given to *infants*, and treating them in other reſpects in the ſame manner, it is probable, that more of them die ſoon after being born, than of *all* the other ſpecies of animals, which we ſee in the ſame circumſtances. See the *Comparative View of the State and Faculties of Man with thoſe of the Animal World*, p. 23.—It is, indeed, melancholy to think of the havock made among the human ſpecies by the unnatural *cuſtoms* as well as the *vices*, which prevail in poliſhed ſocieties. I have no doubt, but that the cuſtom, in particular, of committing infants, as ſoon as born, to the care of *foſter-mothers*, deſtroys more lives than the ſword, famine and peſtilence put together.

(*b*) The ingenious and excellent writer quoted in the laſt note, obſerves, that the whole claſs of diſeaſes which ariſe from catching cold, are found only among the civilized part of mankind, p. 51.—And, concerning that

jured by every breath of air, and that rottenneſs of conſtitution which is the effect of intemperance and debauchery, were never intended by the author of nature; and it is impoſſible, that they ſhould not lay the foundation of numberleſs ſufferings, and terminate in premature and miſerable deaths.— Let us then value more the ſimplicity and innocence of a life agreeable to nature; and learn to conſider nothing as ſavageneſs but malevolence, ignorance and wickedneſs. The order of nature is wiſe and kind. In a conformity to it conſiſts health and long life; grace, honour, virtue and joy. But nature turned out of its way will always puniſh. *The wicked ſhall not live out half their days.* Criminal exceſſes embitter and cut ſhort our *preſent exiſtence*; and the higheſt authority has taught us to expect, that they will not only kill the *body*, but the *ſoul*; and deprive of an EVERLASTING EXISTENCE.

loſs of all our higher powers which often attends the decline of life, and which is ſo humiliating to human pride; he obſerves, that it exhibits a ſcene ſingular in nature, and that there is the greateſt reaſon to believe, that it proceeds from adventitious cauſes, and would not take place among us if we led natural lives, p. 62.

APPENDIX.

Note (A). See Queſtion III. Page 11.

LET E be any given expectation of life; and $\frac{4E-x}{4E} \times px$ will be the number of perſons alive at the end of x years, ariſing from p perſons left annually as widows, (or added annually to a town or ſociety) at the age whoſe *expectation* is E. The *maximum*, therefore, is always pE—. In Mr. *De Moivre's Hypotheſis*, E is always $\frac{1}{2}$ the difference between the given age and 86. See the note page 2, and the latter end of the note in page 37. See likewiſe the beginning of the Firſt Eſſay, and note (L) in this Appendix, where the inveſtigation of this rule will be given.

It will not be amiſs to give the following example of the application of this rule.

At the time of the commencement of the ſcheme, among the miniſters and profeſſors in SCOTLAND, for making proviſion for their widows, it was neceſſary, that a calculation ſhould be made of the number of widows that would be upon the ſcheme at the end of every year, till they came to a *maximum*, on the ſuppoſition that, (agreeably to what particular enquiry had ſhewn to have happened for many preceding years,) 20 new widows would be left every year. In order to make this calculation, let 4 of the 20 widows be ſuppoſed to be under 32 years of age when left; and let 28 be supposed their mean age. Let the same number be left between 32 and 39, and let 35 be their mean age; between 39 and 47, and 43 their mean age; between 47 and 57, and 52 their mean age; between 57 and the extremity of life, and 63 their mean age. The number in life together, to which, in 10 years, 4 widows left annually at the age of 28 will grow, is, by the rule, (E being 29) $\frac{116-10}{116} \times 40$, or 36.55——The number alive at the end of 20 years, will be $\frac{116-20}{116} \times 80$, or 66.2. At the end of 30 years, the number alive will be 89; of 40 years, 104.82; of 58 years 116——These numbers, found in the same way, for the 2d class, (E being 25.5), at the end of 10, 20, 30, 40, and 51 years, will be 36.7—64.31—84.7—97.25—102——for the 3d class, (E being 21.5) at the end of 10, 20, 30, 40, and 43 years, 35.34—61.4—78.13—85.6—86——For the 4th class, (E being 17) at the end of 10, 20, 30, and 34 years, 34.11—56.47—67—68——For the 5th class, (E being 11.5) at the end of 10, 20, and 23 years, 31.3—45.2—46——The whole number, therefore, consisting of all the classes, will come to a *maximum* nearly in 58 years; and the totals in life, at the end of 10, 20, 30, 40, 50, and 58 years, will be 173.37—293.58—364.83—401.67—418.

These determinations suppose none to marry. In 10 years, from 1757 to 1767, I have been informed, that but 9 widows married. Let us then suppose, that one widow of the first class marries every year; and let all that marry, be supposed to continue, one with another, 5 years in widowhood before they marry. On these suppositions, the foregoing totals will, at the end of the ſame periods of years, be 169.23—282—347.5—380.47—394.

Theſe calculations are made from Mr. *De Moivre*'s Hypotheſis. Had they been made exactly from Dr. *Halley*'s table, or any other of the Tables I have given at the end of this work, except the *London* one, the reſults would have been very nearly the ſame.—It appears, that the probabilities of life, among theſe widows, are greater than thoſe given by theſe tables. See the Laſt Eſſay, pages 263, 264 266, 270, &c. The effect of this muſt be, to raiſe the *maximum* without ſenſibly increaſing the numbers in life for the firſt 20 or 25 years: and its effect *may* be, to raiſe the *maximum*, and at the ſame time even to diminiſh theſe numbers.

Twenty-five years have now elapſed ſince the commencement of this ſcheme; and the number of widows living every year have, in fact, correſponded to the laſt numbers I have given, as nearly as could poſſibly be expected in an affair of this nature.

Note (B). Queſtion VI. Page 21.

LET r ſignify the ſum of 1*l.* and its intereſt, for one year. The value of a life, whoſe complement is n, being (by Mr. *De Moivre* on *Annuities*, 4th edition, page 14. and p. 100.) $\frac{n-1}{nr} + \frac{n-2}{nr^2} + \frac{n-3}{nr^3} + \frac{n-4}{nr^4}$, &c. the preſent value of the remainder of it after *two* years muſt be $\frac{n-3}{nr^3} + \frac{n-4}{nr^4}$, &c. which is equal to $\frac{1}{r^2} \times \frac{n-2}{n} \times \overline{\frac{n-3}{n-2r} + \frac{n-4}{n-2r^2} + \frac{n-5}{n-2r^3}}$, &c.

Now $\frac{1}{r^2}$ is the preſent value of 1*l.* due at the end of two years. $\frac{n-2}{n}$ is the probability that a life, whoſe complement is n, ſhall continue two years, and $\frac{n-3}{n-2r} + \frac{n-4}{n-2r^2} + \frac{n-5}{n-2r^3}$, &c. is the value of a life two years older than the life whoſe complement is n. And, therefore, (ſince any number of years leſs than n may be ſubſtituted for two years) the firſt rule given in this queſtion is right.

The ſame proceſs, applied to joint lives, will demonſtrate what is ſaid in the *Scholium*.

Note (C). See Queſtion VII. Page 22.

LET the complements of any two aſſigned lives be n and m. The preſent value of the firſt poſſible payment of an annuity to be enjoyed by the life whoſe complement is n, provided *both* lives continue 7 years, and the life, whoſe complement is n, ſurvives the other *after* that term, is the probability, that the life of the expectant ſhall continue 8 years, and the other life 7 years and then fail in the 8th year, multiplied by $\frac{1}{r^8}$, or by 1*l.* diſcounted for 8 years.—The probability that the life of the *expectant* ſhall continue 8 years is $\frac{n-8}{n}$. The probability that the *other* life ſhall continue 7 years is $\frac{m-7}{m}$. The probability that it ſhall continue 7 years, and fail in the 8th year, is $\frac{m-7}{m} \times \overline{1-\frac{m-8}{m-7}} = \frac{1}{m}$. The probability, therefore, that the life of the *expectant* ſhall continue 8 years, and the other life 7 and fail in the 8th year, is $\frac{n-8}{n} \times \frac{1}{m}$; and the preſent value of the firſt poſſible payment of the annuity ſuppoſed, is $\frac{n-8}{nr^8} \times \frac{1}{m}$. See *The Doctrine of Annuities* by Mr. *Simpſon*, p. 6—15, or his *Select Exerciſes*, p. 315, &c.—— In like manner, the preſent value of the 2d payment, at the end of the 9th year, may be found to be $\frac{n-9}{nr^9} \times \frac{m-7}{m} \times \overline{1 - \frac{m-9}{m-7}}$, or $\frac{n-9}{nr^9} \times \frac{2}{m}$. and the present value of all the possible payments, $\frac{1}{r^7} \times \overline{\frac{n-8}{nr} \times \frac{1}{m} + \frac{n-9}{nr^2} \times \frac{2}{m} + \frac{n-10}{nr^3} \times \frac{3}{m}, \&c.}$ But this series is equal to $\frac{1}{r^7} \times \frac{n-7}{n} \times \frac{m-7}{m} \times \overline{\frac{n-8}{\overline{n-7}\,r} \times \frac{1}{m-7} \times \frac{n-9}{\overline{n-7}\,r^2} \times \frac{2}{m-7} + \frac{n-10}{\overline{n-7}\,r^3} \times \frac{3}{m-7}, \&c.}$ Now $\frac{n-8}{\overline{n-7}\,r} \times \frac{1}{m-7} + \frac{n-9}{\overline{n-7}\,r^2} \times \frac{2}{m-7}$, &c. is the value of an annuity for a life seven years older than the expectant, after another life seven years older than the life whose complement is m. $\frac{n-7}{n} \times \frac{m-7}{m}$ is the probability that both the assigned lives shall continue 7 years. And $\frac{1}{r^7}$ is the value of 1*l.* due at the end of 7 years. The rule, therefore, given for solving this question, is right.

This demonstration, as well as that in the last note, is, for the sake of more ease and clearness, applied to the hypothesis of an equal decrement of life. It does not, however, depend upon it, but may be applied to any table of observations.

Note (D). Question IX. Page 29.

LET the complement of any two assigned lives be n and m, and the given term be *seven* years, as in note (C). The probability that the former life (supposed to be the life in expectation) shall last 8 years, is, by Mr. *De Moivre's* Hypothesis, $\frac{n-8}{n}$; and the probability that the latter life shall fail in 8 years, is $\frac{8}{m}$; and the first payment of the annuity mentioned in this question, depends on the happening of *both* these events, the probability of which is $\frac{n-8}{n} \times \frac{8}{m}$.

The present value, therefore, of the first possible payment of the annuity is $\frac{n-8}{nr^8} \times \frac{8}{m}$.——In like manner; the present value of the *second* possible payment is $\frac{n-9}{nr^9} \times \frac{9}{m}$; and of all the payments, $\frac{n-8}{nr^8} \times \frac{8}{m} + \frac{n-9}{nr^9} \times \frac{9}{m} + \frac{n-10}{nr^{10}} \times \frac{10}{m}$, &c. But $\frac{n-8}{nr^8} \times \frac{8}{m} = \frac{n-8}{nr^8} \times \frac{1}{m} + \frac{n-8}{nr^8} \times \frac{7}{m}$; and $\frac{n-9}{nr^9} \times \frac{9}{m} = \frac{n-9}{nr^9} \times \frac{2}{m} + \frac{n-9}{nr^9} \times \frac{7}{m}$. The foregoing series, therefore, is equal to the two series's $\frac{1}{r^7} \times \overline{\frac{n-8}{nr} \times \frac{1}{m} + \frac{n-9}{nr^2} \times \frac{2}{m} + \frac{n-10}{nr^3} \times \frac{3}{m}}$, &c. and

$$\frac{1}{r^7}\times\overline{\frac{n-8}{nr}\times\frac{7}{m}+\frac{n-9}{nr^2}\times\frac{7}{m}+\frac{n-10}{nr^3}\times\frac{7}{m}}\text{, \&c. or}$$

$$\text{to }\frac{1}{r^7}\times\frac{n-7}{n}\times\frac{m-7}{m}\times\frac{n-8}{\overline{n-7}\,r}\times\overline{\frac{1}{m-7}+\frac{n-9}{\overline{n-7}\,r^2}\times\frac{2}{m-7}+\frac{n-10}{\overline{n-7}\,r^3}\times\frac{3}{m-7}}\text{, \&c.}+\frac{1}{r^7}\times\frac{7}{m}\times\frac{n-7}{n}\times\overline{\frac{n-8}{\overline{n-7}\,r}+\frac{n-9}{\overline{n-7}\,r^2}+\frac{n-10}{\overline{n-7}\,r^3}}\text{, \&c.}$$

which is the very rule given for solving this queſtion, as will appear from notes (B) and (C).

Note (E). See the Scholium to Quest. X.

ACCORDING to the calculations, the time in which the first yearly payment of a reversionary *annuity* becomes due, is the end of the year in which the event happens that entitles to it, however little or much of the year may then happen to be unelapsed. And this, likewise, is the time when a reversionary *sum* becomes due. Those who know how the calculations of the values of reversions are instituted, must know this. But an annuity, the first payment of which is to be made at the same time with another payment of a sum in hand, sufficient to buy an equal annuity, is worth one year's purchase more than the sum. For instance. Reckoning interest at 4 per cent. and *r* being 1*l.* increased by its interest for a year, or 1.04, $\frac{1}{r}+\frac{1}{r^2}+\frac{1}{r^3}$, &c. = 25*l.* is the present value of an estate of 1*l.* per annum for ever. That is, it is the value of it, supposing the first rent of it is to be paid a year hence.——If the first rent is to be received immediately, or at the same time with another payment of 25*l.* it is worth one year's purchase more, or equivalent to 26*l.*——I have not found, that any of the writers on annuities and reversions, have attended to this observation. It suggests a correction necessary to be applied to the common solutions of several important problems: particularly to the 21st and 22d in Mr. *Simpson's Treatise on Annuities*, and the 26th, 27th, 32d, 33d, and 40th problems in his *Select Exercises*; and to all other problems of the same kind in other writers. There can be no great occaſion for being more explicit. It will not, however, be amiſs to add the following demonſtration: —— $\frac{1}{n}$ is the preſent probability that a life, whoſe complement is n, will fail in any one aſſignable year of its duration. $S \times \overline{\frac{1}{nr} + \frac{1}{nr^2} + \frac{1}{nr^3}}$, &c. ($n$), or the preſent value of 1*l.* per annum for n years, multiplied by $\frac{S}{n}$, is the preſent value of the ſum or legacy denoted by S, payable at the failure of the given life. Therefore, (n being 56; the life 30; intereſt 4 per cent. $r = 1.04$; the ſum 25*l.*) the value of the expectation, by Mr. *De Moivre*'s hypotheſis, is 9.919.

Further. The value of 1*l.* to be received at the end of a year, provided the life whoſe complement is n fails, is the probability of the failure of the life multiplied by 1*l.* diſcounted for a year, or $\overline{1 - \frac{n-1}{n}} \times \frac{1}{r}$. In like manner; the value of 1*l.* to be received at the end of 2 years, if the ſame life fails in 2 years, is $\overline{1 - \frac{n-2}{n}} \times \frac{1}{r^2}$. And, therefore, the value of all the *poſſible* payments of an eſtate or annuity of 1*l.* for ever, to be entered upon after the given life, is $\overline{1 - \frac{n-1}{n}} \times \frac{1}{r} + \overline{1 - \frac{n-2}{n}} \times \frac{1}{r^2} + \overline{1 - \frac{n-3}{n}} \times \frac{1}{r^3}$, &c. ($n$) $+ \frac{1}{r^{n+1}} +$

$\frac{1}{r^{n+2}}$, &c. or $\frac{1}{r}+\frac{1}{r^2}+\frac{1}{r^3}$, &c. $-\overline{\frac{n-1}{nr}+\frac{n-2}{nr^2}+}$ $\overline{\frac{n-3}{nr^3}}$, &c. that is, the value of the life ſubtracted from the perpetuity; or, in this example, 14*l*. 684, (the value of a life at 30) ſubtracted from 25; that is, 10*l*. 316. But 10.316 is to 9.919, in the ſame ratio with 104 to 100, or 26 to 25, agreeably to the rule in the *Scholium*.

Note (F.) Queſtion XIII. Page 44.

WHEN I here call 48 the mean age of all married men, and 40 the mean age of married women, I do not intend to ſuppoſe, that there are as many married perſons who exceed theſe ages, as there are who fall ſhort of them. It is likely that the latter are moſt numerous; and it is neceſſary that this ſhould be the caſe, to render the ſuppoſition I make juſt——If all marriages commenced at 33 for the man, and 25 for the woman, one half of them would be diſſolved by the time the men were 50, and the women 42; for (by the *Hypotheſis*, and alſo nearly by the *Breſlaw*, *Norwich*, and *Northampton* tables) there is an equal chance for the joint continuance of two lives, whoſe ages are 25 and 33, *ſeventeen* years. Forty-two and fifty then would be properly the mean ages at which widowhood would commence; meaning by theſe, "the "ages on each ſide of which equal numbers are "left widows and widowers."——But, tho' in this caſe half the marriages of every year would be diſſolved in 17 years, they would not be *all* diſſolved in twice that time. So far would this be from happening, that about a 7th part would continue beyond twice 17 years; nor would it be *certain*, that they would be all diſſolved till near the extremity of the poſſible extent of life. Tho', therefore, an equal number of marriages would be diſſolved, or an equal number of widows and widowers left *before* 50 and 42, and *afterwards*, yet the ages of the latter would, one with another, much more exceed 50 and 42, than the ages of the former (that is, of the widows and widowers left *before* 50 and 42) would fall short of them. And the number of marriages also in the world, among persons of greater ages than these, would be much fewer than among persons of lesser ages——In other words: the period, at which the marriages that have been contracted are half dissolved, is not the period at which the number of marriages constantly existing is equally divided, but this period falls some years sooner; and the period I have in view, falls in that part of the interval between these two periods, where the greater ages of the marriages on one side, are just enough to compensate (in such a calculation as that I have given) their deficiencies in number, compared with the number of marriages on the other side.

In short. Suppose 35 marriages every year, between persons 33 and 25. In 12 years there would be half as many in the world, as could possibly arise from such a number of yearly weddings. In 17 years, half every set would be extinct. The *expectation* of every marriage would be 19 years, by prob. 21 of Mr. *De Moivre's Treatise on Annuities*, or by the note p. 299: that is, taking them all together, they would exist just as long as an equal number of *single* persons, supposed to be sure of living just 19 years, and no more; or, as long as an equal number of single persons, all 48 years of age, supposed to be subject to the common laws of mortality. One with another, then, they will be all extinct in 19 years: the marriages which continue beyond this term, tho' fewer in number, enjoying among them just as much *more* duration, as those that fall short of it enjoy *less*. *Widows*, then, at a medium, will commence widowhood at 44 (that is, 25 increased by 19) years of age, and *widowers* at 52. The values, therefore, of the lives of the *former*, when they commence widowhood, will, one with another, be the same with the value of a life at 44; or, (reckoning interest at 4 per cent.) 12.5 years purchase, in present payment, (the annuity to begin at the end of a year); and their *expectations* of life will be 21 years, or half the difference between 44 and 86. The value of the lives of the *latter* will be 10.92, and their *expectation* 17 years—The whole number of marriages constantly existing, which would result from 35 supposed to commence annually, would be 19×35, or 665; and 53 years (the difference between 33 and 86) would be the time in which they would increase to this number——The chance of survivorship would be 69 to 53, by prob. 18th, Mr. *De Moivre on Annuities*; that is, in 53 years, 35 relicts of these marriages would be left every year, and the number of *widows* would be to the number of *widowers*, as 69 to 53; or 19.8 *widows* would be left annually, and 15.2 *widowers*. The *maximum* of widows in life together, if none married, would be 21×19.8, or 416; and they would increase to this number in 114 years (or 61 years after the number of marriages had attained to a *maximum*)——The *maximum* of *widowers* would be 15.2×17, or 258; and they would increase to this number in 106 years.

An easy method may be hence deduced of solving the question which occasions this note——If the number of the members of the establishment I have supposed, is 665, and the mean ages at which marriage may be deemed to commence are 25 and 33, 19.8 widows will (it has just appeared) be left every year; and the values of their lives, when they commence widowhood, will be, one with another, 12½ years purchase. An annuity of 20*l.* will, therefore, be worth, to each widow, 250*l.* and 19.8 such annuities must be worth 4950*l.* which, consequently, is the annual income necessary for the support of the establishment, the first payment to be received immediately: or *l.* 7.44 from each of the 665 members; which answers nearly to the determination in page 44.

In the Last Essay, p. 296, it has been shewn, that observations determine the chance of survivorship in favour of the wife in marriage, to be really so great as 3 to 2; and in some circumstances greater. I have also there observed, that in order to account for this, from the difference of age between men and their wives, this difference must be at least 12 years, and the mean ages of all who marry annually, must be supposed to be about 23 and 35. In this case, 19, as before, will nearly be the *expectation* of all marriages. The mean age at which widows and widowers will commence such will be 42 and 54. The number of annual marriages necessary to keep up 665 marriages constantly existing, will be 35. The number of widows left annually, by such a number of marriages, will be 21; and the values of their lives, at the time they commence widowhood, will be 12.85 years purchase by Table VI: and therefore, the whole annual income necessary for the support of the supposed establishment, will be 5397*l.* or an annual payment, beginning immediately, of *l.* 8.11 from each member—The number of widows on such an establishment will, in 63 years, grow, if none marry, to 462; and the number of widowers to 224.——It may be depended on, that all this would happen as far as Dr. *Halley*'s table, or the tables for *Norwich* and *Northampton*, exhibit the true state of human mortality.

Among the miniſters and profeſſors in SCOTLAND, the number of married men being 667, or nearly that here mentioned, the number of annual weddings has, for many years, been at an average 32, and the number of widows left annually 20; and, therefore, the chance of ſurvivorſhip in favour of the wife, as 20 to 12, or 5 to 3. See Eſſay IV. p. 269. This is not more different, from the reſults I have given, than might have been expected; and the chief reaſon of the difference is, that the *expectations* of *ſingle* and *joint* lives among the miniſters and their wives in SCOTLAND, are greater than thoſe given by Dr. *Halley*'s, and the other tables of obſervation——Theſe tables give the expectations of lives as they are among the bulk of mankind in moderate towns. The expectations of lives among the better ſort of men, living moſtly in country villages and pariſhes, are much greater. The fact is, that among the miniſters in *Scotland*, the expectation of a *ſingle* life at the age of 27, is three years and an half greater; and, conſequently, of *joint* lives, above two years greater, than the ſame expectations by Dr. *Halley*'s Table. Ibid, page 264.

I cannot help juſt mentioning another remark here.——It may be obſerved, that ſuppoſing no ſecond marriages, and, at the ſame time, that the odds for the woman's ſurviving in marriage is 3 to 2, the number of *widows* in the world would be *double* the number of *widowers*. But it has been found, in fact, that the number of widows is five times the number of widowers. How this is to be accounted for, I have ſhewn in the Eſſay juſt referred to, page 270, 271.

Note (G). Question XIV. Page 48.

LET r be 1*l.* increased by its interest for one year; t the given time or number of years for which the assurance is to be made; a, b, c, &c. the *probabilities* taken out of a table of observations, that the person whose age is given shall live 1, 2, 3, &c. years; and P the probability that he shall live t years. Then

$$\frac{1-a}{r} + \frac{1-b}{r^2} + \frac{1-c}{r^3}, \&c.\ (t-1) + \frac{1-P}{r^t} + \frac{1-P}{r^{t+1}} + \frac{1-P}{r^{t+2}} \&c. = \frac{1}{r} + \frac{1}{r^2} + \frac{1}{r^3}, \&c.\ (t) - \overline{\frac{a}{r} + \frac{b}{r^2} + \frac{c}{r^3}, \&c.\ (t-1) + \frac{P}{r^t}} + \frac{1-P}{r^t} \times \overline{\frac{1}{r} + \frac{1}{r^2} + \frac{1}{r^3}, \&c.}$$

will be the exact value of an annuity to be entered upon at the failure of the given life, provided it happens in t years. And the rule is nothing but this value expressed in words. In a similar manner may be demonstrated the other rule for finding the values of assurances, for a given time, on two joint lives, or the longest of two lives.

Note (H). Queſtion XV. page 56.

LET r ſignify as before; S the given ſum to be aſſured; t the given time; N and n the number of the living in the table of obſervations, at the age of A and B reſpectively; A, B, C, &c. and a, b, c, &c. the number of the living in the table, at the end of 1, 2, 3, &c. years from the ages of A and B; D, $D_{\prime}$, $D_{\prime\prime}$, $D_{\prime\prime\prime}$, &c. and d, $d_{\prime}$, $d_{\prime\prime}$, $d_{\prime\prime\prime}$, &c. the decrements of life in the table, at the end of 1, 2, 3, &c. years from the ſame ages. Then, by reaſoning in the ſame manner with Mr. *Simpſon*, in p. 316, &c. *Select Exercifes*, it will appear that

$$S\times\overline{\frac{A\times d}{Nnr}+\frac{B\times d_{\prime}}{Nnr^2}+\frac{C\times d_{\prime\prime}}{Nnr^3},\ \&c.\ (t)}+S\times\overline{\frac{Dd}{2Nnr}+\frac{D_{\prime}d_{\prime}}{2Nnr^2}+\frac{D_{\prime\prime}d_{\prime\prime}}{2Nnr^3},\ \&c.\ (t)}=\frac{S}{n}\times\overline{\frac{Ad}{Nr}+\frac{Bd_{\prime}}{Nr^2}+\frac{Cd_{\prime\prime}}{Nr^3},\ \&c.\ (t)}+\frac{S}{2N}\times\overline{\frac{Dd}{nr}+\frac{D_{\prime}d_{\prime}}{nr^2},\ \&c.\ (t)}.$$

This is the exact anſwer to Queſtion XV. and the rule is as near an aproximation to it as there is reaſon to deſire.

In the ſame manner, retaining all the ſame ſymbols, it may be found, that the anſwer to Queſtion XVI. is

$$S\times\overline{\frac{Dd}{2Nnr}+\frac{D_{\prime}d}{Nnr^2}+\frac{\overline{D+D_{\prime}}\times d_{\prime\prime}}{Nnr^3}+\frac{\overline{D+D_{\prime}+D_{\prime\prime}}\times d_{\prime\prime\prime}}{Nnr^4}\ (t),\ \&c.}+S\times\overline{\frac{D_{\prime}d_{\prime}}{2Nnr^2}+\frac{D_{\prime\prime}d_{\prime\prime}}{2Nnr^3}+\frac{D_{\prime\prime\prime}d_{\prime\prime\prime}}{2Nnr^4},\ \&c.}$$

$$(t-1) = \frac{S}{nr} \times \overline{\frac{Dd_{\prime}}{Nr} + \frac{\overline{D+D_{\prime}}\times d_{\prime\prime}}{Nr^2} + \frac{\overline{D+D_{\prime}+D_{\prime\prime}}\times d_{\prime\prime\prime}}{Nr^3}},$$

$$\text{\&c. } (t-1) + \frac{S}{2N} \times \overline{\frac{Dd}{nr} + \frac{D_{\prime}d_{\prime}}{nr^2} + \frac{D_{\prime\prime}d_{\prime\prime}}{nr^3}}, \text{ \&c. } (t).$$

But $\frac{D}{Nr} + \frac{D+D_{\prime}}{Nr^2} + \frac{D+D_{\prime}+D_{\prime\prime}}{Nr^3}$, &c. $(t-1)$ is the ſame with the exceſs of the value of an annuity *certain* for a number of years leſs by one year than the given term, above the value of an annuity on the life of A, for the ſame number of years; from whence the reaſon of the rule for ſolving this queſtion, may be eaſily diſcovered.

Note (I). Page 119, &c.

LET *t* be any given term of years; *p* the value of 1*l.* due at the end of the given term; A the value of an annuity certain for the ſame term; *n* the *complement* of a given life; G the value for the given term, of two joint lives, both equal to the given life; (to be found by Queſt. VI.) P the perpetuity; *r*, 1*l.* increaſed by its intereſt for one year.

Then $\overline{A-G} \times \overline{n+t} \times p \times P - A \times P \times r$ will be the preſent value of 1*l.* 2*l.* 3*l.* &c. (*t*) payable at the end of 1, 2, 3, &c. (*t*) years; but ſubject to failure when the given life fails.

If ſuch a courſe of payment is to begin immediately, and to be made at the beginning of every year, till $t+1$ payments are made in *t* years; add to the preceding value, the value increaſed by unity of an annuity on the given life for *t* years, found by Queſtion VI. and the *ſum* will be the value ſought. And this value, divided by the preſent value of what may happen to remain of the given life after *t* years, found by Queſtion VI. will give the *ſtanding annuity* to which ſuch a ſeries of increaſing annual payments, beginning immediately, will entitle, for the remainder of the given life after *t* years.

With the aſſiſtance of this theorem, all that is ſaid in page 119, &c. may be inveſtigated. It would be too tedious to enter into a more minute account.

Note (K). Page 149.

LET d signify the *difference* between the *complements* of the youngest and the oldest life in the body of Annuitants, here described, at the time they enter; let S signify the sum of these *complements*; n any given number of years not greater than $\frac{S}{2} - \frac{d}{2}$; and x the ratio of the whole number of Annuitants to $\frac{S \times d}{2}$. Then

$x \times d$ will be the number that will die the 1st year;

$x \times \overline{d + \frac{2d}{S}}$ the number that will die the 2d year;

$x \times \overline{d + \frac{4d}{S} + \frac{4d}{S^2}}$, 3d year;

$x \times \overline{d + \frac{6d}{S} + \frac{8d}{S^2} + \frac{8d}{S^3}}$, 4th year;

$x \times \overline{d + \frac{8d}{S} + \frac{12d}{S^2} + \frac{16d}{S^3} + \frac{16d}{S^4}}$, 5th year;

and $x \times \overline{nd + \overline{n^2 - n} \times \frac{d}{S} + \overline{n - 2 + \overline{n-2}|^2} \times \frac{2d}{S^2} + \overline{n - 3 + \overline{n-3}|^2} \times \frac{4d}{S^3} + \overline{n - 4 + \overline{n-4}|^2} \times \frac{8d}{S^4}}$, &c. (n)

will be the whole number dying in n years. When n is greater than $\frac{S}{2} - \frac{d}{2}$, this series is greater than the whole number dying in n years; but in all other cases it gives this number exactly, supposing the probabilities of life to decrease uniformly.——

In the present inſtance, the youngeſt life being 30, and the oldeſt 60, the two complements are 56 and 26. $S = 82$. $d = 30$. $\frac{Sd}{2} = 1230$. And therefore $x = \frac{33,333}{1230} = 27.1$. Take $n = 30$ years, and the foregoing ſeries will be $27.1 \times \overline{900 + 318.2 + 7.242 + .164} = 33.214$, which is a little greater than the whole number dying in 30 years, but at the ſame time leſs than the whole number of Annuitants.

Note (L). See Essay I. Page 169, 170, 172.

THE *sum* of the probabilities that any given lives will attain to the end of the 1st, 2d, 3d, &c. *years* from the present time to the utmost extremity of life (for instance, $\frac{45}{46} + \frac{44}{46} + \frac{43}{46}$, &c. to $\frac{1}{46} = 22\frac{1}{2}$ for lives of 40, by the *hypothesis*) may be called their *expectation*, or the number of payments due to them, as *yearly annuitants*. The sum of the probabilities that they will attain to the end of the 1st, 2d, 3d, &c. *half years* (or, in the particular case specified, $\frac{91}{92} + \frac{90}{92} + \frac{89}{92} + \frac{88}{92}$, &c. $= \frac{91}{2}$ *half* years, or $22\frac{3}{4}$ *years*) is their expectation as *half yearly annuitants*. And the sums just mentioned of the probabilities of their attaining to the end of the 1st, 2d, 3d, &c. *moments* (equal in the same particular case to 23 years) is properly their *expectation of life*, or their *expectation* as annuitants secured by land.

Mr. *De Moivre* has omitted the demonstrations of the rules he has given for finding the *expectations* of lives, and only intimated, in general, that he discovered them by a calculation deduced from the method of fluxions. See his *Treatise on Annuities*, page 66. It will, perhaps, be agreeable to some to see how easily they are deduced in this method, upon the hypothesis of an equal decrement of life.

Let $\dot{x}$ stand for a moment of time, and n the *complement* of any assigned life. Then $\frac{n-\dot{x}}{n}$, $\frac{n-2\dot{x}}{n}$, $\frac{n-3\dot{x}}{n}$, &c. will be the *present* probabilities of its continuing to the end of the 1st, 2d, 3d, &c. moments; and $\frac{n-x}{n}$ the probability of its continuing to the end of x time. $\frac{n-x}{n} \times \dot{x}$ will therefore be the *fluxion* of the sum of the probabilities, or of an *area* representing this sum, whose *ordinates* are $\frac{n-x}{n}$, and *axis* x.—The *fluent* of this expression, or $x - \frac{x^2}{2n}$, is the sum itself for the time x; and this, when $x = n$, becomes $\frac{1}{2}n$, and gives the *expectation* of the assigned life, or the sum of all the probabilities just mentioned for its whole possible duration.——In like manner: since $\frac{\overline{n-x}^2}{n^2}$ is the probability that two equal joint lives will continue x time, $\frac{\overline{n-x}^2}{n^2} \times \dot{x}$ will be the *fluxion* of the sum of the probabilities. The *fluent* is $x - \frac{x^2}{n} + \frac{x^3}{3n}$, which, when $n = x$, is $\frac{n}{3}$, or the expectation of two equal joint lives.——Again: since $\frac{n-x}{n} \times \frac{2x}{n}$ is the probability that there will be a survivor of two equal joint lives at the end of x time, $\frac{n-x}{n} \times \frac{2x}{n} \times \dot{x}$ will be the *fluxion* of the sum of the probabilities; and the *fluent*, or $\frac{x^2}{n} - \frac{2x^3}{3n^2}$ is (when $x = n$) $\frac{1}{3}n$, or the *expectation* of survivorship between two equal lives; which, therefore, appears to be equal to the *expectation* of their joint continnance. The expectation of two *unequal* joint lives, found in the same way, is $\frac{m}{2} - \frac{m^2}{6n}$, m being the *complement* of the oldest life, and n the *complement* of the youngest. The whole expectation of survivorship is $\frac{n}{2} - \frac{m}{2} + \frac{m^2}{3n}$. The expectation of survivorship, on the part of the oldest is $\frac{m^2}{6n}$; and the expectation, on the part of the youngest, is $\frac{n}{2} - \frac{m}{2} + \frac{m^2}{6n}$. It is easy to apply this investigation to any number of joint lives, and to all cases of survivorship.

It may be observed, concerning the first of the fluents here given, that it expresses not only the expectation of a given life for the time x, and therefore its whole expectation when $x = n$, but likewise, the number of persons alive, to which one person added annually to a society, at a given age, will increase in x time.——Thus: Suppose one annuitant, whose age is 28, (and whose *complement* of life, therefore, is 58, or *expectation* of life 29) to come upon a society every year; the number of annuitants alive, deduced from hence, will, in x years, be $x - \frac{x^2}{4 \times 29}$, or $\frac{4 \times 29 - x^2}{4 + 29} \times x$; and, therefore, the number of annuitants alive, deduced in the same time from p annuitants left annually at the same age, will be $\frac{4 \times 29 - x^2}{4 \times 29} \times px$.——In like manner, the 2d fluent, or $\frac{x^3}{3n^2} - \frac{x^2}{n} + x$, gives the number of marriages in being together, that will, in *x* years, grow out of *one* yearly marriage, between perſons of *equal* ages, whoſe complement of life is *n*. If they are of *unequal* ages, and the complement of the oldeſt life is *m*, and of the youngeſt *n*, this number will be $\frac{x^3}{3nm} - \frac{\overline{n+m} \times x^2}{2nm} + x$. And if the number of years is required, in which any given number of yearly marriages, between men and women at given ages, will increaſe ſo far as to be in any given proportion to the greateſt number that can poſſibly grow out of ſuch marriages, this expreſſion muſt be made equal to the *expectation* of the joint lives, or of each marriage, multiplied by the fraction expreſſing the given proportion; and the root of the equation will be the anſwer. Thus: it may be found, that one marriage every year, between perſons 33 and 25 years of age, would in 10 years increaſe to 8.35; in 15 years, to 11.38; and in 53 years, to 19, or their greateſt poſſible number: and, conſequently, that 35 ſuch yearly marriages would, in 10 years, increaſe to 292; in 15 years, to 398; and in 53 years, to 665.——And if it is enquired in what number of years 35 ſuch yearly marriages would increaſe to half the number in being together, poſſible to be derived from them, the value of *x*, in the cubic equation $\frac{x^3}{3nm} - \frac{\overline{n+m} \times x^2}{2nm} + x = \frac{m}{2} - \frac{m}{6n} \times \frac{1}{2}$, muſt be found; which, in the preſent inſtance, is nearly 12.

I have, in ſome parts of this work, had occaſion to make ſuch deductions as theſe. See note (A), p. 277; and note (F), p. 288; and Queſtions III, and XIII.

Note (M). Essay II. Page 226.

LET r signify 1*l*, increased by its interest for one year.

V the PERPETUITY.

n the difference between the age of the youngest life, and 86; or its *complement*.

m the complement of the oldest life.

P the value (in Table II.) of an annuity certain for m years.

And the exact value of any two given joint lives, according to the hypothesis of an equal decrement of life, will be $V - \frac{V+1}{n} \times \overline{\overline{n - m - 2v - 1} \times \frac{P}{m} + 2v}$. Example:

Let the ages be 27 and 38; and the rate of interest 4 *per cent.* Then $n = 59$. $m = 48$. $V = 25$. $P = 21.195$. $n - m - 2v - 1 = -40$. $\overline{\overline{n - m - 2v - 1} \times \frac{P}{m} + 2v} = 50 - 17.660 = 32.340$. And

$V - \frac{V+1}{n} \times \overline{\overline{n - m - 2v - 1} \times \frac{P}{m} + 2v} = 25 - \frac{26}{59} \times 32.340 = 10.748$, the value of two joint lives whose ages are 27 and 38.

Note (N). Essay III. Page 232.

IT is plain, that the purchaser of A's right, as stated in the first of the questions, to which this note refers, cannot get into possession, till the year when A and B shall be both dead; nor then, unless A happens to die *last*. Now, supposing the common complement of life n; the probability that A and B shall be *both* dead at the end of the *first* year, and A die last, is $\overline{1-\frac{n-1}{n}} \times \overline{1-\frac{n-1}{n}} \times \frac{1}{2} = \frac{1}{2} - \frac{n-1}{2n} - \frac{n-1}{2n} + \frac{\overline{n-1}|^2}{2n^2}$.——In like manner, the probability that they shall be *both* dead at the end of the 2d, 3d, &c. years, and A survive, is $\frac{1}{2} - \frac{n-2}{2n} - \frac{n-2}{2n} + \frac{\overline{n-2}|^2}{2n^2}$; $\frac{1}{2} - \frac{n-3}{2n} - \frac{n-3}{2n} + \frac{\overline{n-3}|^2}{2n^2}$, &c. The *present* value, therefore, of the 1st, 2d, 3d, &c. rents of the reversionary estate is $\frac{1}{2r} - \frac{n-1}{2nr} - \frac{n-1}{2nr} + \frac{\overline{n-1}|^2}{2nr}$, $\frac{1}{2r^2} - \frac{n-2}{2nr^2} - \frac{n-2}{2nr^2} + \frac{\overline{n-2}|^2}{2n^2r^2}$, $\frac{1}{2r^3} - \frac{n-3}{2nr^3} - \frac{n-3}{2nr^3} + \frac{\overline{n-3}|^2}{2n^2r^3}$, &c. Supposing r to signify 1*l.* increased by its interest for a year; and the estate to be 1*l. per annum*. And the *sum* of these terms continued *in infinitum*, is the value *required*.——But $\frac{1}{2r} + \frac{1}{2r^2} + \frac{1}{2r^3}$, &c. is *half*

the perpetuity. And $\frac{n-1}{2nr} + \frac{n-1}{2nr} - \frac{\overline{n-1}|^2}{2n^2r} +$
$\frac{n-2}{2nr^2} + \frac{n-2}{2nr^2} - \frac{\overline{n-2}|^2}{2n^2r^2} + \frac{n-3}{2nr^3} + \frac{n-3}{2nr^3} - \frac{\overline{n-3}|^2}{2n^2r^3}$, &c. is *half* the value of the *joint* lives, ſubtracted from *half* the ſum of the values of the two *ſingle* lives; that is, *half* the value of the *longeſt* of the two lives.

A ſimilar demonſtration may be applied to the other queſtion.

Note (O). Essay IV. Page 262.

LET r be 1*l.* increased by its interest for one year.

Let S represent any given interval of time, or number of years, during which the decrements of life in a table of observations continue equal.

a the number of the living in the table at the beginning of the first year of that interval.

b the number of the living in the table at the beginning of the year immediately following the same interval.

P the value of an annuity certain for S years.

p the value, in Table I. of 1*l.* due at the end of S years.

Q the value, in Table VI. of an annuity for the life of a person whose age wants S years of 86.

N the value, in strict agreement with the given table of observations, of an annuity on the life of a person whose age is S years greater than the age at which the interval of equal decrements begins. Then

$Q + \frac{b}{a} \times \overline{P - Q}$ will be the value, according to the table of observations, of an annuity for S years, on a life of the same age with that at which the interval of equal decrements begins. And

$Q + \frac{b}{a} \times \overline{\overline{P - Q} + pN}$ will be the value of an annuity on the whole duration of that life.

When S represents *one* year, Q vanishes, and the last expression becomes $\frac{b}{ar} \times \overline{1 + N}$; which is the rule for finding, from the value given of any life, the value of a life one year younger.

These Theorems save much labour in calculating the values of life-annuities from tables of observations.

The first of them, with its investigation, may be found in page 341, 3d edition, of Mr. *De Moivre's Treatise on the Doctrine of Chances.* But it is necessary to observe, that the direction Mr. *De Moivre* has given for finding the value of Q is wrong. In consequence of calculating agreeably to this direction, he gives the value of a life at the age of 42, by Dr. *Halley's* table, greater than the value of the same life by his own hypothesis; whereas, it is evident, that the probabilities of living after 42, being all along less in Dr. *Halley's* table, than in the hypothesis, the *value* of the life must be also less.

The mathematical reader may easily satisfy himself, that the value of Q ought to be taken from Table VI. as I have directed.

An easy and accurate method of finding the values of singles lives, agreeably to any given table of observations, is given by Mr. *Dodson* in his *Mathematical Repository*, vol. II. page 161.

There is also in Mr. *Simpson's Select Exercises*, page 275, a very easy rule for approximating to the values of single lives, according to Dr. *Halley's* table. But this rule must not be depended on; for I have found it $\frac{1}{2}$ a year's purchase, and sometimes three-quarters of a year's purchase wrong.

To prevent the danger of mistaking the Theorem I have given, I have thought proper to subjoin the following example.

Let the table of observations be the *Breslaw* Table, or Table III. The value of a life at 78, by this

Table, is $\frac{49}{58r}+\frac{41}{58r^2}+\frac{34}{58r^3}$, &c. to the end of life. The number of terms in this series being small, it may be easily found to be 3.514, supposing interest at 4 *per cent.* and $\frac{1}{r}$, $\frac{1}{r^2}$, $\frac{1}{r^3}$, &c. being the values, in Table I. of 1*l.* at the end of 1, 2, 3, &c. years.——From 78 to 74 the decrements of life continue equal; and therefore S=4. $a=98$. $b=58$. P=3.6298, by Table II; $p=$ .8548, by Table I; Q=1.406, by Table VI; N=3.514. $P-Q+pN=5.227$; and $Q+\frac{b}{a}\times\overline{P-Q+pN}=4.500$, or the value of a life at 74.

From 74 to 70 there is another interval of equal decrements; and, by a like easy operation, the value of a life at 70 will be found to be 5.595.

TABLE I.

The present Value of 1*l.* to be received at the end of any number of years, not exceeding 100; discounting at the rates of 3, 3½, 4, 4½, 5 and 6 *per cent.* compound interest.

	3 per Ct.	3½ per Ct.	4 per Ct.	4½ per Ct.	5 per Ct.	6 per Ct.
1	,970874	,966184	,961538	,956938	.952381	,943396
2	,942596	,933511	,924556	,915730	,907029	,889996
3	,915142	,901943	,888996	,876297	,863838	,839619
4	,888487	,871442	,854804	,838561	.822702	,792094
5	,862609	,841973	,821927	,802451	.783526	,747258
6	,837484	,813501	,790315	,767896	,746215	,704961
7	,813092	,785991	,759918	,734828	.710681	,665057
8	,789409	,759412	,730690	,703185	,676839	,627412
9	,766417	,733731	,702587	,672904	,644609	,591898
10	,744094	,708919	,675564	,643928	,613913	,558395
11	,722421	,684946	,649581	,616199	,584679	,526788
12	,701380	,661783	,624597	,589664	,556837	,496969
13	,680951	,639404	,600574	,564272	,530321	,468839
14	,661118	,617782	,577475	,539973	,505068	,442301
15	,641862	,596891	,555265	,516720	,481017	,417265
16	,623167	,576706	,533908	,494469	,458112	.393646
17	,605016	,557204	,513373	,473176	,436297	,371364
18	,587395	,538361	,493628	,452800	,415521	,350344
19	,570286	,520156	,474642	,433302	,395734	,330513
20	,553676	,502566	,456387	,414643	.376889	,311805
21	,537549	,485571	,438834	,396787	,358942	,294155
22	,521893	,469151	,421955	,379701	341850	,277505
23	,506692	,453286	,405726	,363350	.325571	.261797
24	,491934	,437957	,390121	.347703	,310068	,246979
25	,477606	,423147	,375117	,332731	,295303	,232999
26	,463695	.408838	,360689	,318402	,281241	,219810
27	,45[illegible]189	,395012	,346817	,304691	,267848	,207368
28	,437077	,381654	,333477	,291571	,255094	,195630
29	,424346	,368748	,320651	,279015	,242946	,184557
30	,411987	,356278	,308319	,267000	,231377	,174110
31	,39[illegible]987	,344230	,296460	,255502	,220359	,164255
32	,388337	,332590	,285058	,244500	,209866	,154957

TABLE I. Continued.

	3 per Ct.	3½ per Ct.	4 per Ct.	4½ per Ct.	5 per Ct.	6 per Ct.
33	377026	,321343	,274094	,233971	,199873	,146186
34	,366045	,310476	,263552	,223896	,190355	,137912
35	,355383	,299977	,253415	,214254	,181290	,130105
36	,345032	,289833	,243669	,205028	,172657	,122741
37	,334983	,280032	,234297	,196199	,164436	,115793
38	,325226	,270562	,225285	,187750	,156605	,109239
39	,315754	,261413	,216621	,179665	,149148	,103056
40	,306557	,252572	,208289	,171929	,142046	,097222
41	,297628	,244031	,200278	,164525	,135282	,091719
42	,288959	,235779	,192575	,157440	,128840	,086527
43	,280543	,227806	,185168	,150663	,122704	,081630
44	,272372	,220102	,178046	,144173	,116864	,077009
45	,264439	,212659	,171198	,137964	,111297	,072650
46	,256737	,205468	,164614	,132023	,105997	,068538
47	,249259	,198520	,158283	,126338	,100949	,064658
48	,241999	,191806	,152195	,120898	,096142	,060998
49	,234950	,185320	,146341	,115692	,091564	,057546
50	,228107	,179053	,140713	,110710	,087204	,054288
51	,221463	,172998	,135301	,105942	,083051	,051215
52	,215013	,167148	,130097	,101380	,079096	,048316
53	,208750	,161496	,125093	,097014	,075330	,045582
54	,202670	,156035	,120282	,092837	,071743	,043001
55	,196767	,150758	,115656	,088839	,068326	,040567
56	,191036	,145660	,111207	,085013	,065073	,038271
57	,185472	,140734	,106930	,081353	,061974	,036105
58	,180070	,135975	,102817	,077849	,059023	,034061
59	,174825	,131377	,098963	,074497	,056212	,032133
60	,169733	,126934	,095060	,071289	,053536	,030310
61	,164789	,122642	,091404	,068219	,050986	,028598
62	,159990	,118495	,087889	,065281	,048558	,026989
63	,155330	,114487	,084508	,062470	,046246	,025453
64	,150806	,110616	,081258	,059780	,044044	,024012
65	,146413	,106875	,078133	,057206	,041946	,022653
66	,142149	,103261	,075128	,054742	,039949	,021370
67	,138009	,099769	,072238	,052385	,038047	,020161
68	,133989	,096395	,069460	,050129	,036235	,019020
69	,130086	,093136	,066788	,047971	,034509	,017943
70	,126297	,019986	,064219	,045905	,032866	016927

TABLE I. Continued.

	3 per Ct.	3½ per Ct.	4 per Ct.	4½ per Ct.	5 par Ct.	6 per Ct.
71	,122619	,086943	,061749	,043928	,031301	,015969
72	,119047	,084003	,059374	,042037	,029811	,015065
73	,115580	,081162	,057091	,040226	,028391	,014212
74	,112214	,078418	,054895	,038491	,027039	,013408
75	,108945	,075766	,052784	,036836	,025752	,012649
76	,105772	,073204	,050754	,035250	,024525	,011933
77	,102691	,070728	,048801	,033732	,023357	,011258
78	,099700	,068336	,046924	,032280	,022245	,010620
79	,096796	,066026	,045120	,030890	,021186	,010019
80	,093977	,063793	,043384	,029559	,020177	,009452
81	,091240	,061636	.041716	,028287	,019216	,008917
82	,088582	,059551	,040111	,027068	,018301	,008412
83	,086002	,057538	,038569	,025903	,017430	,007936
84	,083497	,055592	,037085	,024787	,016600	,007487
85	,081065	,053712	,035659	,023720	,015809	,007063
86	,078704	,051896	,034287	,022699	,015056	,006663
87	,076412	,050141	,032968	,021721	,014339	,006286
88	,074186	,048445	,031700	,020786	,013657	,005930
89	,072027	,046807	,030481	,019891	,013006	,005595
90	,069928	,045224	,029309	,019034	,012387	,005278
91	,067891	,043695	,028182	,018215	,011797	,004979
92	,065914	,042217	,027098	,017430	,011235	,004697
93	,063994	,040789	,026055	,016680	,010700	,004432
94	,062130	,039410	,025053	,015961	,010191	,004181
95	,060320	,038077	,024090	,015274	,009705	,003944
96	,058563	,036790	,023163	,014616	,009243	,003721
97	,056858	,035546	,022272	,013987	,008803	.003510
98	,055202	,034344	,021416	,013385	,008384	,003312
99	,053594	,033182	,020592	,012808	,007985	,003124
100	,052033	,032060	,019800	,012257	,007601	,002957

TABLE II.

The present Value of an Annuity of One Pound, for any Number of Years not exceeding 100, at the several Rates of 3, 3½, 4, 5, and 6*l.* *per Cent.*

Ye.	3 per Ct.	3½ per Ct.	4 per Ct.	5 per Ct.	6 per Ct.
1	.9708	.9662	.9615	.9523	.9433
2	1.9133	1.8997	1.8860	1.8594	1.8333
3	2.8286	2.8016	2.7750	2.7232	2.6730
4	3.7170	3.6731	3.6298	3.5459	3.4651
5	4.5797	4.5151	4.4518	4.3294	4.2123
6	5.4971	5.3286	5.2421	5.0756	4.9173
7	6.2302	6.1145	6.0020	5.7863	5.5823
8	7.0196	6.8740	6.7327	6.4632	6.2097
9	7.7861	7.6077	7.4353	7.1078	6.8016
10	8.5302	8.3166	8.1108	7.7212	7.3600
11	9.2526	9.0015	8.7604	8.3064	7.8868
12	9.9540	9.6633	9.3850	8.8632	8.3838
13	10.6349	10.3027	9.9856	9.3935	8.8526
14	11.2960	10.9205	10.5631	9.8986	9.2949
15	11.9379	11.5174	11.1183	10.3796	9.7122
16	12.5611	12.0941	11.6522	10.8377	10.1058
17	13.1661	12.6513	12.1656	11.2740	10.4772
18	13.7535	13.1897	12.6592	11.6895	10.8276
19	14.3238	13.7098	13.1339	12.0853	11.1581
20	14.8774	14.2124	13.5903	12.4622	11.4699
21	15.4150	14.6980	14.0291	12.8211	11.7640
22	15.9389	15.1671	14.4511	13.1630	12.0415
23	16.4436	15.6204	14.8568	13.4885	12.3033
24	16.9355	16.0584	15.2469	13.7986	12.5503
25	17.4131	16.4815	15.6220	14.0939	12.7833

TABLE II. Continued.

Ye	3 per Ct.	3½ per Ct.	4 per Ct.	5 per Ct.	6 per Ct
26	17.8768	16.8904	15.9827	14.3751	13.0031
27	18.3270	17.2854	16.3295	14.6430	13.2105
28	18.7641	17.6670	16.6630	14.8981	13.4061
29	19.1884	18.0358	16.9837	15.1410	13.5907
30	19.6004	18.3920	17.2920	15.3724	13.7648
31	20.0004	18.7363	17.5884	15.5928	13.9290
32	20.3887	19.0689	17.8735	15.8026	14.0840
33	20.7657	19.3902	18.1476	16.0025	14.2302
34	21.1318	19.7007	18.4111	16.1929	14.3681
35	21.4872	20.0007	18.6646	16.3741	14.4982
36	21.8322	20.2905	18.9082	16.5468	14.6209
37	22.1672	20.5705	19.1425	16.7112	14.7367
38	22.4924	20.8411	19.3678	16.8678	14.8460
39	22.8082	21.1025	19.5844	17.0170	14.9490
40	23.1147	21.3551	19.7927	17.1590	15.0462
41	23.4124	21.5991	19.9930	17.2943	15.1380
42	23.7013	21.8349	20.1856	17.4232	15.2245
43	23.9819	22.0627	20.3707	17.5459	15.3061
44	24.2542	22.2828	20.5488	17.6627	15.3831
45	24.5187	22.4955	20.7200	17.7740	15.4558
46	24.7754	22.7009	20.8846	17.8800	15.5243
47	25.0247	22.8994	21.0429	17.9810	15.5890
48	25.2667	23.0912	21.1951	18.0771	15.6500
49	25.5016	23.2766	21.3414	18.1687	15.7075
50	25.7297	23.4556	21.4821	18.2559	15.7618
51	25.9512	23.6286	21.6174	18.3389	15.8130
52	26.1662	23.7958	21.7475	18.4180	15.8613
53	26.3749	23.9573	21.8726	18.4934	15.9069
54	26.5776	24.1133	21.9929	18.5651	15.9499
55	26.7744	24.2641	22.1086	18.6334	15.9905

TABLE II. Continued.

Ye.	3 per Ct.	3½ per Ct.	4 per Ct.	5 per Ct.	6 per Ct.
56	26.9654	24.4097	22.2198	18.6985	16.0288
57	27.1509	24.5504	22.3267	18.7605	16.0649
58	27.3310	24.6864	22.4295	18.8195	16.0989
59	27.5058	24.8178	22.5284	18.8757	16.1311
60	27.6755	24.9447	22.6234	18.9292	16.1614
61	27.8403	25.0674	22.7148	18.9802	16.1900
62	28.0003	25.1859	22.8027	19.0288	16.2170
63	28.1556	25.3004	22.8872	19.0750	16.2424
64	28.3064	25.4110	22.9685	19.1191	16.2664
65	28.4528	25.5178	23.0466	19.1610	16.2891
66	28.5950	25.6211	23.1218	19.2010	16.3104
67	28.7330	25.7209	23.1940	19.2390	16.3306
68	28.8670	25.8173	23.2635	19.2753	16.3496
69	28.9971	25.9104	23.3302	19.3098	16.3676
70	29.1234	26.0004	23.3945	19.3426	16.3845
71	29.2460	26.0873	23.4562	19.3739	16.4005
72	29.3650	26.1713	23.5156	19.4037	16.4155
73	29.4806	26.2525	23.5727	19.4321	16.4297
74	29.5928	26.3309	23.6276	19.4592	16.4431
75	29.7018	26.4067	23.6804	19.4849	16.4558
76	29.8076	26.4799	23.7311	19.5094	16.4677
77	29.9102	26.5506	23.7799	19.5328	16.4790
78	30.0099	26.6190	23.8268	19.5550	16.4896
79	30.1067	26.6850	23.8720	19.5762	16.4996
80	30.2007	26.7488	23.9153	19.5964	16.5091
81	30.2920	26.8104	23.9571	19.6156	16.5180
82	30.3805	26.8700	23.9972	19.6339	16.5264
83	30.4665	26.9275	24.0357	19.6514	16.5343
84	30.5500	26.9831	24.0728	19.6680	16.5418
85	30.6311	27.0368	24.1085	19.6838	16.5489

TABLE II. Continued.

Ye.	3 per Ct.	3½ per Ct.	4 per C.	5 per Ct.	6 per Ct.
86	30.7098	27.0887	24.1428	19.6988	16.5556
87	30.7862	27.1388	24.1757	19.7132	16.5618
88	30.8604	27.1873	24.2074	19.7268	16.5678
89	30.9324	27.2341	24.2379	19.7398	16.5734
80	31.0024	27.2793	24.2672	19.7522	16.5786
91	31.0703	27.3230	24.2954	19.7640	16.5836
92	31.1362	27.3652	24.3225	19.7752	16.5883
93	31.2002	27.4060	24.3486	19.7859	16.5928
94	31.2623	27.4454	24.3736	19.7961	16.5969
95	31.3226	27.4835	24.3977	19.8058	16.6009
96	31.3812	27.5203	24.4209	19.8151	16.6046
97	31.4380	27.5558	24.4431	19.8239	16.6081
98	31.4932	27.5902	24.4646	19.8323	16.6114
99	31.5468	27.6234	24.4852	19.8403	16.6145
100	31.5989	27.6554	24.5050	19.8479	16.6175

TABLE III.

Shewing the Probabilities of the Duration of Life, as deduced by Dr. *Halley* from Observations on the Bills of Mortality of BRESLAW.

Ages	Persons living.	Decr. of Life.	Ages.	Persons living.	Decr. of Life.	Ages	Persons living.	Decr. of Life
1	1000	145	31	523	8	61	232	10
2	855	57	32	515	8	62	222	10
3	798	38	33	507	8	63	212	10
4	760	28	34	499	9	64	202	10
5	732	22	35	490	9	65	192	10
6	710	18	36	481	9	66	182	10
7	692	12	37	472	9	67	172	10
8	680	10	38	463	9	68	162	10
9	670	9	39	454	9	69	152	10
10	661	8	40	445	9	70	142	11
11	653	7	41	436	9	71	131	11
12	646	6	42	427	10	72	120	11
13	640	6	43	417	10	73	109	11
14	634	6	44	407	10	74	98	10
15	628	6	45	397	10	75	88	10
16	622	6	46	387	10	76	78	10
17	616	6	47	377	10	77	68	10
18	610	6	48	367	10	78	58	9
19	604	6	49	357	11	79	49	8
20	598	6	50	346	11	80	41	7
21	592	6	51	335	11	81	34	6
22	586	7	52	324	11	82	28	5
23	579	6	53	313	11	83	23	4
24	573	6	54	302	10	84	19	4
25	567	7	55	292	10	85	15	4
26	560	7	56	282	10	86	11	3
27	553	7	57	272	10	87	8	3
28	546	7	58	262	10	88	5	2
29	539	8	59	252	10	89	3	2
30	531	8	60	242	10	90	1	1

TABLE IV.

Shewing the Probabilities of Life at NORTHAMPTON. See page 255, 256.

Ages.	Persons living.	Decr. of Life.	Ages.	Persons living.	Decr. of Life.	Ages.	Persons living.	Decr. of Life.
0	1149	300	31	428	7	62	187	8
1	849	127	32	421	7	63	179	8
2	722	50	33	414	7	64	171	8
3	672	26	34	407	7	65	163	8
4	646	21	35	400	7	66	155	8
5	625	16	36	393	7	67	147	8
6	609	13	37	386	7	68	139	8
7	596	10	38	379	7	69	131	8
8	586	9	39	372	7	70	123	8
9	577	7	40	365	8	71	115	8
10	570	6	41	357	8	72	107	8
11	564	6	42	349	8	73	99	8
12	558	5	43	341	8	74	91	8
13	553	5	44	333	8	75	83	8
14	548	5	45	325	8	76	75	8
15	543	5	46	317	8	77	67	7
16	538	5	47	309	8	78	60	7
17	533	5	48	301	8	79	53	7
18	528	6	49	293	9	80	46	7
19	522	7	50	284	9	81	39	7
20	515	8	51	275	8	82	32	6
21	507	8	52	267	8	83	26	5
22	499	8	53	259	8	84	21	4
23	491	8	54	251	8	85	17	4
24	483	8	55	243	8	86	13	3
25	475	8	56	235	8	87	10	2
26	467	8	57	227	8	88	8	2
27	459	8	58	219	8	89	6	2
28	451	8	59	211	8	90	4	2
29	443	8	60	203	8	91	2	1
30	435	7	61	195	8	92	1	1

TABLE V.

Shewing the Probabilities of Life at NORWICH.

See page 256, 257.

Ages	Persons living.	Decr. of Life.	Ages	Persons living.	Decr. of Life.	Ages	Persons living.	Decr. of Life.
0	1185	320	32	392	6	63	174	9
1	865	160	33	386	6	64	165	9
2	705	60	34	380	6	65	156	9
3	645	32	35	374	6	66	147	9
4	613	23	36	368	6	67	138	9
5	590	20	37	362	6	68	129	9
6	570	16	38	356	6	69	120	9
7	554	13	39	350	7	70	111	9
8	541	11	40	343	6	71	102	8
9	530	9	41	337	6	72	94	8
10	521	7	42	331	6	73	86	8
11	514	6	43	325	7	74	78	8
12	508	6	44	318	7	75	70	8
13	502	5	45	311	7	76	62	7
14	497	5	46	304	7	77	55	7
15	492	5	47	297	7	78	48	6
16	487	5	48	290	7	79	42	5
17	482	5	49	283	7	80	37	5
18	477	5	50	276	7	81	32	4
19	472	5	51	269	7	82	28	4
20	467	6	52	262	7	83	24	4
21	461	6	53	255	8	84	20	3
22	455	6	54	247	8	85	17	3
23	449	6	55	239	8	86	14	3
24	443	6	56	231	8	87	11	2
25	437	6	57	223	8	88	9	2
26	431	7	58	215	8	89	7	2
27	424	7	59	207	8	90	5	2
28	417	7	60	199	8	91	3	2
29	410	6	61	191	8	92	1	1
30	404	6	62	183	9	93	1	1
31	398	6						

TABLE VI. (*a*).

Shewing the present Values of an Annuity of 1*l.* on a single life, according to Mr. *De Moivre*'s hypothesis; and, therefore, nearly, according to the probabilities of life at BRESLAW, NORWICH, and NORTHAMPTON. See p. 2, and p. 262.

Age.	3 per Ct.	$3\frac{1}{2}$ per Ct.	4 per Ct.	$4\frac{1}{2}$ per Ct.	5 per Ct.	6 per Ct.
8	19,736	18,160	16,791	15.595	14,544	12,790
9	19,868	18,269	16,882	15,672	14,607	12,839
10	19,868	18,269	16.882	15,672	14.607	12,839
11	19,736	18,160	16,791	15,595	14,544	12,790
12	19,604	18,049	16,698	15,517	14,480	12,741
13	19,469	17,937	16,604	15,437	14,412	12,691
14	19,331	17,823	16,508	15,356	14,342	12,639
15	19,192	17,707	16,410	15,273	14,271	12,586
16	19,050	17,588	16,311	15,189	14,197	12,532
17	18,905	17,467	16,209	15,102	14,123	12,476
18	18,759	17,344	16,105	15,015	14,047	12,419
19	18,610	17,220	15,999	14,923	13,970	12,361
20	18,458	17,093	15,891	14,831	13,891	12,301
21	18,305	16,963	15,781	14,737	13,810	12,239
22	18,148	16,830	15,669	14,641	13,727	12,177
23	17,990	16,696	15,554	14,543	13,642	12,112
24	17,827	16,559	15,437	14,442	13,555	12,045
25	17,664	16,419	15,318	14,340	13,466	11,978
26	17,497	16,277	15,197	14,235	13,375	11,908
27	17,327	16,133	15,073	14,128	13,282	11,837
28	17,154	15.985	14,946	14,018	13,186	11,763
29	16,979	15,835	14,816	13,905	13,088	11,688
30	16,800	15,682	14,684	13,791	12,988	11,610
31	16,620	15,526	14,549	13,673	12,855	11,530
32	16,436	15,367	14,411	13,553	12,780	11,449
33	16,248	15,204	14,270	13,430	12,673	11,365

(*a*) This Table is the same with Mr. *De Moivre*'s Table of the values of single lives, published in his *Treatise on Life Annuities*, and carried as far as the age of 79 to three places of decimals by Mr. *Dodson* in his *Mathematical Repository*, vol. ii. p. 169.

TABLE VI. Continued.

Age.	3 per Ct.	3½ per Ct.	4 per Ct.	4½ per Ct.	5 per Ct.	6 per Ct.
34	16,057	15,039	14,126	13,304	12,562	11,278
35	15,864	14,871	13,979	13,175	12,449	11,189
36	15,666	14,699	13,829	13,044	12,333	11,098
37	15,465	14,524	13,676	12,909	12,214	11,003
38	15,260	14,345	13,519	12,771	12,091	10,907
39	15,053	14,163	13,359	12,630	11,966	10,807
40	14,842	13,978	13,196	12,485	11,837	10,704
41	14,626	13,789	13,028	12,337	11,705	10,599
42	14,407	13,596	12,858	12,185	11,570	10,490
43	14,185	13,399	12,683	12,029	11,431	10,378
44	13,958	13,199	12,504	11,870	11,288	10,263
45	13,728	12,993	12,322	11,707	11,142	10,144
46	13,493	12,784	12,135	11,540	10,992	10,021
47	13,254	12,571	11,944	11,368	10,837	9,895
48	13,012	12,354	11,748	11,192	10,679	9,765
49	12,764	12,131	11,548	11,012	10,515	9,630
50	12,511	11,904	11,344	10,827	10,348	9,492
51	12,255	11,673	11,135	10,638	10,176	9.349
52	11,994	11,437	10,921	10,443	9,999	9,201
53	11,729	11,195	10,702	10,243	9,817	9,049
54	11,457	10,950	10.478	10,039	9,630	8,891
55	11,183	10,698	10,248	9,829	9,437	8,729
56	10,902	10,443	10,014	9,614	9,239	8,561
57	10,616	10,181	9,773	9,393	9,036	8,387
58	10.325	9,913	9,527	9,166	8,826	8,208
59	10,029	9,640	9,275	8,933	8,611	8,023
60	9,727	9,361	9,017	8,694	8,389	7,831
61	9,419	9.076	8,753	8,449	8,161	7,633
62	9.107	8,786	8,482	8,197	7,926	7,428
63	8,787	8,488	8,205	7,938	7,684	7,216
64	8,462	8,185	7,921	7,672	7,435	6,997
65	8,132	7,875	7,631	7,399	7,179	6,770
66	7.794	7,558	7,333	7,119	6,915	6,535
67	7,450	7,234	7,027	6,831	6,643	6,292
68	7,099	6,902	6,714	6,534	6,362	6,040
69	6,743	6,565	6,394	6,230	6,073	5,779
70	6.378	6.219	6,065	5,918	5,775	5,508

TABLE VI. Continued.

Age.	3 per Ct.	$3\frac{1}{2}$ per Ct.	4 per Ct	$4\frac{1}{2}$ per Ct	5 per Ct.	6 per Ct.
71	6,008	5,865	5,728	5,596	5,468	5,228
72	5,631	5,505	5,383	5,265	5,152	4,937
73	5,246	5,136	5,029	4 926	4.826	4,636
74	4,854	4,759	4,666	4,576	4.489	4,324
75	4,453	4,373	4,293	4,217	4,143	4,000
76	4,046	3,978	3,912	3,847	3,734	3,664
77	3,632	3,575	3,520	3,467	3,415	3,315
78	3,207	3,163	3,111	3 076	3,034	2,953
79	2,776	2,741	2,707	2,673	2,641	2,578
80	2,334	2,309	2,284	2,259	2,235	2,188
81	1,836	1,857	1,850	1,832	1,816	1,783
82	1,429	1,411	1,406	1,394	1,384	1,362
83	0,961	0,955	0,950	0,943	0,937	0,925
84	0,484	0,483	0,481	0,479	0,476	0,472
85	0,000	0,000	0,000	0,000	0,000	0,000

TABLE VII.

Shewing the Value of an Annuity on the joint continuance of two lives, according to Mr. *De Moivre's Hypothesis*; and, therefore, nearly according to the probabilities of life at BRESLAW, NORWICH, and NORTHAMPTON. See Essay II. and p. 2, 3, 226, 262.

Age of the youngest.	Age of the eldest.	Value at 3 per Cent.	Value at 4 per Cent.	Value at 5 per Cent.
10	10	15.206	13.342	11.855
	15	14.878	13.093	11.661
	20	14.503	12.808	11.430
	25	14.074	12.480	11.182
	30	13.585	12.102	10.884
	35	13.025	11.665	10.537
	40	12.381	11.156	10.128
	45	11.644	10.564	9.646
	50	10.796	9.871	9.074
	55	9.822	9.059	8.391
	60	8.704	8.105	7.572
	65	7.417	6.980	6.585
	70	5.936	5.652	5.391
15	15	14.574	12.860	11.478
	20	14.225	12.593	11.266
	25	13.822	12.281	11.022
	30	13.359	11.921	10.736
	35	12.824	11.501	10.402
	40	12.207	11.013	10.008
	45	11.496	10.440	9.541
	50	10.675	9.767	8.985
	55	9.727	8.975	8.318
	60	8.632	8.041	7.515
	65	7.377	6.934	6.544
	70	5.932	5.623	5.364

TABLE VII. Continued.

Age of the youngest.	Age of the eldest.	Value at 3 per Cent.	Value at 4 per Cent.	Value at 5 per Cent.
20	20	13.904	12.341	11.067
	25	13.531	12.051	10.840
	30	13.098	11.711	10.565
	35	12.594	11.314	10.278
	40	12.008	10.847	9.870
	45	11.325	10.297	9.420
	50	10.536	9.648	8.880
	55	9.617	8.879	8.233
	60	8.549	7.967	7.448
	65	7.308	6.882	6.495
	70	5.868	5.590	5.333
25	25	13.192	11.786	10.621
	30	12.794	11.468	10.367
	35	12.333	11.095	10.067
	40	11.776	10.655	9.708
	45	11.130	10.131	9.278
	50	10.374	9.509	8.761
	55	9.488	8.766	8.134
	60	8.452	7.880	7.371
	65	7.241	6.826	6.440
	70	5.826	5.551	5.291
30	30	12.434	11.182	10.133
	35	12.010	10.838	9.854
	40	11.502	10.428	9.514
	45	10.898	9.936	9.112
	50	10.183	9.345	8.620
	55	9.338	8.634	8.018
	60	8.338	7.779	7.280
	65	7.161	6.748	6.373
	70	5.777	5.505	5.254

TABLE VII. Continued.

Age of the youngest.	Age of the eldest.	Value at 3 per Cent.	Value at 4 per Cent.	Value at 5 per Cent.
35	35	11.632	10.530	9.600
	40	11.175	10.157	9.291
	45	10.622	9.702	8.913
	50	9.955	9.149	8.450
	55	9.156	8.476	7.879
	60	8.202	7.658	7.172
	65	7.066	6.662	6.294
	70	5.718	5.450	5.203
40	40	10.777	9.826	9.014
	45	10.283	9.418	8.671
	50	9.677	8.911	8.244
	55	8.936	8.283	7.710
	60	8.038	7.510	7.039
	65	6.951	6.556	6.198
	70	5.646	5.383	5.141
45	45	9.863	9.063	8.370
	50	9.331	8.619	7.987
	55	8.662	8.044	7.500
	60	7.831	7.332	6.875
	65	6.807	6.425	6.080
	70	5.556	5.300	5.063
50	50	8.892	8.235	7.660
	55	8.312	7.738	7.230
	60	7.568	7.091	6.664
	65	6.623	6.258	5.926
	70	5.442	5.193	4.964
55	55	7.849	7.332	6.873
	60	7.220	6.781	6.386
	65	6.379	6.036	5.724
	70	5.291	5.053	4.833

TABLE VII. Continued.

Age of the youngest.	Age of the eldest.	Value at 3 per Cent.	Value at 4 per Cent.	Value at 5 per Cent.
60	60	6.737	6.351	6.001
	65	6.043	5.730	5.444
	70	5.081	4.858	4.653
65	65	5.547	5.277	5.031
	70	4.773	4.571	4.385
70	70	4.270	4.104	3.952

TABLE VIII.

Shewing the Probability of the Duration of Life in LONDON, deduced by Mr. *Simpson* from observations on the bills of mortality in LONDON for 10 years, from 1728 to 1737.

Ages	Persons living.	Decr. of Life.	Ages.	Persons living.	Decr. of Life.	Ages.	Person living.	Decr. of Life.
0	1000	320	27	321	6	54	135	6
1	680	133	28	315	7	55	129	6
2	547	51	29	308	7	56	123	6
3	496	27	30	301	7	57	117	5
4	469	17	31	294	7	58	112	5
5	452	12	32	287	7	59	107	5
6	440	10	33	280	7	60	102	5
7	430	8	34	273	7	61	97	5
8	422	7	35	266	7	62	92	5
9	415	5	36	259	7	63	87	5
10	410	5	37	252	7	64	82	5
11	405	5	38	245	8	65	77	5
12	400	5	39	237	8	66	72	5
13	395	5	40	229	7	67	67	5
14	390	5	41	222	8	68	62	4
15	385	5	42	214	8	69	58	4
16	380	5	43	206	7	70	54	4
17	375	5	44	199	7	71	50	4
18	370	5	45	192	7	72	46	4
19	365	5	46	185	7	73	42	3
20	360	5	47	178	7	74	39	3
21	355	5	48	171	6	75	36	3
22	350	5	49	165	6	76	33	3
23	345	6	50	159	6	77	30	3
24	339	6	51	153	6	78	27	2
25	333	6	52	147	6	79	25	
26	327	6	53	141	6			

TABLE IX.

Shewing the *Expectations* of Life in LONDON, according to the preceding Table. See Mr. *Simpson's Select Exercises*, p. 255.

Age.	Expectation.	Age.	Expectation.	Age.	Expectation.
1	27.0	28	24.6	55	14.2
2	32.0	29	24.1	56	13.8
3	34.0	30	23.6	57	13.4
4	35.6	31	23.1	58	13.1
5	36.0	32	22.7	59	12.7
6	36.0	33	22.3	60	12.4
7	35.8	34	21.9	61	12.0
8	35.6	35	21.5	62	11.6
9	35.2	36	21.1	63	11.2
10	34.8	37	20.7	64	10.8
11	34.3	38	20.3	65	10.5
12	33.7	39	19.9	66	10.1
13	33.1	40	19.6	67	9.8
14	32.5	41	19.2	68	9.4
15	31.9	42	18.8	69	9.1
16	31.3	43	18.5	70	8.8
17	30.7	44	18.1	71	8.4
18	30.1	45	17.8	72	8.1
19	29.5	46	17.4	73	7.8
20	28.9	47	17.0	74	7.5
21	28.3	48	16.7	75	7.2
22	27.7	49	16.3	76	6.8
23	27.2	50	16.0	77	6.4
24	26.6	51	15.6	78	6.0
25	26.1	52	15.2	79	5.5
26	25.6	53	14 9	80	5.0
27	25.1	54	14.5		

TABLE X.

Shewing the Value of an Annuity on *One* Life, according to the probabilities of life in LONDON. See Mr. *Simpson's Select Exercises*, p. 260.

Age.	Yrs. purchase at 3 per Cent.	Yrs. purchase at 4 per Cent.	Yrs. purchase at 5 per Cent.	Age.	Yrs. purchase at 3 per Cent.	Yrs. purchase at 4 per Cent.	Yrs. purchase at 5 per Cent.	Age.	Yrs. purchase at 3 per Cent.	Yrs. purchase at 4 per Cent.	Yrs. purchase at 5 per Cent.
6	18.8	16.2	14.1	31	14.8	12.9	11.4	56	10.1	9.1	8.4
7	18.9	16.3	14.2	32	14.6	12.7	11.3	57	9.9	8.9	8.2
8	19.0	16.4	14.3	33	14.4	12.6	11.2	58	9.6	8.7	8.1
9	19.0	16.4	14.3	34	14.2	12.4	11.0	59	9.4	8.6	8.0
10	19.0	16.4	14.3	35	14.1	12.3	10.9	60	9.2	8.4	7.9
11	19.0	16.4	14.3	36	13.9	12.1	10.8	61	8.9	8.2	7.7
12	18.9	16.3	14.2	37	13.7	11.9	10.6	62	8.7	8.1	7.6
13	18.7	16.2	14.1	38	13.5	11.8	10.5	63	8.5	7.9	7.4
14	18.5	16.0	14.0	39	13.3	11.6	10.4	64	8.3	7.7	7.3
15	18.3	15.8	13.9	40	13.2	11.5	10.3	65	8.0	7.5	7.1
16	18.1	15.6	13.7	41	13.0	11.4	10.2	66	7.8	7.3	6.9
17	17.9	15.4	13.5	42	12.8	11.2	10.1	67	7.6	7.1	6.7
18	17.6	15.2	13.4	43	12.6	11.1	10.0	68	7.4	6.9	6.6
19	17.4	15.0	13.2	44	12.5	11.0	9.9	69	7.1	6.7	6.4
20	17.2	14.8	13.0	45	12.3	10.8	9.8	70	6.9	6.5	6.2
21	17.0	14.7	12.9	46	12.1	10.7	9.7	71	6.7	6.3	6.0
22	16.8	14.5	12.7	47	11.9	10.5	9.5	72	6.5	6.1	5.8
23	16.5	14.3	12.6	48	11.8	10.4	9.4	73	6.2	5.9	5.6
24	16.3	14.1	12.4	49	11.6	10.2	9.3	74	5.9	5.6	5.4
25	16.1	14.0	12.3	50	11.4	10.1	9.2	75	5.6	5.4	5.2
26	15.9	13.8	12.1	51	11.2	9.9	9.0				
27	15.6	13.6	12.0	52	11.0	9.8	8.9				
28	15.4	13.4	11.8	53	10.7	9.6	8.8				
29	15.2	13.2	11.7	54	10.5	9.4	8.6				
30	15.0	13.1	11.6	55	10.3	9.3	8.5				

TABLE XI.

Shewing the Value of an Annuity on the joint continuance of Two Lives, according to the probabilities of life in LONDON. See Mr. *Simpson's Select Exercises*, p. 266.

Age of the youngest.	Age of the eldest.	Value at 3 per Cent.	Value at 4 per Cent.	Value at 5 per Cent.
	10	14.7	13.0	11.6
	15	14.3	12.7	11.3
	20	13.8	12.2	10.8
	25	13.1	11.6	10.2
	30	12.3	10.9	9.7
10	35	11.5	10.2	9.1
	40	10.7	9.6	8.6
	45	10.0	9.0	8.1
	50	9.3	8.4	7.6
	55	8.6	7.8	7.1
	60	7.8	7.2	6.6
	65	6.9	6.5	6.1
	70	6.1	5.8	5.5
	75	5.3	5.1	4.9
	15	13.9	12.3	11.0
	20	13.3	11.8	10.5
	25	12.6	11.2	10.1
	30	11.9	10.6	9.5
	35	11.2	10.0	9.0
	40	10.4	9.4	8.5
15	45	9.6	8.8	8.0
	50	8.9	8.2	7.5
	55	8.2	7.6	7.0
	60	7.5	7.0	6.5
	65	6.8	6.4	6.0
	70	6.0	5.7	5.4
	75	5.2	5.0	4.8

Age of the youngest.	Age of the eldest.	Value at 3 per Cent.	Value at 4 per Cent.	Value at 5 per Cent.
	20	12.8	11.3	10.1
	25	12.2	10.8	9.7
	30	11.6	10.3	9.2
	35	10.9	9.8	8.8
	40	10.2	9.2	8.4
20	45	9.5	8.6	7.9
	50	8.8	8.0	7.4
	55	8.1	7.5	6.9
	60	7.4	6.9	6.4
	65	6.7	6.3	5.9
	70	6.0	5.7	5.4
	75	5.2	5.0	4.8
	25	11.8	10.5	9.4
	30	11.3	10.1	9.0
	35	10.7	9.6	8.6
	40	10.0	9.1	8.2
	45	9.4	8.5	7.8
25	50	8.7	7.9	7.3
	55	8.0	7.4	6.8
	60	7.3	6.8	6.3
	65	6.6	6.2	5.8
	70	5.9	5.6	5.3
	75	5.1	4.9	4.7
	30	10.8	9.6	8.6
30	35	10.3	9.2	8.3
	40	9.7	8.8	8.0

TABLE XI. Continued.

Age of the youngest.	Age of the eldest.	Value at 3 per Cent.	Value at 4 per Cent.	Value at 5 per Cent.
30	45	9.1	8.3	7.6
	50	8.5	7.8	7.2
	55	7.9	7.3	6.7
	60	7.2	6.7	6.2
	65	6.5	6.1	5.7
	70	5.8	5.5	5.2
	75	5.1	4.9	4.7
35	35	9.9	8.8	8.0
	40	9.4	8.5	7.7
	45	8.9	8.1	7.4
	50	8.3	7.6	7.0
	55	7.7	7.1	6.6
	60	7.1	6.5	6.1
	65	6.4	6.0	5.6
	70	5.7	5.4	5.1
	75	5.0	4.8	4.6
40	40	9.1	8.1	7.3
	45	8.7	7.8	7.1
	50	8.2	7.4	6.8
	55	7.6	6.9	6.4
	60	7.0	6.4	6.0
	65	6.4	5.9	5.5
	70	5.7	5.4	5.1
	75	5.0	4.8	4.6
45	45	8.3	7.4	6.7
	50	7.9	7.1	6.5
	55	7.4	6.7	6.2
	60	6.8	6.3	5.8

Age of the youngest.	Age of the eldest.	Value at 3 per Cent.	Value at 4 per Cent.	Value at 5 per Cent.
45	65	6.3	5.8	5.4
	70	5.6	5.3	5.0
	75	4.9	4.7	4.5
50	50	7.6	6.8	6.2
	55	7.2	6.5	6.0
	60	6.7	6.1	5.7
	65	6.2	5.7	5.3
	70	5.5	5.2	4.9
	75	4.8	4.6	4.4
55	55	6.9	6.2	5.7
	60	6.5	5.9	5.5
	65	6.0	5.6	5.2
	70	5.4	5.1	4.8
	75	4.7	4.5	4.3
60	60	6.1	5.6	5.2
	65	5.7	5.3	4.9
	70	5.2	4.9	4.6
	75	4.6	4.4	4.2
65	65	5.4	5.0	4.7
	70	4.9	4.6	4.4
	75	4.4	4.2	4.0
70	70	4.6	4.4	4.2
	75	4.2	4.0	3.9
75	75	3.8	3.7	3.6

TABLE XII.

Shewing the Probabilities of Life in LONDON, on the supposition, that all who die in LONDON were born there. Formed from the Bills, for 10 years, from 1759 to 1768. See page 245.

Ages	Persons living.	Decr. of Life.	Ages	Persons living.	Decr. of Life.	Ages	Persons living.	Decr. of Life.
0	1000	240	31	404	9	62	132	7
1	760	99	32	395	9	63	125	7
2	661	42	33	386	9	64	118	7
3	619	29	34	377	9	65	111	7
4	590	21	35	368	9	66	104	7
5	569	11	36	359	9	67	97	7
6	558	10	37	350	9	68	90	7
7	548	7	38	341	9	69	83	7
8	541	6	39	332	10	70	76	6
9	535	5	40	322	10	71	70	6
10	530	4	41	312	10	72	64	6
11	526	4	42	302	10	73	58	5
12	522	4	43	292	10	74	53	5
13	518	3	44	282	10	75	48	5
14	515	3	45	272	10	76	43	5
15	512	3	46	262	10	77	38	5
16	509	3	47	252	10	78	33	4
17	506	3	48	242	9	79	29	4
18	503	4	49	233	9	80	25	3
19	499	5	50	224	9	81	22	3
20	494	7	51	215	9	82	19	3
21	487	8	52	206	8	83	16	3
22	479	8	53	198	8	84	13	2
23	471	8	54	190	7	85	11	2
24	463	8	55	183	7	86	9	2
25	455	8	56	176	7	87	7	2
26	447	8	57	169	7	88	5	1
27	439	8	58	162	7	89	4	1
28	431	9	59	155	8	90	3	1
29	422	9	60	147	8			
30	413	9	61	139	7			

TABLE XIII.

Shewing the *true* Probabilities of Life in LONDON till the Age of 19. See page 249.

Age.	Perfons living.	Decrements of life.
0	750	240
1	510	99
2	411	42
3	369	29
4	340	21
5	319	11
6	308	10
7	298	7
8	291	6
9	285	5
10	280	4
11	276	4
12	272	4
13	268	3
14	265	3
15	262	3
16	259	3
17	256	3
18	253	4
19	249	
20	494	
21	487	
&c.	&c.	

The numbers in the fecond column to be continued as in the laft Table.

TABLE XIV.

Shewing the *true* Probabilities of Life in London for all Ages. Formed from the bills for 10 years, from 1759 to 1768. See page 251.

Ages.	Persons living.	Decr. of Life.	Ages.	Persons living.	Decr. of Life.	Ages.	Persons living.	Decr. of Life.
0	1518	486	31	404	9	62	132	7
1	1032	200	32	395	9	63	125	7
2	832	85	33	386	9	64	118	7
3	747	59	34	377	9	65	111	7
4	688	42	35	368	9	66	104	7
5	646	23	36	359	9	67	97	7
6	623	20	37	350	9	68	90	7
7	603	14	38	341	9	69	83	7
8	589	12	39	332	10	70	76	6
9	577	10	40	322	10	71	70	6
10	567	9	41	312	10	72	64	6
11	558	9	42	302	10	73	58	5
12	549	8	43	292	10	74	53	5
13	541	7	44	282	10	75	48	5
14	534	6	45	272	10	76	43	5
15	528	6	46	262	10	77	38	5
16	522	7	47	252	10	78	33	4
17	515	7	48	242	9	79	29	4
18	508	7	49	233	9	80	25	3
19	501	7	50	224	9	81	22	3
20	494	7	51	215	9	82	19	3
21	487	8	52	206	8	83	16	3
22	479	8	53	198	8	84	13	2
23	471	8	54	190	7	85	11	2
24	463	8	55	183	7	86	9	2
25	455	8	56	176	7	87	7	2
26	447	8	57	169	7	88	5	1
27	439	8	58	162	7	89	4	1
28	431	9	59	155	8	90	3	1
29	422	9	60	147	8			
30	413	9	61	139	7			

OBSERVATIONS

ON

TABLES I. and II.

THESE Tables may be met with in most of the books that treat of compound interest and annuities; but there has been, in this work, so much occasion for referring to them, that it was necessary to save the reader the trouble of turning to other books for them.

The 2d, 3d, 4th, &c. numbers in the *Second* Table, are only the *sums* of the first 2, 3, 4, &c. numbers in the *First* Table. This Table, therefore, is the foundation of the *Second*; and, indeed, of all the common tables of compound interest; and, with the help of it, almost all the questions in compound interest may be easily answered.

The following specimen of this may, I think, be of considerable use.

QUESTION I. "To what *sum* or *annuity* "will any given *sum* or *annuity*, now to be "laid up for improvement, at a given rate "of compound interest, increase, in a given "number of years?"

ANSWER. Divide the given *sum* or annuity by the value of 1*l.* payable at the end of the given number of years, and the *quotient* will be the anſwer.

Example. Let the given ſum be 50*l.* and the given time 18 years. The rate of intereſt 4 *per cent.*—The preſent value, at 4 *per cent.* of 1*l.* payable at the end of 18 years is, by Table I. .4936; and 50*l.* divided by this value, gives *l.*101.296, or 101*l.* 5*s.* the *ſum* to which 50*l.* will increaſe in 18 years. In like manner; 2*l. per annum*, the firſt payment of which is to be made a year hence, will increaſe (intereſt ſuppoſed the ſame) in 18 years, to an *annuity* of *l.*4.05: for 2*l.* the given annuity, divided by .4936, gives *l.*4.05, or 4*l.* 1*s.*

QUESTION II. "To what *ſum* will a "given *annuity* amount, in conſequence of "being forborn and improved, at a given "rate of compound intereſt, for a given "number of years?"

ANSWER. From the *increaſed* annuity, found by the laſt Queſtion, ſubtract the *given* annuity; and multiply the *remainder* by the PERPETUITY, and the *product* will be the anſwer.

Example. 2*l. per ann.* improved at 4 *per cent.* compound intereſt, will, by the laſt Queſtion, increaſe, in 18 years, to *l.*4.05 *per ann.* 2*l.* ſubtracted from 4.05, leaves 2.05, which, multiplied by 25, the *perpetuity*, gives *l.* 51.25, or 51*l.* 5*s*, the *amount* in 18 years. In the ſame manner it may be found, that 10*l.* *per ann.* (intereſt being the ſame) will amount, in 41 years, to 998*l.*

It ſhould be remembered, that the PERPETUITY is 33.33,—28.57,—25—20,—or 16.666, according as intereſt is reckoned at 3,—3½,—4,—5 or 6 *per cent:* And that the *annuity* meant in all theſe Queſtions is an annuity, the firſt payment of which is to be made at the end of a year.

QUESTION III. "In what number of "years will a given *ſum* or *annuity* increaſe "to another given *ſum* or *annuity*, in conſe-"quence of being improved at a given rate "of intereſt?"

ANSWER. Divide the *original ſum* or *annuity* by the *increaſed ſum* or *annuity*; and look for the *quotient*, or the number neareſt to it, in Table I; and the number of years correſponding to it will be the anſwer.

Example. Let the *ſum* be 50*l.* The increaſed ſum *l.* 101.29. The rate of intereſt, 4 *per cent.* The former ſum divided by the latter gives .4936, which ſtands oppoſite in the Table to 18 years, or the time in which 50*l.* will gain the required increaſe.——In like manner, it may be found, that 18 years is the time in which 2*l.* *per ann.* will increaſe to *l.* 4.05 *per ann.*

QUESTION IV. "In what time will any "given *annuity* amount to a *given ſum*, in "conſequence of being forborn and im- "proved, at a given rate of compound in- "tereſt?"

ANSWER. Divide the given *ſum* to which the annuity muſt amount by the PERPETUITY. Add the given annuity to the quotient; and by the quotient ſo increaſed, divide the given annuity; and this *ſecond quotient*, found in Table I. will ſhew the anſwer.

Example. A perſon owes 1000*l.* and reſolves to appropriate 10*l. per annum* of his income towards diſcharging it. In what time will ſuch an appropriation, in conſequence of being improved at 4 *per cent.* amount to a ſum equal to the debt?—— 1000*l.* divided by 25 gives 40*l.* 10*l.* added to 40*l.* makes 50*l*; and 10*l.* divided by 50*l.* gives .2000, which in the Table ſtands oppoſite to 41 years, the required time.

In the ſame manner it will appear, that the ſame annuity, if improved at 5 *per cent.* will amount to 1000*l.* in 37 years.

QUESTION V. "In what time will a "*given principal* be annihilated, by taking "out of it, at the end of a year, a given ſum, "and after that, the ſame ſum annually, to- "gether with its growing intereſts?"

ANSWER. In the ſame time plainly in which an equal annuity would amount to the *given principal.*

A perſon, therefore, poſſeſs'd of 1000*l.* capital, bearing intereſt at 4 *per cent.* would, by Queſtion IV. reduce it to nothing in 41 years, by taking out of it 10*l.* the firſt year, and as much more every following year, as would be neceſſary, together with the intereſt of the remaining capital, to make his annual income conſtantly 50*l.*

Remark. The ſum to which a *given* annuity will amount in a given time, is the ſame with the value of an annuity for the given time, equal to the *given* annuity increaſed by the yearly intereſt of the amount. That is, 1000*l.* is the value of 50*l. per ann.* for 41 years, at 4 *per cent:* And the ſame ſum is likewiſe the value of 60*l. per annum,* for 37 years, at 5 *per cent.* The reaſon is plain: 1000*l.* it has appeared, would, in conſequence of being put out to theſe different rates of intereſt, be juſt ſufficient to pay the annuities.

I have been the more explicit in theſe rules, becauſe they point out a very eaſy method of deducing and examining all I have ſaid, in different parts of this work, and particularly in Chap. III. concerning the increaſe of money at intereſt.——I will juſt mention one inſtance.

400,000*l.* *per annum*, applied in the manner ſuppoſed in Queſtions IV and V. would annihilate 55 millions, bearing intereſt at 5 *per cent.* in 42 years.

In 1716, when the *ſinking fund* was eſtabliſhed, the public debts were near this ſum, and bore 5 *per cent.* intereſt. This fund then, had but 400,000*l.* of it been inviolably applied to the annihilation of the public debts, would, in 1758, have diſcharged all the debts contracted *before* 1716.——And it may be further found very eaſily, by the anſwer to Queſtion IV. that had it been ſuffered to go on in its operation, and been applied, *ſince* 1758, to the redemption of only 3 *per cents* at *par*, it would by this time have diſcharged 104 millions; and ſeven years hence, 140 millions.——The aſſertion, therefore, in page 164, is ſtrictly true. But the following proof of that aſſertion will, perhaps, be more clear and ſtriking.

Suppoſe an annuity of 400,000*l*, beginning in 1716, to have been applied till 1730, to the annihilation of debts bearing intereſt at 5 *per cent*; from 1730 to 1748, to the annihilation of debts bearing intereſt at 4 *per cent.* and from 1748 to 1771, to the annihilation of debts bearing intereſt at 3 *per cent.* In the firſt of theſe periods the annuity would have increaſed to 800,000*l.*; in the *ſecond*, to 1,600,000*l.*; in the *laſt*, to 3,200,000*l.*——In the preſent year, therefore, the nation might have been eaſed of above *three millions per annum* in taxes. And, at the ſame time, (ſuppoſing all the ſame meaſures taken in other reſpects) it would have enjoyed that very *ſinking fund* it now has; and no detriment could have ariſen to the public, from any applications of it to current expences.

As I am now again on the national debt, I will beg leave to add the following proof of another obſervation on this ſubject, in page 140.

The diſburſements, on account of any loans, will be the ſame, whatever different intereſts they bear, ſuppoſing a proviſion made for diſcharging the principal, by applying to that purpoſe ſurpluſſes bearing to one another the ſame proportions with thoſe intereſts.

For Example. Let a million be borrowed at 3 *per cent.* and let a fund be charged with it which brings in 6*s.* *per cent.* *per annum* more than the intereſt; or 33,000*l.* inſtead of 30,000*l.* *per annum.* This ſurplus, applied in the manner I have explained, will annihilate the *principal* in 81 years, as may be gathered from Queſtion V. At the end of this time, the diſburſements on account of the loan will be 33,000*l.* multiplied by 81; that is, 2,673,000*l.*

Let us again ſuppoſe a million borrowed at 6 *per cent.* and let a fund be charged with it producing a ſurplus of 12*s.* *per cent.* *per* *annum*. Such a fund, besides paying the interest, will discharge the principal in 41 years; and the disbursements on account of the loan, will be 66,000*l.* multiplied by 41; that is, 2,706,000*l.* or very nearly the same with the disbursements on account of an equal loan at 3 *per cent.*

It appears, therefore, agreeably to the observation to which I have referred, that were the public, in raising money, to adopt the plan I have proposed, it would be of little consequence what interest was given for money. The practicability of such a plan is self-evident, for it cannot be less easy to apply the *interest* of a sum, to the payment of a debt, than the sum itself: and this plan requires no more.—One particular advantage attending it, already hinted, I will beg leave here to repeat. By keeping the *stocks* steadily at or near *par*, that fluctuation in them would be in a great measure prevented, which now produces so many evils; and which, with the aid of annual lotteries, will, I fear, in time, ruin all honest industry, and turn us into a nation of sharpers and gamblers.

DIRECTIONS for finding the VALUES of TWO JOINT LIVES of given Ages, by TABLE VII.

IF both the ages are given in the Table, the value wanted will be found immediately by inspection.

If the ages are not given in the Table, it will be best to proceed in the following manner.

Suppose the rate of interest 4 *per cent.* and the proposed ages 40 and 66.——It will appear, from inspecting the Table, that the value sought would be 6.556, were the age of the elder life 65; and 5.383, were it 70. Since, therefore, it is 66, the value must be the *first* of four arithmetical means between 6.556 and 5.383, or 6.322.——For the same reason, had the ages of the elder been 68, the value would have been the 3d arithmetical mean between 6.556 and 5.383, or 5.854.——In like manner, were the proposed ages 43 and 65, the value would be the 3d arithmetical mean between 6.556 (the value of two joint lives whose ages are 40 and 65) and 6.425, (the value of two joint lives whose ages are 45 and 65) or 6.478.

Again, let the ages be 43 and 66. That is, let it be supposed, that neither of the proposed ages is given in the Table.

The values corresponding to the ages $\begin{Bmatrix} 40 \\ 45 \end{Bmatrix}$ and $\begin{Bmatrix} 66 \\ 66 \end{Bmatrix}$, are $\begin{Bmatrix} 6.322 \\ 6.200 \end{Bmatrix}$.

The value, therefore, correſponding to the ages 43 and 66, muſt be the 3d mean between 6.322 and 6.200, or 6.250.——

N. B. The 1ſt, 2d, 3d, and 4th of four arithmetical means between two numbers are found by ſubtracting $\frac{1}{5}$, $\frac{2}{5}$, $\frac{3}{5}$, and $\frac{4}{5}$ of the *difference* between the two numbers, from the *greateſt* of them.

Thus. The difference between 6.556, and 5.383, is 1.173. One fifth of this difference is .234; which, ſubtracted from 6.556, leaves 6.322; the firſt of 4 means between 6.556 and 5.383.——In like manner; the difference between 6.322 and 6.200 is .122. *One* fifth of this difference is .024; and, therefore, three-fifths of this difference is .072, which, ſubtracted from 6.322, leaves 6.250, the *third* arithmetical mean between 6.322 and 6.200.

In order to avoid trouble, if the ages are nearly equal, a year or two may be added to the leaſt, and as much ſubtracted from the greateſt; and the value taken by inſpection. But if one of them much exceeds the other, it will in general be ſufficient to take the neareſt number in the Table for the leſſer.

The mean between the values at 3 *per cent.* and 4 *per cent.* may be taken for the value at 3½ *per cent.* without any error of conſequence. And the like may be ſaid of the values at 4½ *per cent.*

The values of the *longeſt* of two lives is found by ſubtracting the value of the *joint* lives from the *ſum* of the values of the two *ſingle* lives.——Thus, the values of two ſingle lives, whoſe ages are 25 and 30, are by Table VI. (intereſt reckoned at 4 *per cent.*) 15.31 and 14.68. The ſum of theſe two values is 29.99; the value of the joint lives is (by Table VII) 11.46; and this value, ſubtracted from 29.99, gives 18.53, or the value of an annuity on the longeſt of the two lives.

The value of *two* joint lives being given, the value of *three* joint lives may be found by the following rule, taken from Mr. *Simpſon's Select Exerciſes*, page 279.

Let A be the youngeſt, and C the oldeſt of the three propoſed lives. Take the value of the two joint lives B and C, and find the age of a *ſingle* life D of the ſame value. Then find the value of the *joint* lives A and D, which will be the anſwer.

Example. Let the three given ages be 25, 30, and 40, and let the rate of intereſt be 4 *per cent.* Then the value of the two oldeſt joint lives B and C, will (by Tab. VII.) be 10.428, anſwering, in Tab. VI. to a ſingle life D of 54 years of age. And the value of the joint lives A and D, which is 8.917 year's purchaſe, will be the value ſought.

FINIS.